CUTTING UP IN THE KITCHEN

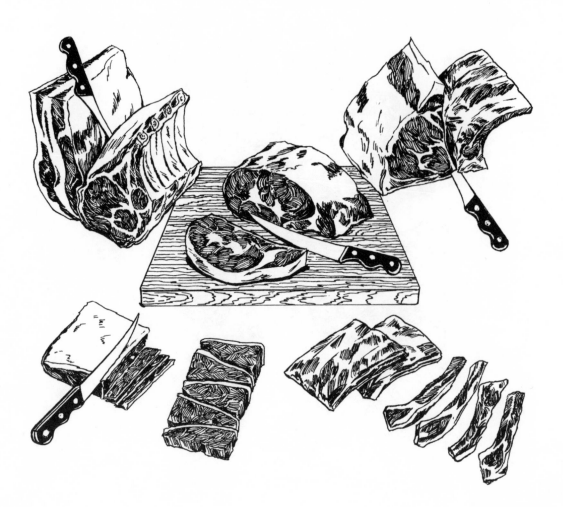

Cutting-up in the Kitchen

THE BUTCHER'S GUIDE TO SAVING MONEY ON MEAT & POULTRY

Merle Ellis

Chronicle Books

Cutting-up in the Kitchen.

Sixth printing, March 1977
Copyright © 1975 by Merle Ellis

Library of Congress Cataloging in Publication Data

Ellis, Merle, 1934-
    Cutting-up in the kitchen.

    Bibliography:
    Includes index.
    1. Meat. 2. Poultry. 3. Cookery (Meat)
4. Cookery. (Poultry) 5. Marketing (Home economics).
I. Title.

TX373.E4 641.3'6 75-26502
ISBN 0-87701-071-4

Chronicle Books
870 Market Street
San Francisco
California 94102

Acknowledgements

To acknowledge all of the people who have helped make this book possible would take a book this big. To all of you, my sincere thank you; you know who you are.

A special thanks to the National Live Stock and Meat Board for its generous assistance over the years and for providing photographs on which many of the illustrations in this book were based; to the American Lamb Council and particularly Mr. Charles Fels for assistance with the chapter on Lamb; to Mr. George Strathearn and the California Beef Council for support, encouragement, consultation and for permission to include as part of this book the valuable consumer *Dictionary of Beef Cuts*.

Last, but certainly not least, a special thanks to Jane Benét, fantastic cook, friend and Food Editor of The San Francisco Chronicle for saying, "Do it—you can do it!"

Designed by Jon Goodchild
Printed in the United States of America

Illustrations by Kay Solomon

Merle Ellis is an odd combination of men. One is the ideal butcher—born in Sioux City, Iowa, youth spent on his grandfather's farm in Nebraska, first started to learn his trade at 13 from his father. Today, a practicing butcher in the quiet and scenic town of Tiburon, a bit north of San Francisco.

That's Merle One. Merle Two is a man of communications, a former television producer for NBC and for his own company, and a highly successful lecturer in person, on radio and TV where he has appeared on several national programs. Now, in a time of high-flying meat prices, he has undertaken a consumer-oriented syndicated newspaper column and this timely book.

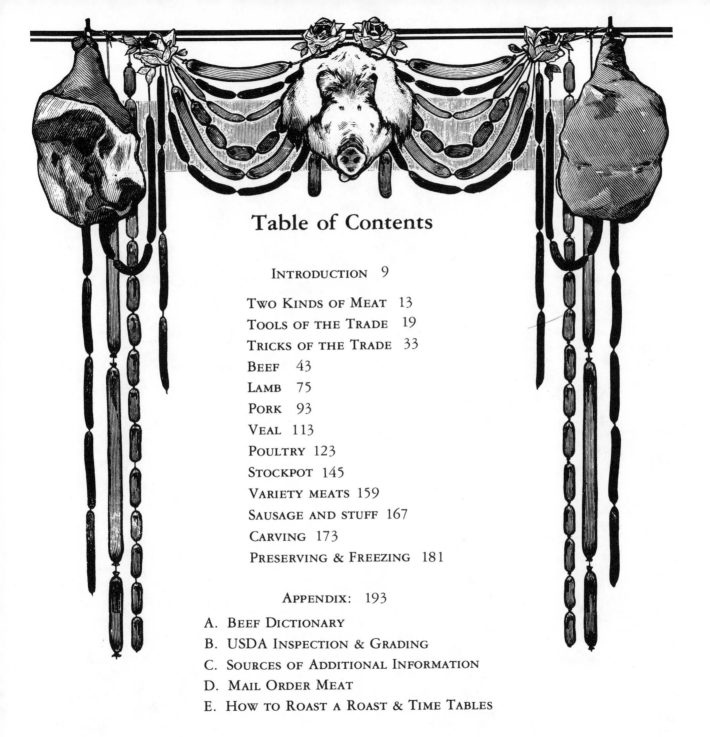

Table of Contents

INTRODUCTION 9

TWO KINDS OF MEAT 13
TOOLS OF THE TRADE 19
TRICKS OF THE TRADE 33
BEEF 43
LAMB 75
PORK 93
VEAL 113
POULTRY 123
STOCKPOT 145
VARIETY MEATS 159
SAUSAGE AND STUFF 167
CARVING 173
PRESERVING & FREEZING 181

APPENDIX: 193

A. BEEF DICTIONARY
B. USDA INSPECTION & GRADING
C. SOURCES OF ADDITIONAL INFORMATION
D. MAIL ORDER MEAT
E. HOW TO ROAST A ROAST & TIME TABLES

INTRODUCTION

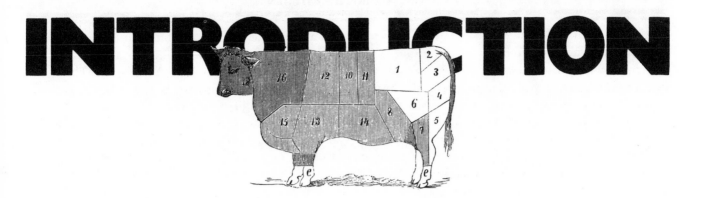

ot too many years ago you could go to the meat counter, recipe in hand, and ask your friendly butcher, "What's the best cut to use for 'Beef Bourguignon'?" or "How long should I cook a three-rib Prime Rib?" and he would know. And if you had six kids and your husband was out of work, he probably knew that too. And then there would always be some cut of meat that was "a real good special today." If you fancied yourself a gourmet, he would "hang back" a Short Loin for an extra week or two, and take pride in presenting it for your inspection—black with "age." In those days the butcher was a trusted friend, looked to for assistance in selecting a good steak, timing a roast of beef or stretching a food dollar.

Times have changed. In the past four decades the trend in the meat industry has been toward prepackaged meat sold in self-service cases. The butcher is still there, but he's not the same friendly guy in the flat-top straw hat that used to inquire about Grandpa's gout or ask Grandma, "How did the Pot Roast turn out?" Now he's part of the fast-paced assembly line team, enclosed in glass, programmed to process the greatest possible volume in the fewest possible man-hours.

Future trends are almost certain to remove the butcher even further from contact with the consumer. It won't be long, according to informed sources within the industry, when much of the meat in your supermarket will be uniformly formed, prepackaged and frozen. It will come from a huge packing plant, adjacent to a huge feed lot, somewhere near the heart of "cattle country."

Today's consumers (not to mention tomorrow's), need to learn or re-learn some of what Grandma knew so they can function effectively and economically in a marketplace more complicated than Grandma could have imagined.

You need to know, as you approach today's meat counter the best cut to use for "Beef Bourguignon." And if that's too expensive, what the alternatives are. If you have six kids and your husband is out of work, *you* need to know which cut is "a real good special today" and how to best take advantage of it.

Armed with a little basic knowledge about meat and a willingness to spend some time in the kitchen doing a little "cutting-up," it is possible to eat extremely well and economically, even in this high cost of living world we live in.

Acquiring basic knowledge used to happen by osmosis back in the days when Grandma was a girl. Things were simpler then. A steer had two front legs, two hind legs, a head, a tail and, in between, a few T-Bones, Porterhouses and a Rib Roast or two. But things aren't so simple anymore.

Part of the confusion can be attributed to regional differences. There is, for example, no such thing as a "New York Steak" in New York City. That term probably had its origin in Kansas City to describe what in Chicago is called a "Shell Strip." On the Sunset Strip in Hollywood it's called a "Club Steak" or a "Top Sirloin" or a "Kansas City Strip," depending on which side of the "Strip" the market is on. And that's just the beginning.

The real confusion arose with the advent of the self-service meat case some time in the mid '40s. Gradually over the years a whole new category of cuts began creeping into the meat case, designed to satisfy

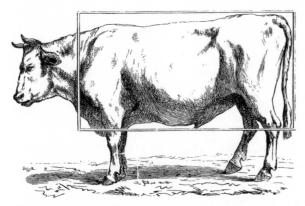

I've seen you hiding out there behind the canned hams surveying the meat case in bewildered confusion, trying to figure out what a "Butterball Steak" is, or a "London Broil," or a "Fluff Steak." I know the cause of your confusion—we in the business call it *merchandising*.

There were at one recent count, some 610 different retail names for various cuts of beef. That is a potential of 610 different labels in your butcher's meat case to designate the component parts of one steer. Add to that a few hundred more for pork, lamb, and veal and you have a situation far more complicated than the "front leg, hind leg and a few T-Bones and Porterhouses" Grandma had to deal with. Terminology in the meat case has become more than confusing; in some cases it borders on ridiculous.

consumer demands without interrupting the butchers' assembly line. You see, every time you ring the bell to ask for something special, it's a little like throwing a monkey wrench into a well-oiled machine. In order to keep you away from that bell, butchers began putting all those "special cuts" in the meat case. After a few people rang the bell to ask for "meat for Stroganoff" or "London Broil," the butcher started putting them in the meat case. They are there now, wrapped in plastic and labeled, along with "Stew" and "Kabobs."

Somewhere along the line the fact seems to have been lost that these items in the meat case are not cuts of meat at all—they're recipe names. Cattle don't have "London Broils," recipe books have "London Broils." Lambs don't have "Kabobs," recipe books have "Kabobs" and they can be made from many different cuts of lamb. Once you have learned to wade through the maze of merchandising terms that confront you in today's meat markets, you'll find that there is very probably a less expensive cut for "Kabobs" than the one the butcher has labeled as such. And, if you buy Top Round and cut it into "Stroganoff" yourself, it will cost you a lot less than the same cut that the butcher has cut and labeled "Stroganoff."

How do you find your way out of the maze? First, by reducing things to their lowest common denominator, the way you did in school when you were learning division. That's what I mean by getting

down to basics. Here's the arithmetic of basic meat-buying: There are only nine basic Primal cuts of beef, not 610. Anybody can handle nine, once they've learned what they are.

The meat industry has even offered to help. The National Livestock and Meat Board has initiated a program encouraging the standardization of meat terminology across the country. It's a voluntary program and it will be a long time, if ever, before all butchers use the recommended terms, but it is a step in the direction of understanding. Several states have passed legislation making the recommended terms mandatory within their jurisdiction, and more are certain to do the same; that's another step toward understanding.

But the final step is yours. The meat industry has said "We think it would be nice if all you butcher-

type guys would call a Chuck Roast a 'Chuck Roast'." State legislatures around the country are saying, "We don't care if it is nice or not—do it!" Now it's up to you. If you're going to become a better buyer—able to shop effectively and for less than a fortune in today's marketplace—you need to know what a "Chuck" is; you need to know what all the primal cuts of meat are, where they come from on the animal, what you can and cannot expect from them in terms of tenderness, and how best to cook them.

I hope this book will help. It gets back to basics. Hopefully, it goes beyond labels to provide a real understanding of the meat we eat, and how, by doing a little "Cutting Up in the Kitchen," we can eat more of it without going broke.

Merle Ellis

TWO KINDS OF MEAT

Chapter 1

To a cowboy on the plains of Texas or a cattleman in the feedlot in Iowa, there are all different kinds of cattle. There are Herefords and heifers, Shorthorns and steers. There are Angus and Brangus and a bunch of exotic breeds most of us haven't even heard of. But to a consumer faced with making intelligent decisions with regard to "what's for dinner," there are but two kinds of cattle, two kinds of any kind of meat for that matter: tough and tender.

That may sound like an oversimplification of the basics but it's a fact. So getting familiar with a few basic facts about what, when and where meat is tough—or tender—can make you a much better buyer. It can help you make daily decisions at the meat counter without fear of disappointment. It may even save you a dollar or two from time to time.

Age

The single most important factor in determining whether a cut of meat will be tough or tender is the age at which the animal was butchered. That's what accounts for the indisputable fact that a six-month-old lamb is more tender than a three-year-old mutton and that an eight-week-old fryer will eat easier than a two-year-old hen. Very simply: the younger the animal the more tender the meat it provides.

Determining the age of the animal at the time of slaughter is not as much of a concern these days as it was back in the days when Grandma was a girl. The meat industry was young then, too, and operated on a much less efficient basis than nowadays. Often cattle, pigs and chickens were old, and therefore tough, before any of them got to the table.

The modern meat industry operates considerably more systematically and with many governmental controls. Virtually all meat offered for sale in this country must be inspected for wholesomeness by the United States Department of Agriculture. In addition, much of the meat we see in the butcher's meat case is graded for quality. Both USDA Inspection and USDA Grading are discussed in detail later in this book. It is enough here to assure you that most of the meat in your butcher's meat case comes from relatively young animals.

Most consumers think they can distinguish between a cut of something young and a cut of something older by the color. At best, this is not too accurate an indication, since there are many other factors that can affect color. Generally speaking, however, there is a darkening of the color of the lean as an animal matures. Young **Prime** quality veal will be almost white, whereas in "yearling" beef the lean is a bright cherry red. A mature cow or bull will have lean that is a deep, dark, almost purple color. The same generally is true with lamb and pork; with an increase in maturity there is a darkening in the color of the lean.

Anatomy

The second most important factor relates to animal anatomy. This *should* concern you. An understanding of basic animal anatomy can help you select just the right cut of meat for any meal. It can give you a pretty good indication of how to cook it. It can make carving a simple task. And it can save you much, much money for the rest of your meat-buying life.

The greatest part of this book is devoted to providing a basic knowledge of animal anatomy as it appears in the butcher's meat case, and then showing you how to use that knowledge, plus a good sharp knife, to your best gastronomic and economic advantage.

Some parts of any animal—it doesn't matter whether it's lamb, beef or buffalo—are just naturally more tender than other parts of the same animal. It has to do with use. Those muscles that get used a lot get tough, those that get little use stay tender. The most tender cuts from any animal are located right in the middle of the back. That part, the Loin, just lies there and stays tender while the rest of the muscles do most of the work involved in stampeding across the plains or moving quietly from one side of the feedlot to the other. From the Loin, in either direction, the cuts of any animal become increasingly less tender. Those cuts at the outer extremes, the Fore Shank, the Hind Shank, the Neck, and the Tail are, in most cases, just plain tough.

Additional Factors

There are other factors that affect or indicate tenderness to one degree or another: (1) the amount of *fat* (marbling) in meat; (2) the *aging* of meat, particularly beef, after slaughter.

Fat—Once, while lecturing to a class of home economics students at one of our local high schools on "How to save money at the meat counter," I shared the program with a nutritionist from the University of California. Now I have never been much concerned with nutrition. My concern has always been with good food that tastes good. But, since more and more people seem concerned with things like "low cholesterol," "high protein," "low carbohydrates," and "unsaturated fats," I decided to get the real nutritional lowdown from an expert. "What sir," I asked, "is the value, if any, of fat in meat?"

"There are a number of fat-soluble vitamins contained in meat fats," he said, then added, "but the major contribution of fat in meat lies in the area of palatability." What that means in down-to-earth language is: *fat makes meat taste good!* Not the excess fat that needs to be trimmed off—that has always been and will always be waste—but the internal fat (marbling) which has for years been one of the contributing factors in judging the quality of beef.

I am convinced that if I put a T-Bone Steak cut from the Loin of a 35-year-old range-fed bull in the meat case next to a similar steak from a young **Prime** steer, the bull would sell first. Why? Because, "It doesn't have all that fat." Somewhere along the line, fat has become a dirty word. That's not really fair—after all, it doesn't even have four letters. Yet the growing consumer demand for "lean" beef is having tremendous effects on the entire beef industry. Ranchers are experimenting more and more with the heavy exotic European breeds—Charolais, Simmental, and Limousin to name a few—which they hope will cross with more familiar Short Horns, Herefords, and Angus to produce a breed of beef that has all the desirable qualities of palatability and cutability, without all that (marbling) fat.

A number of leaders within the beef industry are saying that the USDA should change grading requirements to allow more of the leaner beef to grade **Choice** or even **Prime.** There is even one faction which would like to add a new grade between **Choice** and **Good** to accommodate this leaner beef. They suggest calling it **Select** or **Super Select** or something equally acceptable.

I'm reserving judgment until a few things happen. I'll wait until the nutritionists decide *for sure* what they feel about cholesterol. I'll wait until the breeders come up with that Super Steer, a cross between some breed of bovine and a hybrid jellyfish, that will be all Filet Mignon with no fat and no bone. In the meantime, however, I'm going to stick with the standards I know. When it comes to selecting a steak by that means, look for a little marbling—because paraphrasing the nutritionist from the University of California, "Fat makes meat taste good."

Aging—Lack of proper aging probably causes more people more disappointment with the beef they buy and serve than any other single factor. Even the finest quality **Prime** beef, if not "Well Aged," will lack the flavor and tenderness that makes for a memorable meal.

I remember really well-aged beef from my early days in the meat business. The kind gourmets rave about; the kind that has hung so long it has fuzz on it. I say 'remember' because I don't see it anymore. If it were available, I'd hate to think of the price tag. Aging is a simple process but an expensive one. It requires that meat be stored for two to six weeks, or even longer, at a temperature of between 34 degrees and 38 degrees. This causes two things:

1) the deterioration of the connective tissues holding the muscles together, which helps promote tenderness, and

2) the evaporation of moisture, which causes shrinkage. That's why it's expensive. A side of beef hung for six weeks may lose as much as 12% to 15% of its weight. That's evaporated money, since it will be sold by the pound. The only way to make it up is to charge a higher price per pound.

Only the top grades of beef can be aged effectively. **Prime** and heavy **Choice** beef have a good layer of fat on the outside to protect the meat from spoiling during the aging process. Lesser grades lack this natural cover and will likely turn bad before they turn better. For the same reason, veal cannot be aged to any advantage. Neither can pork. Lamb, however, benefits by "hanging" around in the cooler awhile and mutton demands it.

There are several misconceptions with regard to aging that have grown up over the years. Contrary to what some butchers may have led you to believe, meat cannot be effectively aged in the butcher's meat case. A dark steak is not necessarily a well-aged steak. Probably there is nothing wrong with it, but it's equally probable that it is no better in flavor or tenderness than that nice bright one next to it. It may or may not have been aged. Just as meat will not age in the meat case, it will not effectively age in your refrigerator or on the drain-board of your sink.

It is important to differentiate between aging and tenderizing. You can help tenderize a tough piece of meat, perhaps, by allowing it to rest in a marinade for a day or two. And there are, according to some authorities, some tenderizing benefits to be gained from allowing a steak or roast to come to room temperature before cooking. But that's not aging. Aging helps tenderize, it's true, but it does much more: it develops an incomparable texture and flavor that is sought after by anyone who has ever tasted a good thick Porterhouse cut from a well-hung Short Loin of **Prime** beef.

Two Kinds of Cooking

Once you've learned to recognize a cut of meat as tough or tender you are almost at the point where you need never eat a tough piece of meat again—*ever*. Of course, there are a couple of other basics with which you need to become familiar before you can prove for yourself what every good butcher knows: "There is no such thing as a tough piece of meat . . . *if you cook it right!*"

That statement has been passed down the line from one generation of butchers to the next, very probably since man first put heat to meat. It serves as something of a defense mechanism for the butcher by putting the blame for a tough piece of meat on the cook. But it has survived the test of time for one reason alone: it's true! Even a tough piece of old range-fed bull buffalo can make for some pretty good eating if it's properly prepared.

There is nothing secret or magic about the proper preparation of meat. Tender meat, that which comes from the little-used muscles of the Loin and the Rib on a relatively young animal, can be cooked with *dry heat*. Tough meat, on the other hand, needs *moist heat*.

Roasting, broiling, pan broiling, and frying are the basic dry-heat methods. In hundreds of recipe books you can find thousands of recipes for various cuts of meat under each heading. The thing they all have in common is the fact that they use no moisture to help tenderize the meat. As a matter of fact, dry heat cooking tends to toughen meat if over done. That's why a waiter may cringe if you order a steak well-done. Heat solidifies the protein in meat, so once you get past medium rare you've got some pretty solid protein that gets increasingly hard to chew as it continues to cook.

Moist heat, on the other hand, contributes to the tenderness of meat. Long, slow cooking in liquid breaks down the connective tissue and turns it into gelatin. Moist-heat methods of cooking are listed in

your cookbook as stewing, simmering, braising, or cooking in liquid. Recipes using these methods will outnumber dry-heat recipes by at least ten to one in any cookbook. Presumably this is because there is a lot more tough meat in this world than there is tender. Or perhaps it's because cooking with moist heat offers creative cooks their finest moments. It is my firm conviction that the major reason why the French have developed sauces to their pinnacle of culinary perfection is the fact that their meat is tough. Not that I don't appreciate the French contribution to good eating, I do. But I just can't attribute it to any inborn genius in the kitchen. You don't have to speak French to eat extremely well. It does help a great deal, however, to have a working knowledge of moist-heat cooking, and to realize that much of the flavor of meat can be lost in the "pan drippings." To get them back requires a sauce. Don't let that scare you. Aside from the fancy French name, most sauces are little more than what's left in the pan after you've cooked some meat, mixed with a little imagination. We'll talk of that later, in the chapter on the stockpot.

TOOLS
OF THE TRADE

Chapter 2

According to that great and highly respected encyclopedia of food, wine and cookery *Larousse Gastronomique*, a knife is: "A cutting instrument consisting of a handle and a blade." Now I call that a nice simple, appropriate and concise definition. Easy to grasp, to the point, as sharp and clean as a good knife. But that's just for starters, when it comes to "Kitchen Knives"—things get as cluttered as a Kitchen drawer:

"**Kitchen Knives**—*For the various culinary operations it is essential to have good tools, and in particular very good knives.*

Each of the knives has its proper use. In order of size they are: vegetable knife for peeling vegetables; knife for cutting fish filets, with a larger blade; slicing knife, a tool with a fairly large blade with which it is possible to slice raw or cooked meat perfectly; straight bladed chopper, a tool with which it is not only possible to break bones of a certain size, but also to hash up meat in the same way as with the four blade chopper; the carving knife which is used for cutting bards of fat pork or bacon and which resembles a little the so-called 'English' knife used to carve large joints of beef and hams, but which, instead of having a rounded point is sharply pointed.

"We also must mention the knife for boning meat which is used more especially in butchery but can be used in cooking.

"Among the cutting tools which it is necessary to have in a well-ordered kitchen, are the following: the cleaver, a fairly large instrument with which a carcass can be cut in half; the chopper, with which it is possible to crack the hardest bones; the chopping knife which is made with one, two or four blades; and finally, the whole series of small knives used for chopping vegetables, particularly potatoes, for peeling and paring vegetables, and those for cutting potatoes into ribbons; knives for opening oysters and finally tin-openers, which can be included among cutting tools.

"Little tools such as knives with a fluting device or one for scraping lemon zest, should be mentioned; little instruments for cutting ravioli; special knives for cutting grapefruit; scissors for jointing chicken; the cutlet beater; the butcher's saw; and finally the scraper for the butcher's table."

Now that begins to sound like the typical kitchen "knife drawer" looks; all kinds of cutting instruments consisting of handles and blades designed to do all kinds of jobs from spreading peanut butter to pitting olives.

Most kitchens have at least one drawer like that filled full of knives. There are usually an assortment of serrated edged gems that were part of a set that came as a premium from the gas station; along with several miscellaneous hollow-ground stainless steel goodies "guaranteed" to hold an edge forever. But in most drawers in most kitchens there is not one good *sharp knife*. For the work we have to do in *"Cutting Up in the Kitchen"* we need few tools—but they must be **sharp!**

I have watched in awe the merchants of San Francisco's Chinatown filet an ocean perch in a second and a half or dice a cooked duck in less time. Not with an array of implements like those of a surgeon but with a Chinese cleaver—a good *sharp* Chinese cleaver.

Cooks in the restaurants of Chinatown use the same type of cleaver for all the slice-slice, chop-chop that is an essential part of Chinese cooking. If you want to start with only one good sharp knife a Chinese type cleaver might be a good choice.

I have made a living cutting meat and done a lot of cooking for years with only two "good sharp knives." Oh, I'll confess to a drawer full of gadgets; cheese cutters, egg cutters, potato peelers, melon ball scoops and the like—but we're not talking about the gadgets, we're talking about the basic tools of the trade and for me there are two:

A 6 inch *Boning Knife* used (as the name implies) for removing the bones from all manner of meat, fish and poultry; as well as for cutting up chickens, dividing an apple exactly in half (when you have two small girls it must be "exactly" in half) or for doing any cutting job that requires a *small* "good sharp knife."

The other is a *large* "good sharp knife." At the meat market it's a 10-inch "Steak Knife" used (again as the name implies) for cutting steaks; and chops and roasts and anything else that needs to be cut.

There are of course other tools for sawing, chopping, grinding, etc. that range in importance from "need-to-have" to "nice-to-have" and we'll discuss a few of those later in this chapter, but for now and for most of the cutting-up we're going to be doing, two good sharp knives—one big and one small—will do it all.

Selecting the Right Knives

Knives come in a variety of shapes with a variety of different type handles. Whether your small knife is a 5-inch or a 6-inch or 7-inch boning knife with a straight or curved blade and a wooden or pink plastic handle is largely a matter of personal preference.

My preference is for a straight blade, fairly ridged, with a simple wooden handle that has a slight protective knob where the blade and handle meet. The little knob helps keep your hand on the handle and yet such a handle is not so preformed that it dictates how you must hold the knife. As you will see when we discuss how to use a knife, there is more than one way to hold a knife and you will want to be able to make your own decision with regard to that and not have it made for you by the machine that made the knife. Whether the handle you choose is wooden or plastic, avoid the ones with all of the little finger grooves, they only get in the way.

You may find a 10- or 12-inch French chef's knife to be a good choice for your "Big Knife." It will do all the jobs of any of the other types but because of its shape (if you learn to use it) it can do a lot more. You can chop and dice and slice and mince faster than you can imagine—*if* you learn to use it. We'll talk about that later.

Types of Steel

There was a time, not long ago, when it was a simple matter to recommend a knife by the type of steel from which it was made. "Good knives are made of Carbon Steel" was a standard comment not too many years ago. Today such a statement, though still true, is not exclusively true. Good knives are made from *Stainless Steel*, too! There are, however, a ton of junk knives on the market made of stainless steel and you are more apt to get a good knife that will hold an edge for more than a few minutes if you look for *Carbon Steel*. It will stain with use and you may never want to take it to the table to carve that Thanksgiving turkey, but it will hold a good edge.

Types of Edges

The cutting edge is quite naturally one of the more important component parts of any knife and there are again a variety to choose from. Most of the knives available today have one of three basic edges: hollow-ground, serrated or flat ground. Most of the books I have read recommend hollow-ground knives, yet I have yet to see a professional butcher or cook using a hollow-ground or serrated knife. Evidently professionals don't usually write books. Well, times are changing—I'm a "pro" and for my money you can have all the fancy edges—hollow-ground or serrated, guaranteed to stay sharp forever—give me a knife of carbon steel with a plain old "flat edge" that I can keep sharp forever! You keep your guarantees.

Sharpening a Knife

There are three separate and distinct steps involved in getting and keeping a knife sharp; grinding, honing and steeling. A good knife will need grinding once or twice a decade if it's cared for properly. Honing will be required more frequently, once or twice a year perhaps. And steeling, once or twice every 15 minutes when the knife is in use.

Grinding

Seldom if ever does a good knife that has been properly cared for need grinding. The only time grinding becomes necessary is when a knife gets chipped or badly dulled through improper use or storage. When and if grinding becomes necessary it should be done by someone who knows what he's doing and has the equipment to do it right.

My grandfather, God rest him, loved to grind knives and axes and hoes on a big sandstone wheel that sat out by the shed. He could get his axe so sharp he could shave hair off his arm with it and impress the hell out of a lot of little woodsmen looking on in awe. But when it came to Grandma's kitchen knives that sandstone didn't sharpen them, it *ate* them. A dull 12-inch cook's knife was converted in no time to a dull 4-inch paring knife. If you have a knife that needs grinding, take it to a "pro," it's much, much cheaper in the long run.

Modern Sharpeners

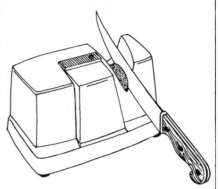

Modern electric knife sharpeners that come attached to the top of modern electric can openers and the like, are a little like the old sandstone Grand Dad used to use. They can sharpen a knife fast, keep it sharp for as long as it lasts, but they don't let a knife last very long—they eat it!

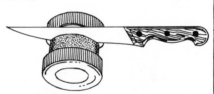

Roll type sharpeners do essentially the same thing, but perhaps not quite as fast. Both, in effect, grind knives and if you have a good knife, that needs grinding, it would be much much cheaper in the long run to take it to a "pro."

Use your electric or roll-it type knife sharpener to put temporary edges on all of the other knives in your kitchen drawer. If it doesn't do anything else, it will help you get rid of them.

Honing

A bright shiny brand new knife of the finest steel is not sharp and ready for immediate use the minute you unwrap it. Most new knives do not need further grinding, but without exception, they will need "honing" before they are sharp enough to qualify as a "good sharp knife."

Honing is done most effectively on a fine carborundum stone on which water or oil is used to maintain a scum-free abrasive surface. You can buy such a stone very inexpensively at almost any hardware store, usually they will come with a "coarse" textured surface on one side and a "medium" or "fine" on the other. The stone should be placed on a damp towel when using it to keep it from sliding. Use the coarse side first then the fine side.

To hone a knife, grasp the handle firmly in the right hand. Place the heel of the blade on the right end of the stone. With the finger tips of the left hand hold the blade firmly against the stone. The blade should be tilted so that the beveled cutting edge makes contact. Draw the blade gently across the stone from right to left. Then turn the knife over and repeat the process from left to right.

Take your time and be patient with this part of the sharpening process. If it's done right it only needs doing every three months or so to keep a kitchen knife in a beautiful condition.

Steeling

Certainly the most important of the three sharpening steps is "steeling." Once you have a good sharp knife you should never take it from the drawer or rack without also taking out and often using a "steel." The steel doesn't get a knife sharp, it keeps it sharp and if you learn to use a steel effectively you will seldom need to "sharpen" your knives.

To steel a knife the way you've watched your butcher do it with swift sure strokes requires a little very careful practice. The trick is to keep the elbows equi-distant one from the other and let the wrist and forearm do the work. If you don't it can hurt.

Grasp the steel firmly in the left hand with your thumb on top of the handle, that helps keep it out of the way. If you don't it most certainly will hurt.

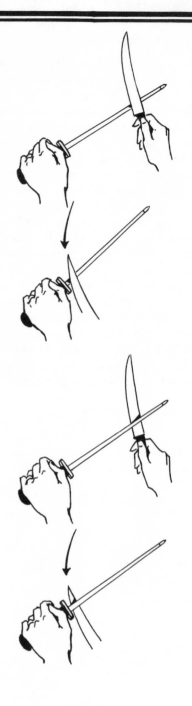

Place the heel of the knife blade against the tip of the steel at about a 20 degree or a 25 degree angle and draw the blade against the tip of the steel toward the left hand with a swift but careful motion of the wrist and forearm. Remember, keep your elbows still. The entire length of the blade should pass lightly over the steel.

Bring the knife back to the starting position—this time on the opposite side of the steel. Repeat the process on the alternate side of the steel until you have a good true edge.

There are a couple of other ways of using a steel which, while not quite as effective as the standard described earlier and no where near as flashy, can get the job done without the fear of getting "hurt."

1) Hold the steel out in front of you like a stick you are whittling and whittle it or pretend to take a slice out of the top of the steel; then the bottom. It is a little more difficult to maintain the ideal 20 degree angle this way but there is a little less likelihood of nicking the knuckle.

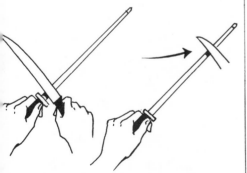

2) Put the point of the steel on the cutting board and hold it as you would if you were going to pound it into the wood. Run the knife down the steel first on one side then the other until the task is accomplished. Again, be careful of the angle and try to keep it at around a 20 or 25 degree angle. If you don't you're defeating your purpose.

To test the sharpness of a knife hold a sheet of paper between the thumb and forefinger and take a slice out of it with the full edge of the blade. A sharp knife will cut through the paper like a whiz, a dull knife will tear. After you have a bit of experience you can test for sharpness by moving the ball of your thumb lightly over the edge, but this is not recommended for amateurs. If you do a good job with the steel but have a heavy touch with the thumb, it can definitely hurt!

Types of Steels

There are several different types of steels and almost certainly the one you have, the one that came with the carving set, is the wrong type. Most "home-type" steels are much too rough and give the knife a saw-toothed edge.

The steel that hangs off a hook on the belt of a guy who makes his living boning necks in a packing house is as smooth as a mirror and the knife he uses is as sharp as a razor.

Between the rough steel that came with the carving set and the mirror smooth finish of a packing house steel, there is just the right steel for your purpose. It has a medium surface, not smooth but nearer to that than coarse. It is 10 or 12 inches in length and may be either round, flat or oval in shape.

Seldom in this book have I or will I recommend anything by specific brand name. There are almost always many more than one good product to fill the bill. I'm sure such is the case with steels—there are many good ones. And yet, I wouldn't be telling it as I feel it, if I didn't single out one company which has, since the beginning of time (as I know it), been making the best steel going. They make a good knife too, but there are lots of those. For my money there is but one steel →F. DICK. Ask any butcher you know who made his steel.

Knife Racks

One of the *most* important pieces of equipment used to keep a sharp knife sharp, an absolute must in any kitchen where there is a good sharp knife, is some kind of some place to keep it that way. Bouncing around in a drawer full of kitchen gadgets is enough to take the edge off any knife. There are all kinds of good knife racks available that can do the job and at the same time blend into your kitchen decor.

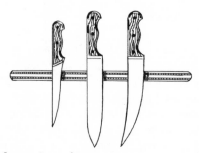

Magnetic racks are inexpensive and easy to install, but most of those I have seen would best be used for your lightweight paring knives and not your good sharp 10- or 12-inch "Big Knives." Make sure the magnet has a good strong pull if you expect it to hold your big knives.

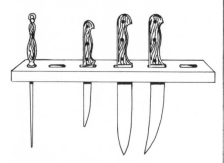

Old-fashioned "slotted wood racks," like the kind that used to hang on the side of the butcher block, are my favorite type of knife rack. They are available in most hardware and department stores but they are also very easy to construct on your own with a few pieces of hardwood. They have the obvious advantage over the magnetic rack in that once a knife is in place, it's not going to fall off. Most of them also have the added advantage of a special place to keep your steel. Once you get used to using good sharp knives, you will want that steel handy all of the time.

Knife racks come in all sizes and shapes so finding one to do the job should not be difficult. However, should all else fail, here is an effective method of storing knives in your kitchen drawer.

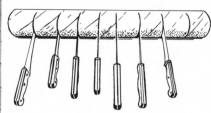

Take the cardboard tube from the center of the roll of paper towels. Make slots in it at appropriate intervals, clear a spot in your kitchen drawer and use the cardboard tube as a rack to keep your good sharp knives protected and away from all that other junk.

Cleaning

We have established the fact that bouncing around in a drawer full of kitchen gadgets is not too good for a good knife. It is equally true of bouncing around in a sink full of dirty dishes. Not only is that not good for the knife, it is very dangerous for whoever is doing the dishes.

The best way to clean a good sharp knife is carefully—very carefully, after each use. Simply wipe the blade with a damp cloth or sponge. Hold the knife so that the back of the blade is toward the palm of your hand and wipe from the handle to the tip. Dry it the same way with a dry towel and put it away.

Knives with wooden handles require a bit of special tender loving care from time to time—but for my money they're worth it. *Never* soak a knife with a wooden handle in water and never *ever* put it in the dishwasher. There are good knives with plastic handles that can stand up to that kind of treatment but not wooden handle knives. Even under the best and most gentle cleaning care, a wooden handle will eventually become a bit dry and discolored. This is because with use the natural oils have been washed out of the wood. Every once in awhile, when the wooden handles of your good sharp knives begin to look a little grey and dried out—oil them. Simply rub a drop of cooking oil into the handles with the palm of your hand. They will look like new again and they will last much longer. If you take care of your knives, they'll last you a lifetime!

Chopping Blocks

Little thought is given to the surface upon which a knife is used. And yet, nothing has more effect on the duration of a cutting edge. One swipe of a good sharp knife blade across the edge of a china serving platter and that "good sharp knife" is just a "good knife," the "sharp" got lost somewhere.

The only surface upon which meat should be cut, carved, disjointed, dissected or whatever you want to call it, is *wood*. Some type of carving board, cutting board, chopping block or wooden work table should be a standard part of any well equipped kitchen. These need not be expensive, although a real "butcher's block" or a fancy maple counter is likely to be. My Grandmother used a cross-section from an old mulberry tree for years. The typical Chinese or Japanese chopping block is to this day, nothing more than a good thick slice of hard wood.

There is an advantage to using a cutting board made of a cross-section of a tree or one with a "butcher block" type surface, where the wood is laminated together in such a way that the *cross cut ends* of the wood provide the cutting surface.

A cutting board or chopping block so constructed like the cross-section of a log allows the knife to cut into the surface of the wood with no damage to the knife or to the wooden surface.

The grains of the wood separate to allow the cutting edge to penetrate and return to their original position when the blade is removed.

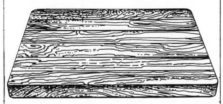

Cutting boards constructed so that the knife cuts across the grain of the wood are a good second choice. They are apt to be a little less expensive, but they wear out faster, since the surface once cut into is permanently scarred. Even so, a good one will last the better part of a lifetime if you take care of it.

Care of a Cutting Board

In the market we throw a handful of clean sawdust on the block and scrape it with a wire brush, then a "block scraper." Finally it gets wiped with a damp cloth. Seldom, if ever, does it get wet. That kind of cleaning works fine in the meat market where the only thing you use the chopping block for is cutting meat.

But in the kitchen, where you are apt to use the same cutting board for cutting meat, making salads, rolling out pie dough, etc., it is extremely important that you wash it well with hot soapy water after using it to cut fresh meat. Don't soak it in water, that softens the wood, but do wash it well. Then dry it immediately before putting it away.

Of course it is impossible to keep a cutting board from absorbing some water in the on-going process of use and cleaning over the years. Eventually even with the best of care you may have to "Salt It." "Salting" is an old butcher's trick to keep a block from getting soft. After a few months or years of good hard use, even with proper care, a block will begin to soften. The knife will begin to sink deeper than it should when you cut against the surface of the block. To harden it up again "Salt It."

Spread a thick layer of ordinary table salt over the entire surface of the block and let it stand overnight.

The next day scrape it off and clean as usual. The salt draws the moisture out of the block and hardens it for another few months or years of use.

Plastic Cutting Boards: The magic of modern science and industry is having its effect on the traditional wooden butcher blocks of the meat industry, just as it is on the old fashion butcher himself. Most modern meat markets don't have wooden blocks anymore, they have blocks made of plastic. Plastic is easier to keep clean; you don't ever have to salt it or scrape it, just scrub it. In many parts of the country local Health Departments have made them mandatory in meat markets. But somehow the old market isn't the same without the old wooden butcher block.

Plastic blocks are available now for kitchen use. They come in all colors and you can even run them through the dishwasher. But as far as this nostalgic butcher is concerned, they have all the charm of a paper plate.

Need to Have

Aside from the basic tools of the trade, there are a few items that you Need to Have in any kitchen where there is a concern for saving money on meat:

Meat Grinder

One of the best money-saving gadgets that you'll find in any kitchen, you'll not find in many kitchens today. Back in the days when Great Grandma was a girl they were as common as butter churns and used as often, but today if you find one at all, it will very likely be buried at the back of the bottom cupboard and seldom ever used. Now I'm not one to recommend a lot of kitchen gadgets, most of them are (for my money) a waste of money.

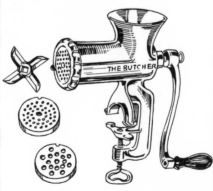

A good old-fashioned meat grinder is one of the few that are worth the price. It doesn't have to be one of the new fangled electric things that doubles as a mixer, knife sharpener, shoe polisher, and vibrator; a simple inexpensive hand-crank type not only will do, but it will probably do it better. Grandmother used to use hers to make her own sausage and head cheese and souse. She made her own mincemeat for Thanksgiving pies and ground up goose livers for pâtés. But what good, you ask, will one do you? Let me count the ways:

• Use it to make creative and economic use of leftovers.

• Grind up leftover Beef or Corned Beef roasts for hash or croquettes.

• Turn leftover ham into ham salad to stuff a tomato or spread on a sandwich.

• If you're one who likes to have your meat ground fresh while you watch, you'll get more of what you pay for if you buy the cut you like and grind it yourself. Most commercial meat grinders are so large that several ounces of whatever the butcher ground last will remain in the grinder to be pushed out first when he grinds yours.

- When Chuck Roast is on special in your local supermarket at a particularly good price, buy a couple, bone them out, make a good rich soup from the bones and grind the meat a couple of times through your old-fashioned meat grinder for some of the best Ground Chuck you've ever tasted and at a very good price.

- Bologna by the chunk is always less expensive than sliced bologna. You can make a sandwich spread guaranteed to make a hit with the kids by grinding up chunk bologna followed by a few sweet gherkins and a half an onion. Mix it all with enough mayonnaise to moisten and check the price of sandwich spread next time you're in the market to see how much money you saved.

If your Great Grandmother didn't leave you a grinder, and you'd better check the back of the bottom cupboard just to be sure, there are some very good and inexpensive ones on the market today. Look for the kind that had the interchangeable face plates, so that you can choose between course, medium and fine grinds as your needs dictate. While you're at it, pick up a sausage stuffing tube to fit on the front—just in case you get inspired someday.

Stockpot

Another simple money-saving gadget that is a must in any kitchen where good food and saving money are trying to "make it" together, is a good big Stockpot. They used to be a standard fixture in every kitchen, and in any kitchen where keeping costs down is at all a concern they still are. Stockpots come in all sizes, but to do any good as far as making stock is concerned, as well as to be of any use for a lot of other uses, you will need at least an eight-quart size.

The best place to find one selling for less than an arm and a leg is in a restaurant supply store. It doesn't need to be anything fancy like copper or have a pretty purple enamel exterior or anything. Just a plain big old heavy aluminum pot with a lid will work fine. Don't kick too much if the cost is a bit more than you expected, a good heavy stockpot will last long enough to pass on to your grandchildren and it can save you money for generations.

Meat Thermometer

Another gadget that can save you money on the meat you buy *if* you use it, is a Meat Thermometer. They come in three different styles and any one of the three is far better than none at all. As unfortunately is so often the case, the best kind is the most expensive. That's why I don't have one. That's the kind that you don't leave in the meat you simply use it to take an instant testing of the internal temperature whenever you think the time is right. As I said these are expensive, but they can't be beat for accuracy.

The other two types work essentially the same way, and which you choose is largely a matter of personal preference. One has a dial face, the other is a glass thing with red stuff in it like the one the doctor puts under your tongue. Of the two the dial faced one is the easier to read, but the glass one with the red stuff inside is perhaps a bit more accurate.

We will discuss how to use a meat thermometer later, at this point the point is to encourage you to have one.

Nice To Have

Aside from the few tools that are absolutely essential and a few more that you "need-to-have," there are a number that, while it's possible to do without them, are "nice-to-have."

Wooden mallets are nice for whopping and pounding all kinds of things into thinner things or a bit more tender things. Meat tenderizers are available to make your own cube steaks; a meat saw is nice, they come in a variety of sizes and, like most butcher equipment, they are available from butcher supply stores. You can, however, do a lot of kitchen cutting-up with a plain old hack saw.

If you plan on stuffing anything —don't laugh, you may before we're through—you'll need a stuffing tube. They come to fit most meat grinders, or you can get hand stuffers for stuffing stuff by hand.

It may sound like an extravagance, but an electric meat slicer might be a good investment, particularly if you do a lot of entertaining. It is possible with one of these modern gadgets to slice Roast Beef, for example, considerably thinner than it is possible to do by hand, even with a good sharp knife. You can, therefore, get many more servings per pound; they're "nice to have."

A good heavy meat cleaver is also a "nice-to-have," it looks great hanging on the wall. It is, however, not really essential. We have several hanging on the wall at the market but they haven't been used much since the invention of the electric saw, except for opening cans.

One thing that probably should be categorized with the "need-to-have's" rather than here with the "nice-to-have's," is a ball of cotton string. It's a *must* for doing any roast rolling or "stuff" stuffing, and we'll be doing a lot of both. Any good strong cotton string is fine, even kite string is okay as long as it's not coated with something that will melt when you cook it.

For carving it is not only "nice" but a big saving as far as knives are concerned to have a few wooden inserts for your carving platter. These are inexpensive and useful for much more than they were designed to be used for. They are great for serving cheese, fruit, bread or a fruit cake at Christmas, besides being inserted under the goose to be carved.

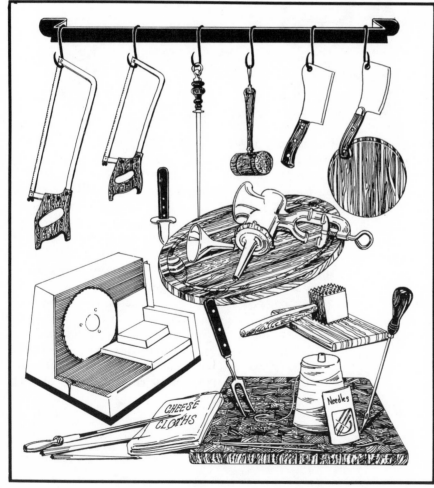

Larding Needles

These are "nice-to-have" these days and they may become absolutely essential before long. Larding needles were a standard piece of kitchen equipment back in the days when Grandma was a girl. Back in those days, meat was considerably leaner and tougher than it is today; and anyone who was concerned with good meat-eating understood the basic fact that—"fat makes meat taste good." Therefore, in those days every good cook had and made regular use of a Larding Needle.

You won't find them in many kitchen drawers these days; they haven't been needed for years. Most of the meat that has come to market since the end of World War II has been adequately "marbled" with fat and there was little need to insert more for flavor's sake. In recent years many consumers have become more concerned with cholesterol than with quality. As a result the meat industry is producing leaner meat. If you are one who wants good flavor, you may do well to do what Grandma did—get a larding needle and use it.

They come in a variety of forms, but the simplest to use is one with a wooden handle and a long trench-shaped steel blade. The fat to be inserted is simply laid in the trough and pushed through the meat. When the needle is withdrawn, the fat is left in the meat where it can add some flavor.

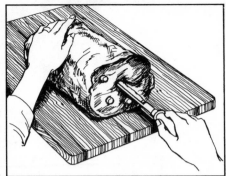

Probably the best fat for larding a Roast of Beef is the fresh back fat of pork. It's smooth and solid, and cuts nicely into "lardoons"—that's fancy French for strips of fat. If your local butcher doesn't have back fat, salt pork or bacon can be used, but you may want to "blanch" it before larding.

Larding can add all manner of interesting flavors to the middle of meat. One of the tastiest Beef Roasts I've ever tasted was a boneless Sirloin tip larded with anchovy filets. Larding can also add a bit of visual interest to a roast, providing a surprise and attractive design inside the meat. But primarily, larding is to provide the fat that is needed for flavor.

While we're on the subject of fat, I should point out the difference between "Larding" and "Barding." Both involve fat, but one (larding) puts the fat *inside* the meat where it flavors the meat; while the other (barding) puts the fat on the *outside* where the best it can do is flavor the gravy. Many markets around the country make a practice of tieing a sheet of fat around the outside of a roast "to keep it from drying out during cooking." All they're doing is selling you fat at Beef Roast prices! Fat on the outside does little to flavor the meat inside. Don't pay good money for fat that does you little good. If you are among those of us who appreciate the fact that fat makes meat taste good and the meat you are buying doesn't have much natural "marbling," put some fat where it does the most good, *in* the meat not on it. Use a larding needle, they're "nice to have!"

Speaking of needles, a couple of regular sewing needles are handy to have around the kitchen for trussing and sewing up things. You can buy needles specially for sewing meat, but almost any needle with an eye big enough to hold your kitchen string will work fine.

One final word about tools. When you buy them, buy them for your grandchildren. If a piece of basic kitchen equipment doesn't look like it will last at least that long, don't buy it. It's too expensive!

TRICKS OF THE TRADE

Chapter 3

There really aren't any tricks, no magic, no mysteries to cutting meat, in the meat market or in the kitchen, but there are a few things that we as butchers have learned over the years that make the whole project easier. I think I can pass along a few without fear of giving out trade secrets.

How to Keep Your Fingers!

A nick on the finger now and then is something of an occupational disease to a butcher. But most of them will tell you they usually get cut when they get careless. If you keep your knives sharp, take your time and watch what you're doing, there is no need to get "wounded in action." A couple of words of precaution:

1) Don't leave a knife lying on the block where it can get covered with anything. A knife you can't see is dangerous! For the same reason, don't drop a sharp knife into a sink full of dish water and then stick your hand in to feel for it.

2) Don't try to catch a knife if it falls. If you drop one or it gets knocked off the counter, throw your hands in the air, as if somebody had a gun in your ribs, and let it fall. For some reason, when a knife falls the blade suddenly becomes 14 times as large as the handle. Your chances of catching it without cutting yourself are totally non-existent. Don't try!

After you get the hang of holding a knife it will become almost like an extension of your arm. You will know where the tip and the edge are at all times and you'll be able to keep them away from your fingers. That's when you need to be careful. Don't let your confidence make you careless!

How to Hold a Knife

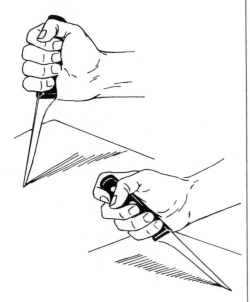

Everybody knows that you hold a knife by the handle just like you hold a hammer or a hoe, but there are a few subtleties that can save you some time and energy. For much of the cutting and boning we'll be doing with the small boning knife, it will help if you learn to reverse the direction of the knife in your hand so that you can push and pull and cut toward you and away from you. It's easier to turn the knife than to be continually turning the meat.

There isn't the need to hold your big knife in the variety of ways you do your boning knife. A good firm grip on the handle will do the job. It does help, however, in cutting through a piece of meat with your big knife, to push before you pull.

Start by pushing down and forward, then finish the cut by pulling back. Keep the downward pressure constant and you will make a nice clean cut without a lot of rough, jagged edges.

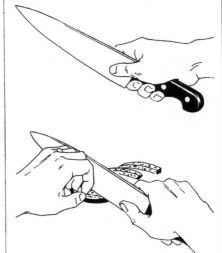

Making a French Chef's knife do all the magic it is capable of doing requires a different kind of grip. Hold it with your hand over the handle so that your fingers can control the angle of the blade. Then, by tucking the fingers of your other hand under and out of the way, you can rest the blade of the Chef's knife against your fingers and chop away with amazing speed and safety. The knife is constructed in such a way that you can rock it on its tip, using the back half of the blade for cutting. There's a bit of a trick to it, but it's well worth practicing a bit. Once you've mastered using one you can dump half a drawer full of kitchen gadgets.

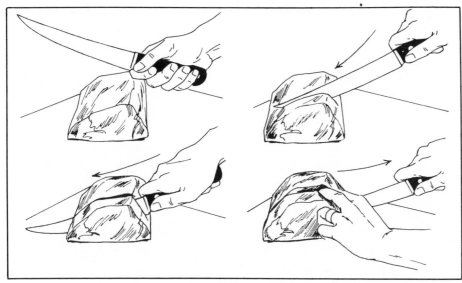

How to Tie a Butcher's Knot

You can roll a roast or tie up a turkey with almost any kind of knot, but the "butcher's knot" can save you time. It goes fast once you get the hang of it.

1) Holding the end of the string in your right hand, run the string under the roast.

2) Bring the string down across the top of the roast and transfer the bottom string to your right hand.

3) Holding both strings in your right hand, reach under the bottom string and grasp the top string between your thumb and first two fingers.

4) Bring the top string down and under the bottom string, at the same time twist your left hand around to form a loop in the string.

5) Put the end of the string through the loop, forming a slip knot.

6) Cinch the knot up tight.

7) Then to hold the knot in place, form another loop around the thumb and forefinger of your left hand, grasp the end of the string and pull it through.

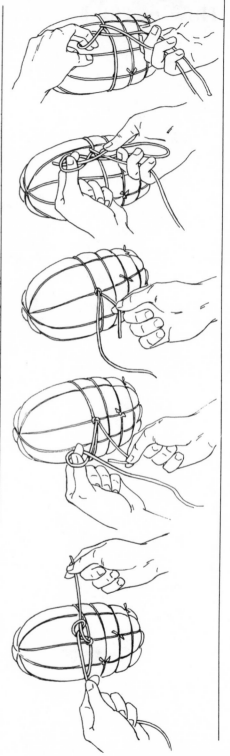

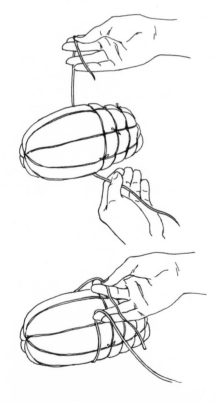

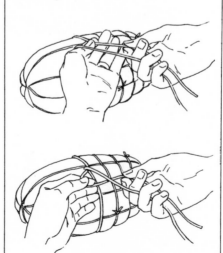

How to Sew a Crooked Seam

There will be times with certain cuts of meat that you may want to roll or stuff or stuff and roll, when simply tieing won't hold it all together. You'll need to sew it up. The stitch described below, works on all kinds of stuff; a seamstress may recognize it as an "edging" or "buttonhole" stitch.

1) First run the needle and string through both pieces of meat to be sewed together and secure with a knot.

2) Now, start sewing. A couple of inches from where you first put the needle through, do it again.

3) Now, catch the string as shown, move an inch or so and sew another stitch. Keep on sewing, pulling each stitch tight as you go, until you are all the way around whatever you're going around.

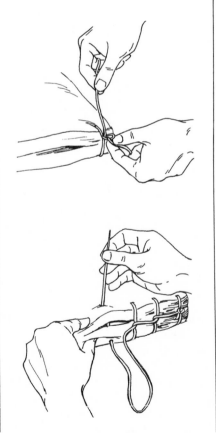

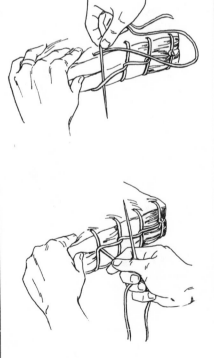

A Bit About Bones

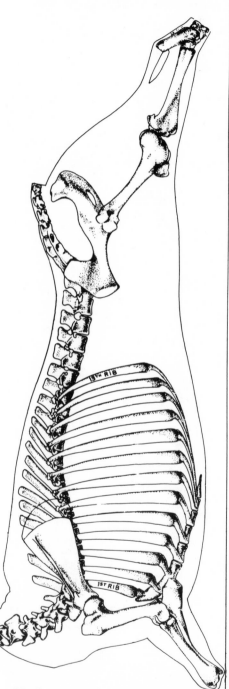

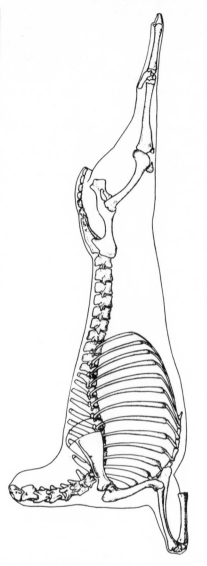

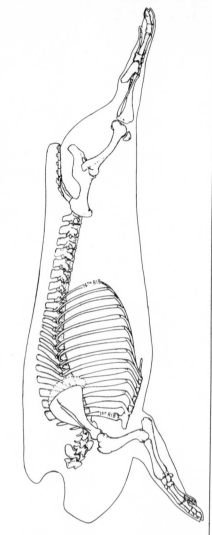

Nat'l Livestock and Meat Board.

Whether you're faced with carving a Leg of Lamb, boning out a Shoulder of Pork, or simply selecting the best Sirloin Steak from the pile in the supermarket meat case, knowledge of the basic bone structure of the meat can be a big help. It's not really as difficult as it may seem. Once you've boned-up on one kind of animal, you've got it all because the basic bone structure of beef, lamb, veal and pork is about the same.

Beyond the obvious fact the knowledge of bone structure tells you where to put your knife, there are other advantages. It can be equally important when you're shopping for meat. It can tell you where best to put your money. The shape of the bone can tell you where a particular cut came from on the carcass—a major factor in judging how tough or tender it is likely to be.

Those most tender cuts from the

Loin, whether from beef, pork, lamb or veal, all have the same shaped bones. Porterhouse and T-Bone Steaks from the beef, as well as Loin Chops of lamb, veal or pork, all contain a cross section of the backbone.

The backbone has three main parts: the *feather* bone and *chine* bone which are both part of the spine, and the *finger* bone which extends out from

of pork, for example, that have been cut from between two ribs and contain no rib bone.

Rib section cuts, like those of the Loin, consist of the feather bone and the chine bone, but the finger bone is replaced by the rib.

So far, learning a bit about bones is fairly simple stuff, but it gets a little more complicated as we move from the back of the animal to the hip and shoulder. And it's in these areas where your need to know is

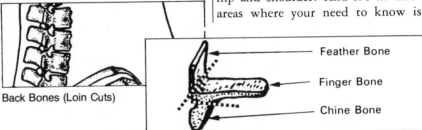

Back Bones (Loin Cuts)

Feather Bone

Finger Bone

Chine Bone

the spine separating the top loin muscle from the tenderloin underneath. It's important that you get a fix on these parts of the backbone. Before we have you boning out a Loin of Lamb or performing other wonders of the butcher's art, we need to be speaking the same language.

most critical. As you move away from the back of any animal, either forward to the shoulder or aft to the rump, the meat attached to the bones becomes increasingly less tender. By knowing which cut came off the animal closest to the tender stuff, you can best select the cuts apt to be less tough.

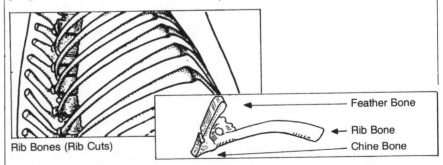

Rib Bones (Rib Cuts)

Feather Bone

Rib Bone

Chine Bone

Cuts from the Rib portion of any animal most often contain one or more rib bones, although it is possible, on occasion, to find Rib Chops

Cuts from the Shoulder, for example, all contain some portion of the shoulder blade. The shape of the blade bone indicates how close to the tender Rib portion it was located, and therefore how tender it is likely to be.

In the cut nearest the Rib section, the blade bone is long and flat, per-

Shoulder Blade (shoulder cut)

haps with a bit of white cartilage at the narrow end. Toward the center section of the shoulder, the blade bone shortens and a ridge appears along the top side. As it progresses toward the less tender neck, the blade bone takes on an appearance vaguely resembling a figure "7," which accounts for cuts (particularly beef) taken from this section being called "7 Bone" cuts.

On the other end of the animal, the Sirloin section, the bone structure is complicated by the presence

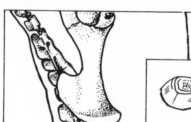

Hip Bones (Sirloin Cuts)

of the hip bone. Here again you can tell which cut originated nearest to the tender Loin portion by the appearance of the bone.

The hip bone first makes its appearance right next to the Loin and in nearly every cut from there to the leg, it has a different shape. The one nearest the Loin contains what is called the pin bone, the next cut or two contain the flat bone, then the round bone and finally nearest the leg, the wedge bone.

7-Bone (near neck)   Blade Bone (center cut)   Blade Bone (near rib)

Cuts from the leg of any animal contain the least bone, also the most simple one: one small round bone.

Pin Bone (near short loin)   Flat Bone and Round Bone (center cuts)   Wedge Bone (near round)

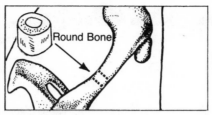

Round Bones (Leg Cuts)

The only indication a round bone gives of the tenderness of the meat around it is in its size. The less tender cuts near the knee will have a larger bone than those from the center of the Round.

The cuts from the front leg (or arm) of any animal also have a round bone. They may also have three or four rib bone pieces, although most often these are removed before selling, leaving only a round bone very similiar to that in the leg. The meat around the round bone of the arm is generally less tender, however, than the meat around the leg. Distinguishing one from the other requires more than a bit of knowledge about bones, it requires an understanding of basic animal anatomy. We will consider that—in detail—in the following chapters.

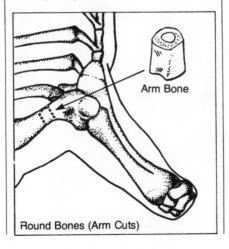

Round Bones (Arm Cuts)

41

BEEF

Chapter 4

"When I first began
To cut up oxen
I would see before me
The whole ox
All in one mass.
After three years
I no longer saw this mass,
I saw the distinctions. . . ."

That quotation is from an ancient Chinese Taoist poem entitled, *"Cutting Up An Ox."* Undoubtedly, the poem is meant to be taken symbolically. But, being a butcher by profession, I prefer to take it literally.

Prince Wen Hui's cook, he's the man quoted, saw what we all need to see if we are to shop wisely in the marketplace for today's oxen, which you can translate as beef. He "saw the distinctions."

He saw before him, on four legs and very likely with horns, the same Porterhouses, T-Bones, Beef Roasts and Briskets that you see in the meatcase of your supermarket.

But—since you don't have to worry about working around the horns and since most of the "mass" has already been cut up for you—it

43

shouldn't take you anywhere near three years to begin to "see the distinctions."

Why should you bother? Because the ability to distinguish one cut of meat from another in your butcher's meat case is a start toward becoming a better meat buyer. It enables you to make the kinds of decisions at the meat counter that can save you money and make you a better cook. These decisions involve choices and choosing means making distinctions.

Prince Wen Hui's cook had to study the whole ox though, before the distinctions became evident. We should, too. So it will help, I think, to begin by examining our "Ox" in the mass. Not "on the hoof," but as it appears to your butcher when it comes from the packing house. Beef comes to the back door of most meat markets in one of two forms, either as "carcass beef" or in "primal cuts."

Beef Primal Cuts

Beef never comes to the market with the whole carcass intact. Rather it is split into two "sides," in turn divided into "quarters," before leaving the packing house. A carcass of beef then, consists of four quarters: two forequarters—"fores"—and two hind-quarters—"hinds." Back in the days when Grandma was a girl, all of the cutting and processing necessary to get beef from this carcass stage to the meat case was done by the retail butcher. Increasingly in recent years, part of the "breaking" and cutting process is done at the packing house, producing what are known as primal or wholesale cuts.

There are nine primal cuts on a side of beef. On the "fore" there is the 1) *Chuck*, 2) *Rib*, 3) *Shank*, 4) *Brisket* and 5) *Short Plate*. The "hind" includes the 6) *Short Loin*, 7) *Sirloin*, 8) *Round* and 9) *Flank*. Understanding the relationship of one primal cut to another and which retail cuts come from which primal is a giant step toward knowing which are tough and which are tender, as well as which are your best retail buys.

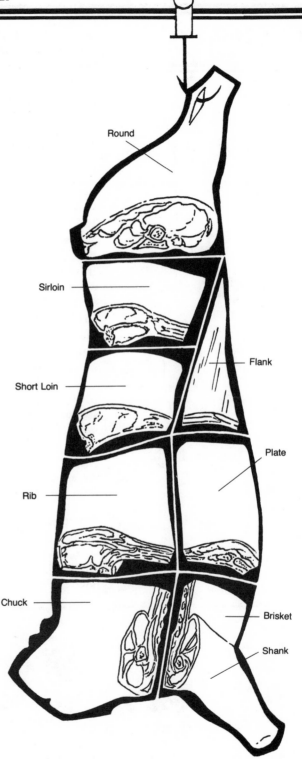

45

Short Loin

Let's begin our anatomical discussion with the Short Loin, the most naturally tender portion of the animal. The Short Loin lies between the small end of the Rib and the pin bone portion of the Sirloin. It is right in the middle of the back and does little more than lazily lie there and stay tender. As a result the Short Loin is the source of the best steaks the "Ox" has to offer. The Porterhouse, the T-Bone, the New York, Filet Mignon, Tournedos, Club Steaks, Kansas City Strips, Chateaubriand, to name a few, all come from the Short Loin. Considering that this most tender of all wholesale cuts comprises less than 10% of the carcass, the number of terms that have evolved to describe the various steaks cut from this portion of the animal seems inordinately voluminous.

If the Short Loin is merchandised with the bone in, the resulting cuts are easy for the consumer to recognize. Traditionally they are Porterhouse, T-Bone and Club Steak. The points of division between the three are somewhat arbitrary and may vary from one market to another.

Porterhouse is cut from the large end of the Short Loin next to the Sirloin and contains the largest portion of the tenderloin muscle. Depending on how thick they are cut, there will usually be only three or four Porterhouse Steaks on a Short Loin.

The *Club Steak* comes from the small end next to the Rib and contains no tenderloin muscle.

Somewhere in-between, with a portion of the tenderloin that varies from large to nonexistent, is the *T-Bone*.

The terms Porterhouse and T-Bone are often used interchangeably, with the only differences between the two being the thickness of the cut and perhaps the amount of "tail" left on the steak. Left meaning untrimmed. It's important to pay attention to the trim when buying any cut of meat, but considering the prices you pay for cuts of the Short Loin, trim becomes even more important. Most of us are on the lookout for large chunks of fat and bone that are obviously waste and avoid them. But we often pay a premium for a tough piece of T-Bone tail.

The tail on a Porterhouse or T-Bone is actually part of the Flank and not nearly as tender as the other muscles (the tenderloin and top loin muscles) of the same steak. They will broil to the desired degree of doneness in exactly the same time, but the tail will take considerably longer to chew. It may be money saved to pay a few pennies more per pound for T-Bone or Porterhouse with the tail completely

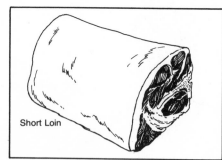

Short Loin

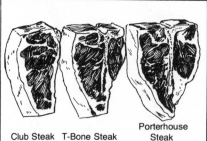

Club Steak   T-Bone Steak   Porterhouse Steak

removed.

When the butcher bones out the Short Loin and sells the boneless or nearly boneless cuts separately, merchandising madness begins. What was a Porterhouse becomes, with a flick of the blade, part and parcel of a lavish array of tender terminology.

Depending upon the part of the country you're in—and sometimes even which side of the street the market is on, the tenderloin muscle becomes Filet Mignon, Chateaubriand, Tournedos, Medallions or Filet de Boeuf depending on how well the butcher speaks French. Chateaubriand! Doesn't that term have class? It even sounds tender. It conjures up in the mind a meal by candle light with wine, soft music and beautiful company. It suggests elegance in a way that Hamburger couldn't possibly. Even T-Bone or Porterhouse sound somewhat second rate by comparison. It is definitely a classy tender term. You would expect, therefore, to pay more for it wouldn't you? You do! Most meat markets offering tender terms like that charge a bit more for them. It makes them taste better.

Actually Chateaubriand, like so many of those fancy tender sounding names in the meat case of your local supermarket, is NOT a cut of meat at all—it's a recipe. Unfortunately, far too many of my fellow butchers like those tender terms too well. They pick them up from cook books or fancy gourmet magazines and use them, often rather indiscriminately, to label cuts of meat in their meat cases. I have seen the term Chateaubriand used to label more than one cut of meat, and more often than not, not the same cut of meat called for in the classic recipe for Chateaubriand. In some markets Chateaubriand is a thick cut of boneless Top Sirloin, in others I have seen that "tender term" labeling a thick cut of Sirloin Tip.

It seems to me that if American butchers are going to use fancy French terms to "merchandise" meat, they should use them to label the *same* cut of meat called for in the fancy French cook book from which the name came. That seems only fair, doesn't it? Well, according to one of the most authoritative of fancy French cook books—*Larousse Gastronomique*, "Chateaubriand" is "a method of preparing a beef Filet." The recipe calls for a thick slice from the large section of a Beef Tenderloin. In America the whole Beef Tenderloin is often mis-

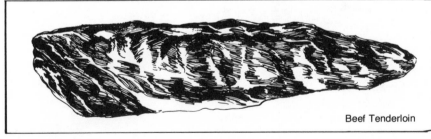

Beef Tenderloin

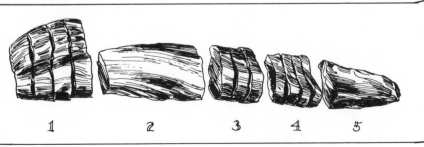

1   2   3   4   5

labeled according to fancy French standards. Here any cut of the Tenderloin is apt to be labeled Filet Mignon. That term in France applies only to the small end of the Tenderloin (5). Other cuts of the French Tenderloin are: (1) Bifteck, (2) Chateaubriand, (3) Filet Steak and (4) Tournedos.

The Tenderloin is the most tender cut of meat you will find in the cattle of any country. It is also the most expensive. But when you see one of those fancy French terms in a meat case in this country, *be careful*! Make sure you're not paying extra for little more than a tender term.

The top loin muscle becomes a New York Strip in Kansas City and Kansas City Strip in New York City and on Hollywood's Sunset Strip I've seen it called Delmonico Steak. On your side of the street it could be almost anything: Shell Steak, Hotel Steak, Sirloin Club Steak, Boneless Club Steak or Charlie's Gourmet Special. Whatever it's called, it too will be most definitely on the expensive side.

No matter how they're cut, the steaks of the Short Loin are going to be relatively expensive. However, if and when Filet de Boeuf, Beef Tournedos, Filet Mignon, Beef Tenderloin or any of those tender sounding steaks is on the menu and within your budget, the cut of meat to look for is Porterhouse.

You can save money, even on the most elegant and tender of steaks, if you do a little cutting on your own. When you want a really top quality and naturally tender steak for the most reasonable price, buy a **USDA Prime** or **Choice** Porterhouse. Preferably one at least 1½ or two inches thick, with a little "marbling" and hopefully with some "age." One such steak will amply serve three.

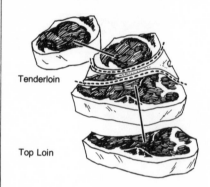

Tenderloin

Top Loin

Simply remove the bone, dividing the steak into A) the tenderloin and B) the top loin. Save the bone for stock. Then divide the top loin in half, making three thick tender steaks ready to broil or sauté to the desired degree of doneness. Serve with a good rich Bordelaise or Bernaise sauce and perhaps stuffed mushrooms. As to a name; since you cut it, call it what you will.

Sirloin—(Bone In)

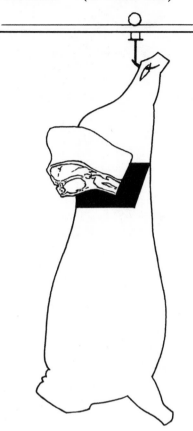

The Sirloin, like the Short Loin, is naturally tender. It lies just aft of the Short Loin between the Porterhouse and the Rump. The steaks from the Sirloin will not be quite as tender as those of the Short Loin—no steaks will—but they do qualify for dry-heat cooking.

Like those of the Short Loin, the various steaks cut from the Sirloin are fairly easy to identify if they are sold with the bone in.

The traditional names are taken from the shape of the hip bone contained in each.

Pin Bone Sirloin is the first steak off the Sirloin, right next to the Short Loin, just the thickness of the knife blade away from the Porterhouse. It has a large portion of the tenderloin muscle, a good-sized section of the top sirloin (a continuation of what was the top loin muscle in the Short Loin) and some portion of the Flank. The bone structure of the Pin Bone Sirloin is very like that of the Porterhouse or T-Bone in that it has a portion of the backbone. What it has (what all of the steaks of the Sirloin have) is a portion of the hip bone. In the Pin Bone Sirloin, the hip bone makes its first appearance. (See Bone Chart.)

Flat Bone Sirloin—As the hip bone widens out toward the tail on one side and the leg socket on the other (see Bone Chart), it flattens and joins with the backbone. In most markets the backbone is removed, leaving only the flat hip bone, explaining the name Flat Bone Sirloin. If the backbone is left in the steak it may be called a Double Bone Sirloin.

Round Bone Sirloin—Where the hip bone heads off in two directions (again see Bone Chart), one side toward the tail and the other side toward the hip socket, there is a Sirloin steak or two with a bone that is round. Hence the name of this cut. If all of the Sirloins in your butcher's meat case are selling at the same price, a Round Bone Sirloin is probably your best Sirloin buy. It has a good ratio of meat to bone and does not contain the gristle that you are apt to find in the next Sirloin Steak.

Wedge Bone Sirloin: As the hip bone widens out to form the socket where the leg bone is attached (back to the Bone Chart), a cross section of the Sirloin has a triangular or wedge-shaped bone. Basic meat market logic being what it is, this cut is called the Wedge Bone Sirloin. It is the least tender of the Sirloin steaks, being the farthest removed from the tender, lazy, middle of the back, known as the Short Loin. It is, therefore, somewhat undesirable unless the price is right. But the Wedge Bone Sirloin still qualifies as a naturally tender steak which can be cooked with dry heat.

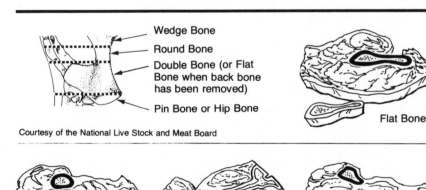

Wedge Bone
Round Bone
Double Bone (or Flat Bone when back bone has been removed)
Pin Bone or Hip Bone

Courtesy of the National Live Stock and Meat Board

Flat Bone

Round Bone   Pin Bone   Wedge Bone

Sirloin—Boneless

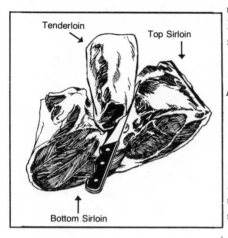

Tenderloin

Top Sirloin

Bottom Sirloin

More and more in recent years, butchers around the country are boning-out the Sirloin portion of the Loin (the Head Loin or Sirloin Butt, as it is sometimes called) and selling the various muscles separately. This makes identification a bit more difficult so *pay attention*.

There are only three basic parts that make up the Head Loin, but these three parts have been called by thirty times three different names. Even an experienced butcher can get lost in the maze of merchandising terminology that is used to describe them. Let's stick to the basics.

with one of those fancy tender French terms, like Filet Mignon or Tornedos, or it is left in one piece and sold as Chateaubriand. Either way it is going to be expensive since, as part of the tenderloin, it is part of the tenderest muscle of the "Ox." The Stub Tender out of a Head Loin will weigh about 1½ to two pounds, making it a perfect size for "Beef Wellington" for four, when and if your budget can afford it.

Top Sirloin: This is the largest muscle of the Sirloin, a continuation of the top loin muscle of the Short Loin. Depending, of course, upon how thick each is cut, the butcher will get three to six steaks from the Top Sirloin. They increase in size but decrease in tenderness as they get farther from the Short Loin and nearer to the Rump. Often the larger steaks are divided into serving-size portions.

Tenderloin: There is in the Head Loin a good-size portion of the tenderloin muscle. This "Stub Tender" or "Head Filet," as it is sometimes called, is either cut into steaks and dubbed

Ball Tip

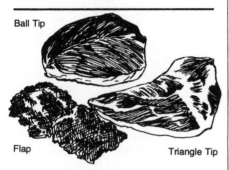

Flap

Triangle Tip

Triangle Tip (Culotte Steaks)

Bottom Sirloin: Actually the Bottom Sirloin is more a part of the Sirloin Tip portion of the Round. The amount of "bottom" left on the Sirloin depends on how the beef is "broke." If the butcher breaks a Chicago Round, more of the "bottom" will be left on the Loin than if he breaks a Diamond Round (see Beef Round illustration, pp. 57). It's particularly important that you get clued-in on the variables in the beef "breaking" process at this point. It can mean some really good savings if you understand what you're looking at. We'll talk more about that when we discuss the Sirloin Tip. Meanwhile, back to the "bottom." If a large portion of the Sirloin Tip is left on the Loin—Chicago-style—the Bottom Sirloin will contain three small muscles that are often sold separately.

The *Flap* is actually part of the Flank and is usually sold for stew meat or ground beef. Or it may be run a time or two through the tenderizing machine and be called a Cube Steak. It has a great flavor, but it's not tender enough to make it as a steak without help.

The *Bell Tip*, sometimes called the Ball Tip or Butcher's Heart, is a small portion of a larger muscle, the remainder of which is in the Sirloin Tip. It has a good flavor and can be broiled or barbecued along with the best of them, but you can probably buy it cheaper in the roast section of the meat counter as a Sirloin Tip Roast. (See page 60.) The Bell is often cubed for Kabobs or Sirloin Tips.

The *Triangle Tip* is a small muscle that, like the rest of the Bottom Sirloin, is often cut up in cubes and called Kabobs. If it is sold as steak, it may be labeled Coulotte Steak. It's a fairly tender muscle that may contain more "marbling" than other muscles of the Bottom Sirloin, and therefore will have a rich beef flavor.

The Rib

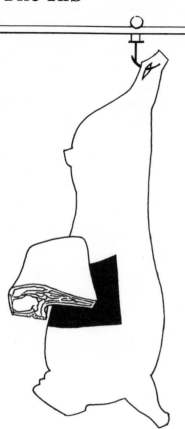

The *Rib* comes off the "Ox" just in front of the Short Loin, between the small end of the Short Loin and the Blade end of the Chuck.

Over the years there has developed a tendency in the trade to refer to this section as the "Prime Rib." Actually that's a misnomer. A Rib is only a Prime Rib if it comes from **USDA Prime** beef and you don't find many of those these days. I prefer to stick to the basic term Rib for our discussion. The Rib qualifies as naturally tender, comparable to the Loin cuts which can be cooked with dry heat. There are thirteen ribs in a whole beef carcass and usually seven of those are contained in the Rib. Here's the arithmetic. The first five ribs are in the Chuck. The thirteenth is left on the Short Loin when the carcass is divided into quarters at the packing house. The wholesale or primal Rib cut, then, contains the sixth through the twelfth rib.

There is much confusion and misunderstanding among butchers themselves as well as among butchers and customers over which rib is which.

Comments such as "I'd like the first three ribs of a Prime Rib," can lead to a lot of misinterpretation.

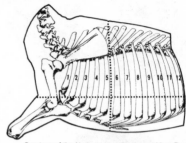

Courtesy of the National Live Stock and Meat Board

The accepted way to count ribs in all meat is to start at the front and count to the rear (See Chart). The first three ribs would then be ribs #6, 7, & 8, right next to the Chuck. That's certainly not what most folks want when they say, "I'd like the first three ribs. . . ." The 10th, 11th, & 12th are nearer the tender Short Loin and therefore the most desirable.

Perhaps a clearer way to keep track of which rib is which is to refer to the "large end" (the end next to the Chuck) and the "small end" (next to the Short Loin). Then, "Three ribs off

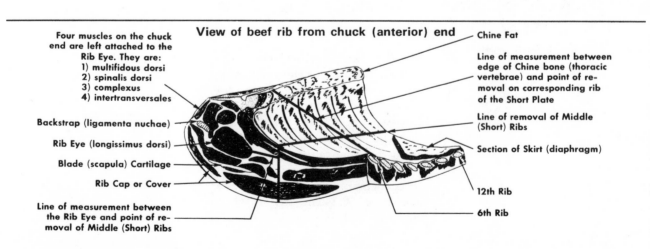

View of beef rib from chuck (anterior) end

Four muscles on the chuck end are left attached to the Rib Eye. They are:
1) multifidous dorsi
2) spinalis dorsi
3) complexus
4) intertransversales

Backstrap (ligamenta nuchae)

Rib Eye (longissimus dorsi)

Blade (scapula) Cartilage

Rib Cap or Cover

Line of measurement between the Rib Eye and point of removal of Middle (Short) Ribs

Chine Fat

Line of measurement between edge of Chine bone (thoracic vertebrae) and point of removal on corresponding rib of the Short Plate

Line of removal of Middle (Short) Ribs

Section of Skirt (diaphragm)

12th Rib

6th Rib

the small end'' will mean the same to butchers everywhere.

The Rib is merchandised in a variety of ways in meat markets around the country. A basic understanding of these merchandising techniques can save you money, particularly when it comes to finding a few great steaks at a bargain price.

Standing Rib—Probably the most common cut, certainly the most recognizable, that comes from the Rib is the Standing Rib Roast. This is the King of beef roasts in this country. In Europe portions of the Loin are often roasted, but in this country the Loin is usually used for steaks and the distinction of being the most naturally tender roast goes to the Rib. As I've mentioned before, the most tender portion of any cut of meat is the portion nearest the Short Loin. It contains a large portion of the tender ribeye muscle and the small end of the Rib is only the thickness of a knife blade away.

In selecting a Standing Rib ask for the small end. It may be a bit more expensive but it is the best. It should be trimmed so that the rib bones are no more than seven or eight inches in length, with the chine bone, feather bones and back strap removed. If not, carving will be a problem.

For a generous serving of Standing Rib, figure on two people per rib. That means if you plan to serve six you should be able to do so with a three rib roast; eight people, four ribs; and so forth. Don't even bother with less than a three-rib roast, any less than that is not a roast but rather a thick steak and would be better treated as such.

Rib Steak—All or part of the Rib is, in most markets, also sold for steaks. If they are sliced off the Rib with the bone in, their price should reflect

View of beef rib from loin (posterior) end

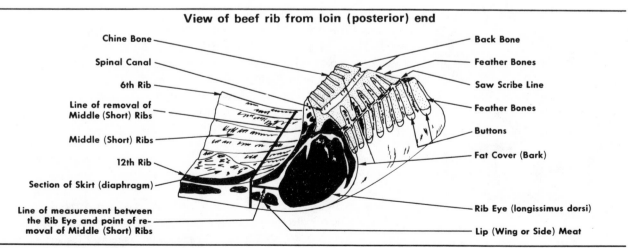

Chine Bone
Spinal Canal
6th Rib
Line of removal of Middle (Short) Ribs
Middle (Short) Ribs
12th Rib
Section of Skirt (diaphragm)
Line of measurement between the Rib Eye and point of removal of Middle (Short) Ribs

Back Bone
Feather Bones
Saw Scribe Line
Feather Bones
Buttons
Fat Cover (Bark)
Rib Eye (longissimus dorsi)
Lip (Wing or Side) Meat

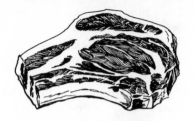

their quality. Those from the small end of the Rib—next to the Short Loin—have a large portion of the tender "eye" muscle and none of the less tender rib cap muscle (see Rib Chart). You would expect to pay more for them than for the larger steaks off the end next to the Chuck. As the steaks from the Rib get larger, the amount of tender Rib "eye" gets smaller. The price you are asked to pay should reflect that. If all of the Rib Steaks in your butcher's meat case are priced the same, don't hesitate to dig through the display in search of the small ones with the big "eye."

Rib Eye—In more and more markets these days, the Rib is being "muscle boned." That means that the various muscles are separated along the natural seams that divide them and all bones are removed. Each muscle is then sold separately, priced according to its desirability and natural tenderness. Without question, the Rib Eye is the most naturally tender and desirable portion of the Rib. The Rib Eye is a continuation of that tender muscle that runs along the back from the shoulder to the hip. In the Sirloin it's called the Top Sirloin, in the Short

Loin it's called the Top Loin; in the Rib, for some incomprehensible reason, it's called the "Eye."

The Rib Eye is sold both as a roast and as steaks. Either way, it is an exceptionally good, tender, tasty piece of meat. The Rib will have a bit more marble than the other cuts of the same animal and, therefore, is apt to have more flavor, since fat and flavor go together. In various parts of the country Boneless Rib Eye Steaks are called Delmonico Steaks, Spencer Steaks, Market Steaks, Beauty Steaks, and Rib Filets, to name a few. Whatever they are called, they will likely be expensive. When the Eye is seamed out for sale as some fancy roast or steaks there results a couple of other spare parts of the Rib that are then also sold separately.

Rib Lifters or *Rib Caps* are the muscles on top of the Eye. They are not as tender as the Eye, and are usually sold as Boneless Short Ribs, or Stew, or they may be added to the lean ground beef trimmings. They are tender enough, however, to be sliced thinly across the grain and used for stir fry or sauté recipes.

Rib Bones: The Rib Bones are often sold as Barbecue Beef Ribs or Beef Back Ribs. My kids love them; they call them "Dinosaur Bones."

It is a common practice in many markets to sell the Rib Roast—small end—at one price and the Rib Roast —large end—at another. When such is the case, the large end will always be the less expensive of the two. You can make some real savings by doing a little of your own cutting-up.

The roast will very likely have had the chine bone and feather bones already removed. If not, ring the bell and ask the butcher to do that for you. The rest you can do yourself.

First, separate the Rib Eye from the cap meat or Rib lifters. This is a simple task, accomplished more by gently pulling the meat apart at the natural seams than by any very fancy knifework. After trimming all the excess fat off the cap meat, set it aside to use for stews or ragouts, or any recipe using moist heat. Or, if the meat is sliced thinly across the grain, it will be tender enough for all kinds of other dishes like Stroganoff, or for Chinese stir-fry recipes.

Next remove the Rib bones. Leave a little meat on them. There probably won't be enough bones from one roast to make a meal, so wrap what you have up and place in the freezer. When a few more accumulate, they'll be great barbecued.

The Rib Eye can be roasted or sliced into steaks of the thickness you like. They'll be every bit as good as the ones the butcher calls "Market Steaks" or "Spencer Steaks." You can be sure they will be a lot less expensive.

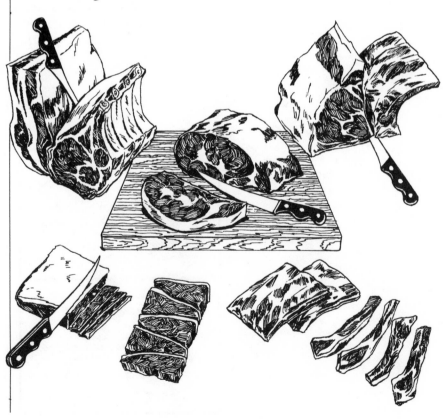

Round

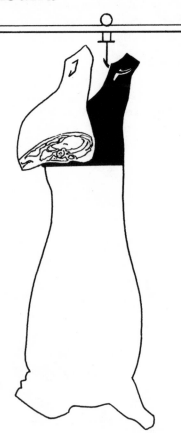

So far, in our discussion of the "Ox," we have been talking about those naturally tender cuts that are usually in great demand and therefore always expensive. The Short Loin, Rib and Sirloin combined comprise less than 30% of the animal, so they are usually in short supply. This helps to account for their high price.

The Round is another story. The primal round alone makes up nearly 25% of the carcass. It is, therefore, in much greater supply. It also falls largely into the category of less tender, and is therefore not so much in demand. Large supply and low demand account for the fact that the Round is often one of the best buys in your butcher's meat case. I would be willing to bet that not a week goes by when some cut of the Round isn't "on special" in a market in your neighborhood. This makes it a good part to get to know.

The Round is the part of the hind leg extending from the wedge bone end of the Sirloin to the ground. It contains four separate muscles, the Top Round, the Bottom Round, the Eye of Round and the Tip. Each varies in tenderness from quite tender, through less tender, to downright tough. It depends upon the proximity to the Short Loin on the Tender side and the ground on the other.

How the cuts of the Round appear in your butcher's meat case depends largely upon how the beef was "broken" at the packing house or in the back room.

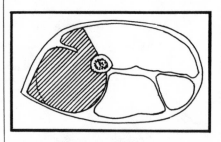

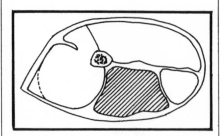

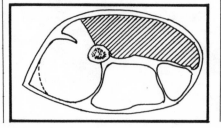

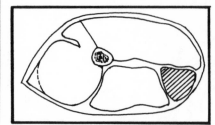

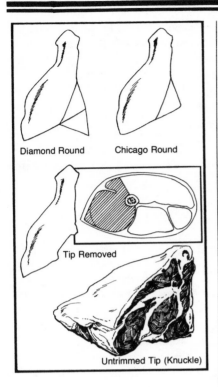

Diamond Round Chicago Round

Tip Removed

Untrimmed Tip (Knuckle)

In the western half of the U.S. it is common to "break" what is known in the trade as a "Diamond Round." That is, when the Loin is separated from the Round, a large portion of the Tip is left on the Round (see illustration). In the East they "break" a "Chicago Round," leaving a larger portion of the Tip on the Loin. In either case the only muscle affected is the Tip, which, in almost all cases, will be removed from the Round and merchandised separately.

The other three muscles, the Top, Bottom and Eye are those most often thought of as the Round. Before we discuss each of these separately, first a bit about bones. The Round contains three major bones, the rump (aitch) bone, the round (leg) bone and the hind shank bone (see Bone Chart). There is also a small amount of tail bone and a piece of the hock, but these never end up in the meat case so we can disregard them.

When the Round is merchandised with the bones in, the various cuts are, as always, easy to identify.

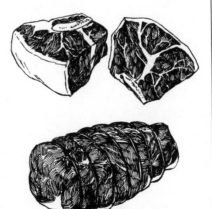

Rump: The whole Rump portion, containing the aitch bone, is removed

and divided into two or three bone-in Standing Rump Roasts. Or, the bone is removed and the Rump is rolled. Either way the Rump is tender enough to be cooked with dry heat, since it comes off the "Ox" right next to the tender Loin portion.

Round Steak: After the Rump has been removed, the Round is cut into steaks. These "Full Cut Round Steaks" are large slabs of meat, each containing a portion of all three muscles of the Round. They vary as far as tenderness is concerned in two ways. 1) Each muscle has its own degree of tenderness and 2) all three become less tender the closer they get to the "heel." The combination of tough and tender within each steak has put Round Steak into the category of less tender in the minds of most cooks, so the recommended cooking procedure usually calls for moist heat. Actually, since there are parts that are tender enough to be cooked with dry heat, there is an increasing tendency for butchers to merchandise the three muscles of the Round separately.

Top Round: The Top Round is the most tender part of the Round. It lies on the inside of the leg and therefore does less work and stays more tender. When the Top Round is merchandised separately, it is usually sliced into steaks and often labeled with a lot of tender terms. The first cut off the Top Round, the one right next to the Sirloin, is often cut thick, then mislabeled "Butterball Steak" or "London Broil" and sold at a premium. The center cuts are usually cut thinner and called simply Top Round. The "heel" portion of the Top Round is cut up for kabobs or stew or used for ground beef.

Again following that axiom of meat-buying, the closer to the Short Loin, the more tender. In the Top Round, the first cut is the closest and the most tender, the heel is the farthest away and the least tender. You can easily tell where each steak came from on the Top Round if you learn the muscle structure and apply your learning at the meat case. A case in point: about mid-way through the Top Round, a second muscle appears on top of the main muscle (see illustration). While at first it's quite small, it gets larger as the steak gets closer to the heel. So, in selecting a Top Round Steak from a pile, look for the one with the *smallest* amount of that second muscle.

Top Round is generally tender enough to cook with dry heat—if you treat it right. Don't cook it at too high a heat and don't overcook. (Anything past medium rare begins to toughen any muscle, so it is definitely to be avoided here.) But Top Round is a good choice for those recipes that call for thin slices of lean meat to be cooked quickly, such as Stroganoff or sauté and stir-fry recipes.

The *Bottom Round* (Outside Round): More than any other portion of the Round, the Bottom Round varies greatly in tenderness from one end to the other. The pointed Rump end comes off the carcass just a knife blade away from the Sirloin and qualifies for dry-heat cooking. The lower end of the Bottom is pretty close to the ground and can be helped along a great deal in cooking by the addition of a little moisture.

The Bottom is usually merchandised in one of two ways. Either it is sliced into steaks for Swiss Steak or it is left in larger pieces and sold as Rump Roasts or Bottom Round Roasts. The larger pieces usually cost less per pound, so when Swiss Steak is on your menu, check the Roast counter. Very likely, you'll save money.

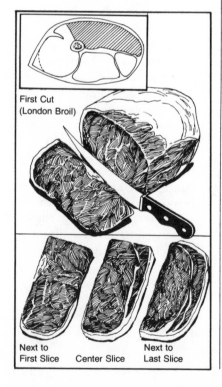

First Cut
(London Broil)

Next to
First Slice   Center Slice   Next to
Last Slice

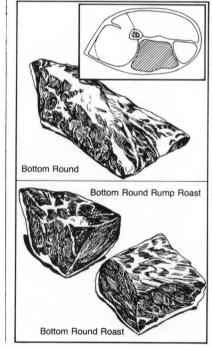

Bottom Round

Bottom Round Rump Roast

Bottom Round Roast

The Bottom Round, being a single, solid muscle, is a good choice when you want thin slices for stuffing and rolling. And again, you'll probably save by buying the roast and doing your own slicing.

Eye of the Round: The Eye is the least tender, the most overrated, and often the most overpriced cut of the Round. The reason, as far as I can tell, is that it looks cute. It's a nice solid, small, cylindrical muscle. It somewhat resembles the tenderloin muscle—but only in appearance, *not* in tenderness. Many markets slice the Eye into thin steaks and call them "Breakfast Steaks" or "Wafer Steaks" and charge a premium for them. You'd be better off buying a less expensive Rump Roast and slicing your own.

Heel of Round: The Heel is a boneless, wedge-shaped cut of the beef Round that contains the toughest ends of all three muscles of the Round. You don't see it in the meat case very often anymore, most butchers use it for Ground Beef. If you do find one it may be labeled "Pike's Peak" or "Denver Pot Roast." Remember, whatever it's called: it is located pretty close to the ground and definitely needs moist heat.

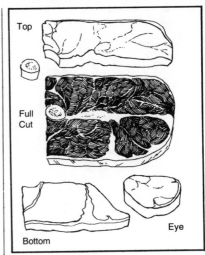

Top

Full
Cut

Bottom

Eye

It boggles my mind when I see, (and I often do), Top Round Steak, Bottom Round Steak, and Eye of the Round Steak displayed right next to Full Cut Round "on special." What I find incredible is not that all four cuts are side by side in the same case, but that any of you would pay a premium, often a rather large premium, for any of the first three. By now, you should know, if you've been paying attention, that Full Cut Round *is* the first three. When you see Full Cut Round on special don't think in terms of one great big steak, think in terms of the component parts and what you can do with each. You don't have to be a master butcher to separate a Round Steak for use in different recipes. Even if what you really wanted were some of the cute little Eye of the Round "Breakfast Steaks," you'd be money and tenderness ahead by buying the Full Cut Round. Even if you went at it with a cookie cutter.

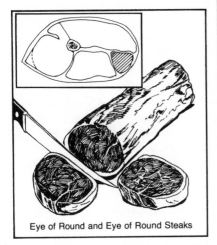

Eye of Round and Eye of Round Steaks

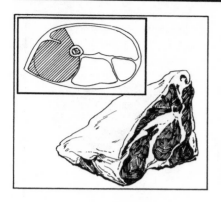

Sirloin Tip

One of the most versatile cuts of beef in your butcher's meat case, and one that offers real money-saving potential for anyone willing to do a little "cutting up in the kitchen," is the Sirloin Tip.

Actually the Tip is a part of the beef Round. It may go by a different name in your neighborhood market; in various parts of the country it is known as the "Knuckle," the "Veiny," the "Round Tip," the "Triangle Tip," and the "Crescent," to quote a few butchers' flights of fancy. The Tip is a cut of boneless meat weighing between 12 and 16 pounds which comes off the beef just aft of the Loin. When the butcher "breaks" a hindquarter of beef into its sub-primal cuts, he first separates the Loin with all of its tender steaks (T-Bones, Sirloins, etc.) from the less tender Round. And that part of the Round which lies just the thickness of a knife blade from the tender Sirloin Steak is the Sirloin Tip.

Butchers do all kinds of magic and wonderful things with the Sirloin Tip. We make from it almost countless different cuts to meet the needs of our meat-buying public. This is called merchandising. We cut the Tip into cubes which we call Kabobs. We slice it thin for Stroganoff. We cut steaks from it and call them London Broil, Essex Steaks, Family Steaks, Wafer Steaks—make up a name, any name, and there is probably a butcher somewhere who sells Sirloin Tip steaks by that name.

But whatever else we may do with the Tip under the name of merchandising, in most markets we also sell at least a portion of it as a roast. Usually in making a roast the whole Tip is trimmed and split down the middle. Then each half is tied into a Rolled Roast weighing between four and eight pounds. Almost without exception, the Sirloin Tip Roast will sell for considerably less than other cuts of the Tip that are hiding out under fancy names in some other part of the meat counter. So when you're in the market for Beef Kabobs or Stroganoff or meat for Sukiyaki, when you want a couple of good tender steaks without taking out a loan, look for a Sirloin Tip Roast.

The Tip is boneless, so you don't have to be a master butcher to do your own magic. You can simply cut a steak or two off the large end. Or, you can dice it, cube it, slice it thick or thin and use it in any recipe that requires lean tender beef. It will be every bit as good as those the butcher cuts—and the cost is apt to be considerably less.

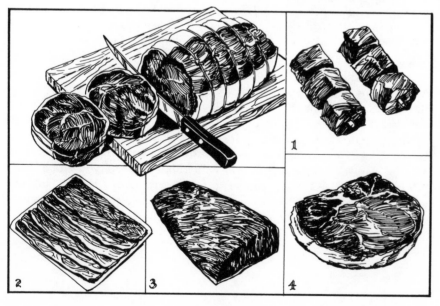

Chuck

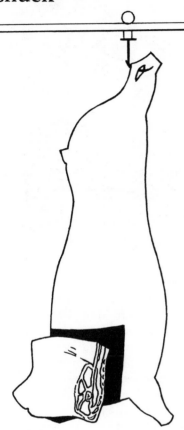

Of all nine primal cuts from the beef carcass, the one that offers the greatest money-saving potential is the Chuck. Since it makes up over 26% of the beef, the operative law of supply and demand determines that cuts from the Chuck are apt to be some of the least expensive in any meat case. Look through the ads in your local newspaper any week and, chances are, you'll find Chuck Roast on sale for a fairly good price in at least one market.

The Chuck is the entire front shoulder section of the beef, including the neck. It comes off the carcass in front of the Rib and above the Brisket and Shank. The methods of merchandising the Chuck are as many and as varied as the imagination of the butcher allows. It would be impossible to describe them all here. What we can do is describe the more common variations.

The way various cuts of the Chuck appear in your butcher's meat case depends largely upon how he "breaks" the forequarter into its primal cuts, and to what extent he "muscle bones" the Chuck. If he "breaks" a Square-Cut Chuck, the predominant method in the eastern half of the United States, many of the resulting cuts will be totally different than those found in the parts of the West where the Chuck is broke California-style.

I'm told by oldtimers on the West Coast that the regional variations in the methods of breaking beef stem from the different nationalities of the "old country" butchers who first began cutting meat in this country. It seems, according to these "old butcher's tales," that the retail meat business in the eastern part of the country was first established by butchers of English descent. They, following the English tradition, generally cut meat across the muscle, with the bone left in. The retail business in California, however, was begun by Continental butchers from France and Italy. Like their fathers before them, *they* made a practice of breaking beef by separating the various muscles, often removing the bones from a cut entirely. The California method of "muscle boning" accounts for the fact that you seldom see "Arm Pot Roasts" in markets in the West, and that the term Cross Rib describes two different cuts, depending upon the section of the country you live in.

Let's discuss the eastern method first, starting with the Square-Cut Chuck.

The Square-Cut Chuck

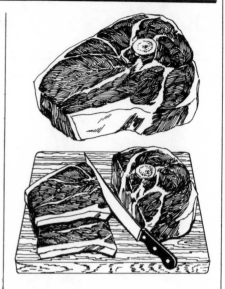

In breaking a Square-Cut Chuck the butcher first divides the forequarter into its primal cuts by separating the Rib from the Chuck between the fifth and sixth ribs. Ribs #1 through #5 remain on the Chuck; #6 through #12 make up the primal Rib. The Shank and Brisket are then removed, leaving a blocky square-shaped Chuck, with the arm and rib bones exposed on one side where it was cut from the Shank section, and the blade bone exposed on the other where it was cut from the Rib section.

From the Square-Cut Chuck the butcher gets all manner of Pot Roasts and Swiss Steaks, most of which are a little less than tender and require moist-heat cooking.

Cross Rib Pot Roast: When an Eastern butcher breaks a Square Cut Chuck, the Cross Rib is cut from the corner where the arm side and the Blade side meet. It contains three ribs (#3, #4, & #5) and the meat which lies across those ribs, hence the name "Cross Rib." This Cross Rib is really little more than three large meaty Short Ribs hooked together and definitely needs moist heat.

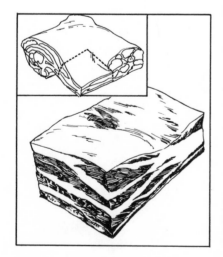

Arm Pot Roast or Steak: After this Cross Rib has been removed, the butcher usually cuts Pot Roasts or Swiss Steaks from the arm side of the Chuck. These contain the round arm bone and possibly a cross section of the remaining two ribs, although it is not uncommon for the rib bones to be removed to make the cut more saleable. The Arm Pot Roast can often provide some money-saving possibilities for a wide-awake shopper.

There is very little bone in an Arm Roast, usually only the small round arm bone. You don't have to be a master butcher to work around that or even remove it altogether. When Stew or Beef Bourguignon or Swiss Steak or Pot au Feu is on your menu, do some price comparisons: How much is the butcher charging for Swiss Steak? What's his price for Stew meat? It's very likely that you may find Arm Pot Roast at a better price per pound in the Roast section of the meatcase.

You can very easily divide the Arm Pot Roast in half; use the boneless half for a couple of Swiss Steaks and pot roast the rest. Or take the bone out entirely and cut the whole thing into cubes for stewing. You may even want to consider grinding your own "Lean Ground Chuck." Whatever you do, don't throw away the bone—save it for the stockpot.

What's left of the Square Cut Chuck, after the Cross Rib or Short Ribs and arm cuts have been removed, is the Blade Chuck. Here Eastern and California-style merge, again, so let's defer discussion of this cut for the moment.

Instead, let's retrace our steps and talk about what happens to the arm portion when beef is broke California-style.

"Muscle-Boned" Chuck

When the Chuck is "muscle boned," the entire shoulder and arm muscle, down to and including the Shank, is lifted away from the ribs in one solid piece following the natural seams between the muscles. The boneless shoulder "clod" is then separated from the arm bone and the Shank, and usually rolled into what Western butchers call the Boneless Cross Rib.

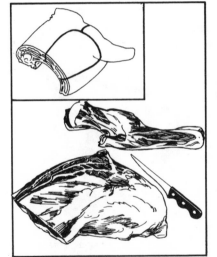

Boneless Cross Rib: A whole Boneless Cross Rib will weigh from ten to fifteen pounds, depending on the size of the beef it came from. It is usually

cut and merchandised as three separate roasts. Since the most tender cut is always the one that comes off closest to the tender middle of the back (the Rib or Loin section), the most tender part of this Cross Rib Roast will be the tapered end which comes off right next to the Rib. This Roast can be very successfully cooked by dry heat. Many markets which sell this type of Cross Rib Roast cut the center portion into steaks and label them "Fluff Steaks," "Patio Steaks," "Family Steaks," "Barbecue Steaks" or some other tender-sounding term.

It is often the case that you can buy a Cross Rib Roast and slice it into steaks in the kitchen to save some money on steaks.

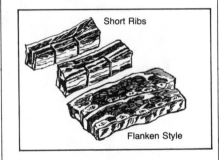

Chuck Short Ribs: After the Cross Rib has been removed, there remains a layer of meat over and around the ribs, usually sold as "Chuck Short Ribs" or "Flanken Short Ribs." These are often leaner but less tender than the Short Ribs from the "middle plate." (See page 69.)

Blade Chuck: Here's where East and West *do* meet. Regardless of how the butcher merchandises the arm portion of the Chuck, there remains that portion containing the shoulder blade. This is the Blade Chuck, a gold mine of money-saving goodies for any consumer.

The blade portion of the Chuck, like every other cut we have discussed, is merchandised both with and without the bone. When the butcher bones out the whole Blade Chuck portion and sells the various muscles separately, he gets three different and distinct pieces, each with unique qualities.

From the top side of the blade bone he gets two small muscles, one from each side of the ridge of the shoulder blade.

On one side is a small triangular-shaped muscle called, by most butchers, the "Flatiron." This is a tender little morsel that is usually sliced into steaks, which are dubbed "Butter Steaks" or "Petite Steaks" or some other cute and tender-sounding name and sold at a premium.

In the first place, there is quite a bit of it so you have the advantage of supply on your side. It has, moreover, gained something of a "Pot Roast" reputation. This puts it in the less desirable, less tender category in most people's minds, which means not much in demand. Plentiful supply, limited demand! That often makes it one of those "hard to move" items for the butcher. As a result the price is almost always good and often downright cheap.

From the other side of the ridge of the shoulder blade comes a small cone-shaped muscle called the "Mock Tender," or "Chuck Tender" or "Scotch Tender," or "Jewish Filet." It resembles the beef tenderloin in shape, if not in tenderness. This cut, like the

Flatiron will very likely be sold at a premium price.

What's left of the Blade Chuck after the blade bone and the two tender little muscles on top of it have been removed is called the "under blade" portion. This is most often trimmed of any ragged edges to form a uniform-sized piece, then rolled and sold as Pot Roast. The lean trimmings are used for Stew or Ground Beef. The boneless Chuck Roll varies in tenderness considerably from one end to the other. The end that came off next to the Rib is tender enough to roast with dry heat, but the closer you get to the neck end the tougher it becomes. Without the bone as a guide it's a little difficult, however, to tell which end is which.

With the bone identifying the various cuts of the Chuck, it's a snap. The shape of the blade bone will tell you exactly where the cut came from on the Chuck, and knowing that can make a great deal of difference when it comes to eating well for a lot less than a fortune.

Blade-Cut Chuck Roast

The first cut of the Blade Chuck comes off the beef right next to the Rib and contains a large portion of the Rib "eye" muscle. This is what ends up in the meatcase labeled "Market Steak" or "Spencer Steak" and selling at a premium.

You can find two nice tender little steaks in a blade-cut Chuck Roast if you know where to look—and have enough left over for three more meals. Here's how:

When the price is right, buy a Blade-Cut Chuck Roast. It will weigh around 3½ to 5 pounds. You can distinguish the Blade-Cut by the shape of the bone. It is long, thin, and shaped something like the blade of a knife, but it gets its name from the fact that it is part of the shoulder blade.

On top of the blade bone is the muscle

that, if boned out and sold separately, would be called Flatiron and go for a premium price. To take it out yourself, simply cut along the bottom of the bone to separate it from the muscle. (Save the bones for the stockpot). The Flatiron is tender enough to slice thin and use for Stroganoff or stir-fry recipes. Or, just cut it into a couple of steaks, as the butcher does.

The tender Rib Eye Steaks we're looking for are just next to the chine bone, that's the bone along the bottom of the Chuck. (Actually, the chine is half of the backbone of the beef where the two halves have been divided.) Keeping the blade of your knife right next to the bone, remove the chine bone and add that to your pile for the stockpot. Next, divide the remaining meat along the natural seam to remove the Rib "eye" muscle from the less tender, coarse-textured

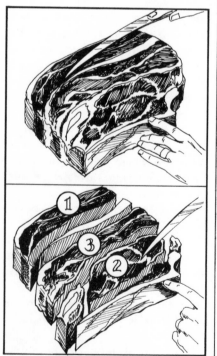

muscle above it. The Rib "eye" can be split to make two small Market Steaks, every bit as tender as those costing three or four times as much in the steak section of your butcher's meat case.

The remaining (middle) muscle is the tough one. It's the one that has given the Chuck Roast a "pot roast" reputation all these years. Use it for Stew or Swiss Steak or any recipe that calls for moist heat. The bone, of course, goes into the stockpot.

So, from one First Cut Blade Chuck Roast we have achieved more than three meals for two people; Steaks, Stew, Stroganoff, with a bonus in the stockpot for soup or sauces.

Center-Cut Chuck

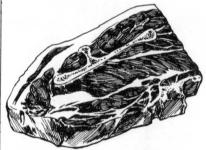

In the center portion of the Chuck, a ridge appears on the top side of the blade bone. The Rib "eye" is all but nonexistent in these "center cuts" but they can still offer some good buys for a kitchen cutter-upper.

The Flatiron muscle is still there, and the meat under the blade is usually quite lean, perfect for cutting into cubes for stewing.

7-Bone Chuck

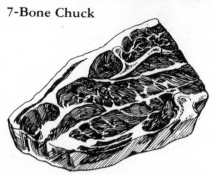

Near the neck the blade bone narrows into a little bone resembling the figure 7—hence the name. The tough muscle under the blade that gives the Chuck Roast a "pot roast" reputation is largest, leanest and toughest in the 7-Bone and the Flatiron on top of the blade is small to nonexistent. But there is a good-sized piece of "Mock Tender" that can make a couple of fair steaks. Since the bone is quite small, you can cut up cubes for Stew with a minimum of stuff fit only for the stockpot.

Flank

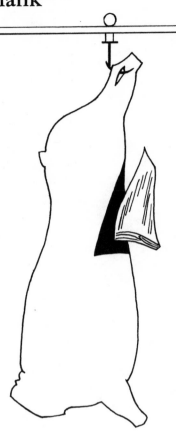

The primal Flank comes off the carcass just under the Short Loin. Well over half of the Flank is fat which winds up in the butcher's "bone barrel." As for the rest, it is mainly a continuation of the muscles that made up the tough "tails" of the T-Bone and Porterhouse steaks, destined to end up in the meat case as Ground Beef. But, in addition, there is one long, thin, fiberous and fairly tough muscle on the Flank that—if you treat it right—is one of the tastiest and most versatile cuts you'll find in any butcher's meat case: the Flank Steak.

Fortunately, Flank Steak is also one of the least expensive steaks. Granted it is not as inexpensive as it once was. I can remember when Flank Steak, Skirt Steak and bones for the dog were priced almost the same. Those days are gone, probably forever, yet Flank Steak is still, as steaks go, a relatively inexpensive steak.

Flank is the ideal simple, quick dinner for that evening when you forgot to take something out of the freezer, don't feel much like cooking, and have guests coming for dinner. It can also be a real money-saver when you have the time to spend in the kitchen doing a little stuffing, rolling and saucemaking.

All of the beef charts and most recipes tell you that Flank Steak requires moist-heat cooking. Not true! There is an exception, a delicious exception. The classic recipe for Flank Steak is "London Broil." This may surprise you, for I'm sure you have seen the term "London Broil" used on a wide variety of different cuts of meat. Included among them are thick-cut Top Round, Sirloin Tip Steak, and thick slices from the center of the Cross Rib Roast.

But, if you will take the time to check any recipe book from Fanny Farmer to James Beard, you will find the first ingredient listed for London Broil is "one Flank Steak."

Many people prefer to marinate Flank Steak in various concoctions for anywhere from three hours to three days before broiling. But I like mine just broiled quickly—four to five minutes on each side—then seasoned with salt and pepper and served, sliced very thin. It can be accompanied perhaps by nothing more than a tomato and onion salad, a rice pilaf and a glass of red wine.

The secret to good tender London Broil is not so much how long it has been soaking in some exotically seasoned marinade, but rather how it is *sliced*. With a very sharp knife held at an angle almost flat to the top of the steak, slice *diagonally* across the grain of the meat, making *thin* uniform slices. A 1½ or two-pound Flank Steak will easily serve four to six people if properly carved.

To make a Flank Steak serve the better part of a small army, stuff it. There are as many methods of stuffing a Flank as there are cuts of meat called "London Broil." Some cooks simply put the stuffing on the Flank, fold it over and sew it up. Others cut a pocket in the Flank to hold the stuffing. But I suggest "butterflying" the Flank Steak.

To butterfly a flank steak, place the meat on a cutting board and put your left hand on top of it. With a sharp knife in your right hand, slice almost through the Flank, parallel to the board. Leave the steak "hinged" along one side so that it can open up to twice its original size. For safety's

sake, be extremely careful to keep the blade of the knife equidistant between the cutting board and the palm of your left hand. If you are lucky enough to have a really "friendly" butcher, perhaps he will do this for you. When the steak has been butterflied, pound it with a mallet, heavy frying pan or a rolling pin. A few good whacks should make it nice and thin. Then spread the Flank liberally with grated cheese (Cheddar, Swiss or whatever you like) and cover with your favorite stuffing. You can even use a stuffing mix, if you like.

Roll the Flank like a jelly roll, secure with tooth picks and lace with string. Sprinkle with seasoned flour, brown in a little hot oil or fat, add a couple of cups of beer, wine, broth or a combination thereof, and simmer for 1½ hours or so.

To serve, slice the Rolled Flank and arrange the slices on a warm platter. Thicken the sauce with a couple of teaspoons of arrowroot dissolved in an equal amount of water. Pour the sauce over the slices of Stuffed Flank and serve with a simple salad, a good French bread and a hearty red wine or whatever is left of the beer.

Plate

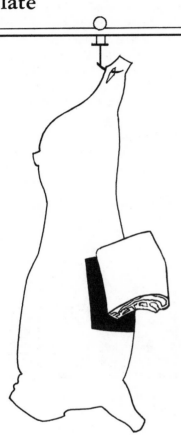

The Plate, which comes off the beef just below the Rib, is a primal cut you will seldom see in the meat case of most markets, at least in any recognizable form. Most Plate meat is boned out and sold as either Stew or Ground Beef. But, depending on how the beef is broken, some portion of the Plate—the "Middle Plate"—will likely be used for Short Ribs.

In some markets the Plate is sold boneless and rolled for a "Yankee Pot Roast." In any case, the Plate needs moist heat and long, slow cooking.

Short Ribs may be displayed in any one of several ways. They may be cut between the ribs so that each piece contains a single rib bone. Or, they may be sawed across the ribs so that each piece contains a small cross-section of several rib bones.

Foreshank and Brisket

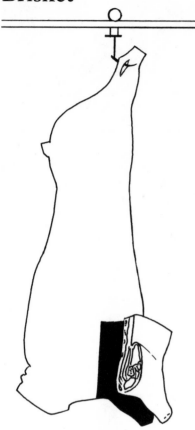

These are two separate and distinct cuts and we'll discuss each individually, but they usually come off the beef together, from below the Chuck and in front of the Plate.

Foreshank: The Foreshank is the front leg of the beef. Like its counterpart on the other end of the Beef, the Hindshank, it is usually boned out and used along with other beef trimmings for Ground Beef.

The Foreshank has a good deal of connective tissue and, therefore, is likely to be about as tender as the sole of an old boot. It does have a great beef flavor, however, and is often sliced into one or two-inch cross sections and sold for making soup. You'll not find a better piece of beef for the purpose.

When simmered slowly in water for a good long time, the tough connective tissue turns to tender gelatin, giving the soup a hearty full body and a rich beefy flavor. For the same reason, the meat from the Shank, when ground one time through the coarse plate of your meat grinder, is unbeatable for making a pot of good homemade Chili.

Brisket: The Brisket is to beef as the Breast is to most other animals. But unlike the Breast of Lamb or Breast of Veal, the Brisket of Beef is usually sold without the bone.

I would guess that most of the Briskets of Beef in this world end up as Corned Beef. But the Brisket can be used for other things. It has a wonderfully rich and well-developed beef flavor, making it excellent for Stew or for pot roasting. Out of **Prime** or **Choice** or "pre-tendered" beef, the Brisket can even be cooked with dry heat *if* you keep the temperature low. One of the tastiest beef roasts I've ever had was Brisket of Beef roasted in a 270 degree oven until just past medium rare. It was served with new potatoes that had been baked in the pan drippings.

The Brisket, either fresh or corned, is usually divided into two separate parts that are sold separately at different prices. The "Flat Cut" will be the more expensive of the two, since it consists of one solid flat muscle with a minimum of fat.

The "Point Cut," with more fat, is usually much less expensive. But the fat, considered undesirable, does give this cut more flavor.

Your best Brisket buy will very likely be the whole Brisket, probably priced somewhere between the two. Don't worry if it's a bit more meat than you need: if the price is right, stock up. There are all kinds of things you can do with boneless Brisket. The flat end makes beautifully uniform-size cubes for stewing. It can be sliced into strips for braising. You might even want to consider making a little of your own Corned Beef. (See page 189.)

Inside Steaks

Now let me give you the inside information on a couple of good steaks. Or perhaps I should say, information on a couple of good inside steaks. Either way, the point is that there are some steaks on the inside of beef that every conscientious consumer should be aware of: the Skirt Steak and the Hanging Tender. You probably won't find them readily available all of the time in most markets and in some you may never see them. But they are well worth keeping an eye out for. Even worth ringing the bell and asking for, if that's the way your meat counter operates, since these steaks are likely to cost a little less, although they have a unique, rich flavor that any beef lover is bound to love.

The *Skirt* is actually the diaphragm muscle. It lies on the inside of the rib cage dividing the abdominal from the chest cavity. It makes a great steak. There are only two Skirts per beef, one on the inside of each forequarter. The standard practice in many markets is to trim the Skirt, flatten it a bit with a mallet, then roll it up jelly-roll fashion and secure it with a couple of wooden skewers. It is then divided into two steaks, each approximately one inch thick. You may have seen them labeled "London Broil" in some markets. But then, in some markets, you're likely to see most anything labeled "London Broil."

The *Hanging Tender* is actually the . . . —well actually I can't tell you what the Hanging Tender is. I've looked in dozens of reference books and talked to scores of butchers, and nobody seems to know just what the thing is. It's just there. It hangs off the kidney just below the tenderloin on the inside of the left hindquarter of the beef; only on the left side, so there is but one Hanging Tender per animal. Don't worry if you've never seen one—there's a good reason.

Over the years the Hanging Tender has come to be known in the trade as the "Butcher Steak." Since there is but one per beef that, after trimming, yields only two steaks, there is rarely enough to make a display in the meat case. So, according to meat market mythology, the butcher traditionally took them home. This one still does, but many modern butchers don't. Instead, they probably end up in a hamburger. It's very possible that you could talk your butcher into saving one or two for you, if you ask real nicely. But don't tell him who told you about them, I don't want every butcher in the business down on me for giving out trade secrets.

Hamburger

Whatever happened to "Hamburger?" Considering the fact that we Americans are reported to eat more of the stuff than any other nation on the face of the earth, I have often wondered why we never see a sign reading "Hamburger" in the meat cases of our local supermarkets anymore.

Today we see Ground Chuck and Ground Round, Ground Beef and Lean Ground Beef, Extra Lean Ground Beef and Super Lean Ground Beef. We even see Ground Sirloin. But never "Hamburger."

I decided to do a bit of research on the subject.

Did you know that what we today call "Hamburger" had its origin in Russia? In medieval times, the Tartar peoples of the Baltic States of Russia liked their beef served raw, chopped fine and seasoned with nothing more than salt and pepper and perhaps a bit of onion juice. It wasn't until ships from the German port of Hamburg began calling on Russian ports in the Baltic, that the recipe for what we call "Tartar Steak" was transported to Hamburg, Germany. There some unnamed but nonetheless ingenious chef first added the heat necessary to turn Tartar Steak into Hamburg Steak. Years later and thousands of miles away, in America, the chopped meat cooked Hamburg-style became known as the "Hamburger." It even evolved into the "Hamburger Sandwich," thanks to the fourth English Earl of Sandwich who liked to gamble, but that's another story. And so much for history.

But whatever became of Hamburger? As a matter of fact, what is Hamburger and how does it differ from all of those other ground meats in today's supermarket meat case?

The United States Department of Agriculture makes the following distinction between "Hamburger" and "Ground Beef" when these products are ground and packaged in a Federally-inspected or State-inspected plant: "Hamburger is ground beef to which seasonings and pieces of beef fat MAY be added while the meat is being ground. No added water, extenders or binders are permitted." In contrast, by USDA standards, "Ground Beef" is just what the name implies; ground beef—no extras, no binders or extenders, no water, not even any extra fat. "Seasonings, however, may be added as long as they are identified on the label." Thus, according to the United States Department of Agriculture, the only difference between "Hamburger" and "Ground Beef" is the optional addition of a bit of extra fat.

But, what of all those other ground things in the meat case? What is the difference between "Ground Beef" and "Ground Chuck?" How much leaner is "Extra Lean?" How come "Ground Sirloin" is so much cheaper than the Sirloin that is still a steak. The USDA doesn't have easy answers for these questions, nobody has. Since there are no standards for meat ground in local supermarkets, contrasted to meat-processing plants, there are *no* standards with regard to how much fat ground beef may contain if your supermarket grinds its own, and it probably does. There are also no standards with regard to what this ground beef is called; a supermarket can label its packages of ground beef as it pleases. In some places it's "Regular," "Lean," and "Extra Lean." In other markets it's "Ground Beef," "Ground Chuck" and "Ground Round." But, no matter what the label says, the only difference between one ground beef and another is the same as the USDA's distinction between "Hamburger" and "Ground Beef"—fat content.

Most meat markets make their ground beef from the trimmings that are a natural part of the meat-cutting process. When a butcher trims the tail off a T-Bone Steak, or "squares-up" a rolled roast, the trimmings go into the ground beef. The less tender portions of the beef, the Plate and Shank and Brisket, those cuts which just won't sell, are trimmed of their excess fat and ground. From these trimmings we get ground beef.

The difference between "Ground Beef" and any of that other ground stuff is (in most markets) a little or a lot of bull. No one adds fat to ground beef to make it "Hamburger" anymore, but it is a common practice to add lean bull meat to ground beef to make it "Lean Ground Beef" or "Ground Chuck"—and a little more and call it "Ground Round." There is nothing wrong with bull meat; it's lean and flavorful. The only problem is, it's tough. But grinding solves that. My objection stems from the almost deceptive practices found in the labeling. Some of the superlatives used to describe ground beef are just that. Perhaps someday there will be standards with regard to ground beef terminology. Until then, if you want "Ground Round" that really is, you'd best buy a Round Steak and grind it yourself.

LAMB

Chapter 5

Like most kids from "Corn-'n-cow country," I couldn't stand lamb when I was a boy. Why those filthy critters caused Tom Mix and Hopalong Cassidy more trouble than the Sioux. They ate the grass too short; they took up all the range; they made a mess of the waterholes; and they didn't smell good like cows do. Any six-year-old cowboy knows that. I know it sounds ridiculous but I really believe that those melodramatic Saturday afternoon movie myths were largely responsible for the fact that I was well into adulthood before I outgrew my unfounded, typically Middle America hang-ups and discovered the gastronomic delights of lamb.

It is interesting to note that throughout the rest of the world, lamb is one of the very few meats against which there are no prejudices. Beef is not consumed in India because of religious taboos. In Ethiopia cattle are hoarded like gold as an indication of wealth, but no one would eat one. Pork is not eaten by Moslems or followers of the traditional Jewish faith. But with the possible exception of fish, there are fewer prejudices against lamb than any other meat. It is, to some, a symbol of purity. This reputation is based at least partly in fact: fewer lambs are condemned by government inspection than any other class of meat animal.

Sheep can be raised on land unsuited for any other domesticated animal. They thrive on sparse natural forage and can produce a crop of high quality lamb on nothing more than grass and mother's milk. Lamb's ability to "finish out" as PRIME or CHOICE without any grain feeding becomes—in this grain-short, hungry world—a real money-saving advantage to the American consumer, provided, as I said, you have no hang-ups against it.

One of the reasons often given for "I don't like lamb," is "It has a bad odor!" Not true! The only thing that can cause a bad odor in lamb is cooking it at too high a temperature. Lamb fat is classed as "hard" fat and burns at a lower degree of heat than other animal fat. Anything that's burnt smells bad. Never roast lamb at a temperature over 325 degrees, preferably 300 degrees.

While we're dispelling a few prejudices about lamb, what about that gland? I'll bet I have removed what people call the "musk gland" from a million legs of lamb for customers who are convinced that it causes odor and strong flavor. *False!* The identical glands are also found in beef and pork and are never removed. They have absolutely no effect on either odor or flavor. The only advantage in removing the gland is that it provides a nice place to put a clove of garlic.

Spring Lamb

The time between the first Monday of March and the first Monday of October has, by law and tradition, been established as Spring as far as lambs are concerned. Actually the term is fairly arbitrary with its foundation more in fantasy than in fact. Back in the days of legend— when a shepherd "wintered his flock in the high country" with the help of a faithful dog and a crooked stick and came trudging down the mountain "after the first thaw," carrying at least one of his new Spring lamb crop nestled in his arms or across his shoulders—the term "Spring Lamb" may have had more meaning. The fact is, in most parts of this country these days, the road to market for a lamb is really a fairly wellpaved path and while there are still shepherds and sheep dogs and probably even crooked sticks, along with "Genuine Spring Lamb" from March to October, it is also a fact that very, very good young tender lamb are on the market all year long.

Lamb are probably raised in all of the fifty states, with well over half of those contributing to the commercial lamb crop. The marketing season for lamb varies in different areas of the country depending largely upon climate. For example, in California, Arizona, certain sections of the South, and to some extent in the Northwest where the climate is fairly mild, lambs are born in the fall and early winter. These become what is called the "early lamb crop" and are ready for market in early spring at about the time the purple ink begins to flow, marking the year's first "Genuine Spring Lamb."

Most lambs, however, are born later in the winter and in the spring. These lambs remain in the "high country" (along with their shepherd, his dog and his crooked stick) all during the lush spring and summer for a period of five or six months. These make up what is called the "late lamb crop," and many don't make it to market until long after the purple ink distinguishing "Spring Lamb" has been retired for the year. That, however, makes them no less desirable as far as good eating is concerned. It is a generally accepted fact within the industry that the lamb crop year is all year long. It starts in May and runs through the following April, with the "milk-fed, grass-finished" season from April through October, and the "grass-fed, grain-finished" season from November through March, with considerable overlap all the way along the line.

The point of all this, in case you've missed it, is that Spring Lamb is about as archaic a term as Spring Chicken. We have delicious, young, tender lamb available to us all year long—with or without the "Genuine" purple stamp.

Lamb Primal Cuts

The anatomy of a lamb is basically the same as that of the "Ox" in miniature. The most tender of all the tender parts of the lamb is (as on the "Ox") the Loin section, right in the middle of the back. It is important to remember, however, that lamb is a young animal, always less than one year old, and often well under that. If you will remember from our earlier discussion of "Tough and Tender," one of the two basic factors which affect the tenderness of meat is "the age of the animal at the time of slaughter." During the five or eight or ten months of the average lamb's short life, the meat doesn't have time to get tough. Therefore, nearly all parts of the lamb qualify for dry heat cooking.

Unlike beef, which is divided into quarters at the packing house, lamb usually finds its way into the meat market all in one piece, and it is left to the butcher to "break" the carcass into primal cuts.

There are as many different styles for doing this as there are butchers. It is of little concern to us here whether your butcher breaks a Long Saddle or a Short Saddle, a Three-Rib Yoke or a Four-Rib Yoke. The basic primal cuts come out about the same and that's what we are concerned with, the basics.

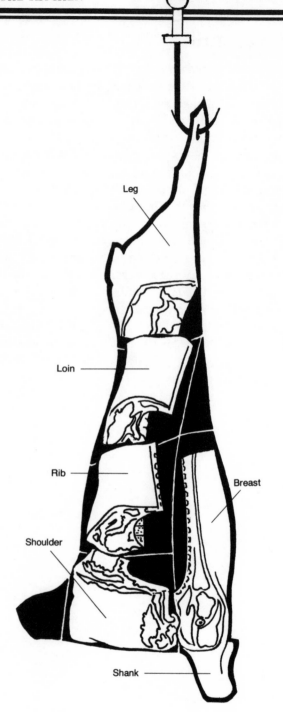

Leg

Loin

Rib

Breast

Shoulder

Shank

The Loin

The Loin is to lamb as the Short Loin is to beef. It is that most tender section from which come the most sought after and therefore most expensive cuts. The muscles of the Loin correspond to those of the T-Bone and Porterhouse; i.e., the top loin, the tenderloin and the flank.

The whole Loin section can be sold for a roast, but in most markets the lamb Loin is merchandised as "Loin Chops" or "Small Loin Chops." The Loin section is split along the backbone (chine bone) and each half is cut into chops that resemble tiny T-Bones. These are all too often cut much too thin; they should be at least an inch thick to be as juicy and delicious as they can be.

Some butchers offer "Double Loin Chops" but they all don't mean the same thing by "double." To some, a "Double Loin Chop" is one cut twice as thick as a regular Loin Chop. To others a "Double Loin Chop" or "English Chop" is cut from a Full Loin which has not been split along the chine bone. Either way the chops from the Loin are by far the finest, and surely the most expensive, the lamb has to offer.

Lamb Saddle: If your butcher sells "Double Loin" or "English Chops," it is probable that you can ask for and get a Saddle of Lamb for roasting. There is no more tender or elegant lamb roast, but they do require a certain expertise when it comes to carving.

While it is unlikely that you will save any money doing your own cutting-up with the Loin of lamb, it is possible to create some delightful and delicious "specialties-of-the-house" at your house if you will make use of a little courage, a cutting board, and your good sharp boning knife.

Boneless Loin Roll: You can make an absolutely elegant rolled lamb roast for the oven or barbecue, or some of the most impressive lamb chops you've ever seen, from a couple of boneless lamb Loins.

Ask your butcher for two lamb Loin Roasts (see illustration). Take them home and "go to." Lay one on the cutting board, fat side down. With your boning knife, cut down along the chine bone to the finger bone, then along the finger bone under the

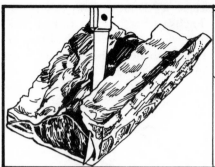

filet. *Got that?* If not go back to page 39 and review a bit about bones —we can't get this job done, or have any fun, if we don't speak the same language. Now, leaving the filet attached, cut along under the bones back to the feather bone, turn down and cut along the feather bone right down to the cutting board and —look what you've done!—you've "boned" a Lamb Loin. Now do the same to the other one—it shouldn't take nearly as long.

Lay the two boneless Loins one on top of the other, so that the large end of one is next to the small end of the other, and tie them together with string at one-inch intervals. You now have a boneless, rolled, double Loin Lamb Roast guaranteed to cost less and taste even better because you did it yourself.

If "Boneless, Rolled, Double Loin Lamb Chops" are more to your liking, simply cut midway between each string.

If you like your lamb chops with a bit of kidney, old-fashioned English fashion, try rolling two or three lamb kidneys between the two halves of the roast.

Sirloin

In most parts of the country the Sirloin portion of the lamb is left on the leg. We will discuss it later as part of the leg. Where it is merchandised separately it will usually be sliced into steaks or chops. There are only three or four slices on the lamb Sirloin and, unlike those of the "Ox," they are not usually named for the shape of the hip bone contained in each. The most common name is "Lamb Leg Sirloin Chops," but in different parts of the country and in various markets on different sides of the street, you may see them labeled: Large Loin Lamb Chops, Leg Chops, Lamb Steak, Chump Chops, Sirloin Steaks, or Loin

End Steaks. Whatever they are called, remember—they come off the lamb right next to the Loin and will be every bit as tender and tasty, but very likely less expensive.

The Leg

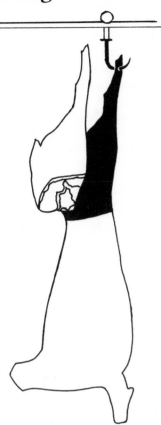

The Leg of Lamb is by far the most popular cut of the carcass. It ranks with the Standing Rib of Beef or a beautifully Baked Ham when it comes to elegant dinner party dining. It can also provide good and inexpensive everyday eating for families large and small. There are dozens of methods for merchandising Legs used by butchers across the country. The following are a few of the most common:

The Full Leg: The Full or Whole Leg contains the Sirloin section complete with the hip bone, aitch bone, chine bone, leg bone, shank bone, with or without the tail bone. All these bones make the Full Leg something of a problem when it comes to carving. They also make for a very long and somewhat unwieldy Leg that may not fit too well in the average roasting pan.

Half Leg: In many markets the Full Leg is divided into two roasts—the Sirloin half and the Shank half. This solves the problem of "will it fit in the pan" and provides Leg of Lamb for a small family, but it also presents the problem of which half is the best half. The Sirloin half is the one closest to the Loin and therefore has a larger percentage of the most tender meat. It also, however, has all of those bones which make carving a problem. The Shank half is easy to carve but contains the less tender Shank. Either way, there is a better way.

Short Leg (3/4 Leg): This Leg of Lamb is, I think, the one most apt to please most families. It has the "classic" look a Leg of Lamb ought to have if it is to star at the dinner party, yet it presents fewer carving problems and is more apt to fit your roasting pan because the Sirloin section has been removed.

American Leg: A more compact, but perhaps less classic-looking Leg is achieved by removing the Shank at the stiffle joint. Legs merchandised in this manner are called American Legs. They are easier to get in the roasting pan but they still contain all those bones that make carving a problem.

Frenched Leg: In the meat business "Frenched" anything means "with a bit of bone exposed." A Frenched Leg of Lamb is one with a small portion of the Shank meat cut away to expose the Shank bone. This can be done to either a Full-Cut or Short-Cut Leg to add a little class to its presentation at the table. Usually Frenched Legs are offered up with a little paper "ruffle" covering the exposed bone.

The big buy may be the best buy

With Leg of Lamb, as with so many other cuts of meat, you can often save money by thinking big. A Full-Cut Leg of Lamb, for example, may be larger than you need but it is very probable that it will sell for less per pound than many of its component parts displayed in some other part of the meat case. Don't pass up a good buy on Leg of Lamb even though you are not planning a fancy dinner party.

A Full-Cut Leg of Lamb can be divided up to provide several family meals for any size family.

Ask the butcher to cut 3 or 4 steaks off the Sirloin end for a separate meal, then roast the Short Leg. If that is still a bit more than you need, have the shank removed for a meal of Lamb Stew or for braising.

Boning a Leg of Lamb

Boning a Leg of Lamb is a feat rather easily accomplished and one that can turn a Leg into all manner of interesting and different meals at considerable savings over what the same meat would cost if the butcher boned it. A boneless Leg of Lamb can be rolled into a beautiful roast that provides absolutely no problems for the carver. Or part of it can be rolled and other parts can be cut into boneless steaks or Kabobs to provide additional meals. Once the bone has been removed only lack of imagination limits what can be done with the meat.

The *Short Loin* or *3/4 Leg* is the easiest to bone. So, if your butcher sells only the Full Leg with the Sirloin section attached, ring the bell and ask him to remove the Sirloin end and cut it into chops. That will give you one meal of three or four Sirloin Chops and a Leg that is much easier to work with.

Put the leg to be boned skin-side down, inside up, on your cutting board.

First remove the tail. Set it aside—don't throw it away! The tail, along with all of the other bones, can go into the stockpot to provide a meal or at very least a first course of "Scotch Broth."

Next remove the aitch bone. This is the only part that may cause you any problem. Just take your time, proceed slowly and don't worry about ending up with a few scraps of meat—they can make an excellent Curry.

Cut down behind the aitch bone, keeping the blade of your knife as close to the bone as you can. After you cut down an inch or so, stop and wiggle the aitch bone a bit. You will

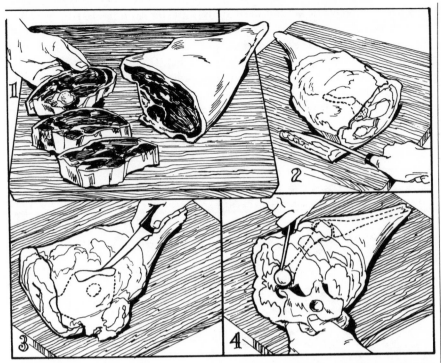

becue grill.

For Kabobs take the leg apart a little more. With your fingers separate the individual muscles along the natural seams. Just as with the Round of Beef, there are three major muscles in the Leg: the top leg muscle, the bottom and the "eye." If you separate them and then cut each muscle separately, your little Kabob cubes will be solid pieces of meat.

If there is more meat than you need on a Leg of Lamb, boning is a great way to make more than one meal out of it. Separate out the top round muscle and save it to be sliced into the meatiest Boneless Lamb Chops you've ever seen, then roll the rest for a roast or cut-up for Kabobs. Once you've learned to bone a Leg you will find all kinds of things you can make of the meat. And you can do it without leftovers.

see where it is attached to the leg bone at the hip socket. Find the space between the joints and cut through. There *is* a space between the joints. Then follow along the aitch bone to free it and lift it out. Set it aside along with the tail for soup. What's left is child's play.

Starting at the round knob end of the Leg bone, make a cut along the bone to the knee joint and then down the length of the shank bone. Once you have the bone marked, simply trim around it and lift it out. Cut away the little "knee cap" bone and you've boned a Leg of Lamb. Easy, wasn't it?

To convert your boneless Leg into a Boneless Rolled Roast simply tuck things back together a bit and tie with string. Or you can pull it apart and flatten it out into what's called a "Butterfly Leg of Lamb" for the bar-

Rib Rack

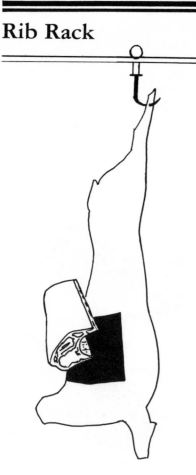

The Rib section of the lamb is known in the trade as "The Rack." It comes off the lamb between the Loin and the Shoulder. Like beef, lamb normally contains thirteen ribs; in the breaking process, however, only four ribs instead of five are left on the shoulder. The Lamb Rack, therefore, usually ends up containing eight ribs rather than the seven common on a Beef Rib. Occasionally, a lamb will have fourteen ribs—don't ask me why—and you will wind up with a nine-rib rack.

The Rack has a large end and a small end, like the Beef Rib. The large end next to the shoulder will contain a portion of the shoulder blade bone which is usually removed by the butcher before putting the Rack on sale.

Rib Chops

The most common method of merchandising Racks is simply to cut them into Rib Chops. The chops may be cut between each rib, yielding approximately one-inch thick chops, or if your butcher likes lamb, they may be "Double Cut" with two ribs per chop. For good juicy chops make sure they are cut no thinner than one inch. Any thinner than that and they tend to dry out under the high heat of broiling or frying.

The first two or three ribs off the large end contain more fat than those closer to the Loin. Often chops are sold separately with those closest to the Loin selling at a premium over the two or three next to the shoulder. Occasionally the more expensive ones will have a bit of rib bone exposed, entitling them to wear a paper ruffle and be called Frenched Lamb Chops.

The Rack makes an excellent roast for three people or for two people when "three's a crowd" and you want something simple and simply elegant. Be sure to ask the butcher to "crack the chine between the ribs," so that you can carve it after it's roasted. And, to

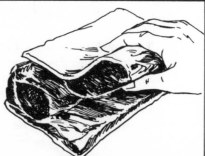

add a little excitement, be sure to have the rack "Frenched."

Making a Rolled Rib Roast from two Racks is considerably easier but the results are no less elegant than making a boneless Loin roll. Simply bone out two Racks. Be sure to remove the "fell" (the thin, paper-like membrane covering the Rack) and the piece of blade bone in the large end if the butcher hasn't done it. Trim away as much of the excess internal fat as possible, leaving only the nice lean Rib Eye muscle. Put the two Rack sections on top of each other, with the small end of one on the large end of the other, and tie up with string. For Boneless Rib Lamb Chops cut between the strings.

You're not apt to see Crown Roasts in the meat cases of your local supermarkets, but at certain times of the year you find them on the cover of nearly every magazine dealing with food. They have become almost as synonymous with good holiday eating as the turkey or the Christmas goose, but they are considerably harder to come by. Most butchers won't take the time and, if they will, they are apt to charge a fortune for making a Crown Roast.

Actually it's very simple. There is nothing magic or secret about the procedure and, while it does take a little time, the results are elegant in the center of a festive holiday table.

Ring the bell at your local supermarket and ask for two or three "8-rib Racks of Lamb." A two-rack Crown will feed six or eight people; three racks will make a Crown big enough for eight to ten. If you plan on feeding more than ten you would be better off making two smaller Crowns.

Ask the butcher to "crack the ribs along the chine bone;" remove the "fell" and "French" them for you, *if* there's no extra charge. Otherwise do it yourself. To remove the "fell" start a corner of the membrane with your fingernail until you can get a good hold, then just peel it off. "To crack the ribs along the chine bone" you'll need a saw. It doesn't have to be a big electric meat saw like the one the butcher uses, it doesn't even have to be a meat saw. A hacksaw with a clean blade will work nicely. After you've sawed through the ribs, remove the chine bone entirely, completing with the knife the cut you or your butcher started with the saw.

To "French" the racks simply remove the meat from an inch or so of the rib bones. Also remove the little bit of blade bone (if there is any) in the large end of the Rack. Repeat the process on the remaining Rack or Racks. Then tie the Racks together loosely, end to end, using strong cotton string and a large needle. There are needles specially made for this sort of thing but you needn't buy one. Any needle with a large enough eye will do; upholstery or rugmaking needles work fine and most needle sets contain one or the other—look in your sewing basket.

After you have the strings in place, bend the racks into the crown shape, tighten the strings and tie. It may make it a bit easier to bend into shape if you make a small cut between each rib at the base of the crown.

There you have it—a Crown Roast of Lamb—every bit as elegant as the one on the cover of any magazine and likely a whole lot less expensive. You did it yourself!

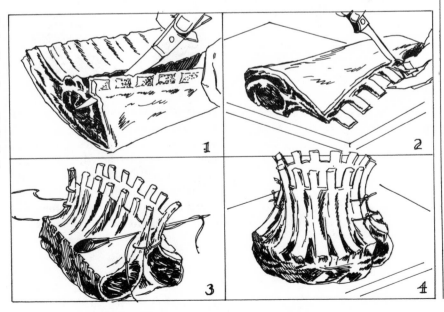

Shoulder

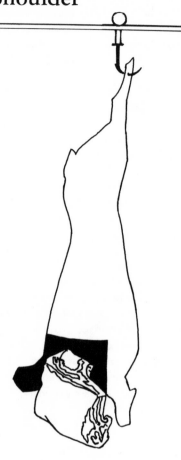

The shoulder is by far the most versatile of all the cuts of the lamb and like its counterpart in the beef, the Chuck, offers some of the greatest money-saving potential for any consumer willing to spend a little time learning all of the many things that can be done with it; then doing it!

The Lamb Shoulder is usually removed from the carcass between the 4th and 5th ribs. But not always. In different parts of the country, some butchers leave as many as seven ribs on the Shoulder, while others may only leave three. The norm however, is four or five. After the Shoulder section (the yoke) is separated from the Rib, the Shank and the Breast are removed. Then the neck is trimmed off. What remains is split down the chine bone leaving what is known in the trade as the "Square-Cut Shoulder." We will discuss the Shank and the Breast as separate primal cuts but first, the Shoulder.

Square-Cut Shoulder: The Shoulder can be merchandised in a variety of ways: sold whole for a roast, bone-in, boneless, or pre-carved; sliced into chops; cubed for Kabobs; even used for ground lamb. The most common merchandising practice is something of a combination of all the above.

Two or three chops will be cut from the round bone side of the Shoulder. The remaining chops will be cut from the blade bone side, leaving only a small portion next to the neck to be cut into cubes for stew. The thickness of the chops can vary from less than an inch to nearly two inches. In some parts of the country the thick-cut shoulder chops are called "Lamb Blocks."

Unfortunately, one of the more common practices in the fast-paced meat markets of our fast-paced world is to slice the Blade Chops and then tie them back together and call it a "Pre-carved Roast." Pre-carved it is, and that's a blessing, since carving a Lamb Shoulder with the bone in is next to impossible. But a roast it is most certainly not—at least not a very appetizing one. When roasted the "pre-carved roast" looks fine on the outside but when you cut the string—*yuk*! The inside chops have an awful color; they very likely will be too well done; they are apt to be dry. All in all, a "Pre-carved Lamb Shoulder" is a bad lamb roast. You would do far better to cut the string and cook the chops separately as chops. You might even save money since the Shoulder Roast will likely be selling for less in most markets than the Shoulder Chops in some other part of the same meat case.

If a good lamb roast is what you want, buy a Leg or bone a Shoulder.

Boning a Shoulder

How do you make of a Shoulder of Lamb all of the great things that can be made of a Shoulder of Lamb? First, it is necessary to take the bone out. And this is possibly the most complicated do-it-yourself boning job we will talk about in this book. It is worth the effort, however, because the result is some of the most fun and fancy meals you can imagine, all from one relatively inexpensive Shoulder of Lamb. There aren't many butchers around these days who will take time to make a "Cushion Shoulder Roast" or "Saratoga Chops," but you can make both and more from a Shoulder of Lamb in your own kitchen.

Ask your butcher for a whole "Square-Cut Shoulder." Even if he doesn't have one in the meat case he will very likely be more than happy to cut one for you since it requires little of his time and gives him an opportunity to sell a whole Shoulder without worrying about how he is going to "move" the slow-selling parts. If he asks you if you would like him to "crack the chine" or "knock off a few chops" tell him, "No, thank you, I'm going to bone it out." He'll probably, at this point, look at you rather strangely. In that look, amazed disbelief will mingle with admiration and respect. You will have become in his eyes a different kind of customer,

one who knows what he is doing, one who "speaks his language," one to whom he can talk. That look may be the beginning of a whole new relationship with your butcher, resulting in shopping for meat being a whole lot more fun. That alone may be worth the effort.

When you get your Shoulder home, put it on the cutting board "fell" side down with the bones up. Look at it for a minute or two. Turn back to the Lamb Chart on page 78 and try to get an idea of what you're working with. There are those long thin rib bones (probably four of them) attached to the chine bone. Then, on the other side of that little trench where the spinal cord was, there are the feather bones. And in front of those a few neck bones. In the middle of the meaty portion on one side is a little round bone; a cross section of the arm bone and on the other side a long flat cross-section of the blade bone. Note on the Bone Chart where these come together. Okay. Now, have at it! All the while you're at it, keep two things in mind; 1) you're saving money and 2) all of the little scraps and bits and pieces that may result as part of the process, either naturally or as a result of your inexperience, make excellent Curry.

First remove the strip of meat from along the chine bone and underside of the neck. Set this aside; it's the beginning of your Curry pile.

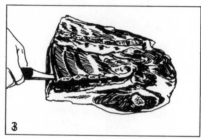

Next, cut along the first rib from the round bone side clear into the chine bone.

Now place the blade of your boning knife under the ribs and cut along the underside ribs clear to the chine bone, up to the feather bones and along the underside of the feather bones.

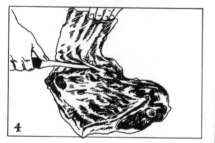

Pull up on the rib bones, using them as a handle, while you trim on down to loosen the meat from around the neck bones, until you can lift the whole bony section off in one piece.

Don't worry about leaving a little meat on the bones. This whole piece can go into the stockpot for a great pot of soup and a little extra meat on the bones means a little extra meat in the soup. If this is too big for your stockpot, divide it up by finding the "spaces between the joints," cutting through with your knife as far as you can and breaking the rest.

Next run your knife in along the top of the blade bone and follow it out to loosen the flap of meat on top of the blade. This flap becomes your handle' for the rest of the job.

Trim back the meat along the top side of the blade bone to expose the joint where it is attached to the arm bone. Then cut along the arm bone and trim around it. Now with the point of your knife cut through the "space between the joints." Loosen the small end of the blade bone with the tip of your knife, then take a good hold and pull; the whole blade bone will pop out. Now all that remains is to remove the round arm bone and you've done it! Stand back and let the joy of the work sink in. . . .

Why, you must certainly be asking by now, would anyone want to go through all of that?

Let me count the reasons:

1. A boneless Shoulder of Lamb can be rolled into a beautiful, easy-to-carve roast—perfect for the oven or rotisserie.

2. It can be made into an old-fashioned "Cushion Roast," which when stuffed with an appropriate dressing, can amply feed at least a small army.

3. It can be divided up, with part of it rolled for a roast, part cut into boneless "Saratoga Chops."

4. All or part of the Shoulder can be cut into cubes for Kabobs or Stew.

5. What you can do with a boneless Shoulder of Lamb is limited by little but your imagination.

Boneless Rolled Shoulder Roast

To make a Rolled Shoulder, trim away any excess fat from the inside of the boneless shoulder. Be sure to remove the clod of fat near the center. It contains the prescapular gland and, while that does not (as is often mistakenly assumed) adversely affect the flavor, it does have a negative effect on the appearance of the roast when you slice into it.

After you have the shoulder nicely trimmed, roll it lengthwise so that the blade side is exposed, with the round bone side tucked underneath.

Tie a couple of strings around the roast lengthwise to hold it in shape, then make cross ties at one-inch intervals to form a neat roll.

Saratoga Chops

The most tender portion of the Boneless Shoulder can be turned into delicious boneless chops which (if the butcher were to do it) would be called "Saratoga Chops" and would sell at a premium price. Once you've gotten the bone out of the Shoulder of Lamb you can easily make your own lamb chops and call them whatever you want, and save money.

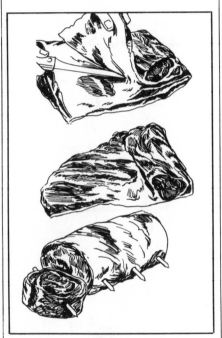

Simply remove the Rib "eye" muscle along with the "flap" meat from on top of the blade by following along the natural seam where you removed

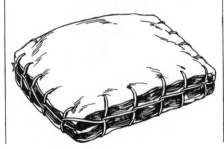

the blade bone. Roll it up with the "flap" meat rolled around the outside of the "eye." Hold the roll in shape with string or wooden skewers and slice into boneless chops. Remember, for the tastiest, juciest chops make them at least one-inch thick. Saratoga Chops—or whatever you choose to call them—can be broiled, grilled, pan-fried or barbecued along with the best of them. For added flavor and a bit of pizzaz, you may want to wrap each chop with a slice of bacon.

The remaining "outer muscle" can be rolled into a roast just the right size for a smaller family or it can be cut into cubes for Kabobs. Or, for special occasions, when you're up to boning *two* Shoulders of lamb, the two outside muscles can be tied together and stuffed to form a more modern version of the old-fashioned "Cushion Shoulder."

Breast and Shank

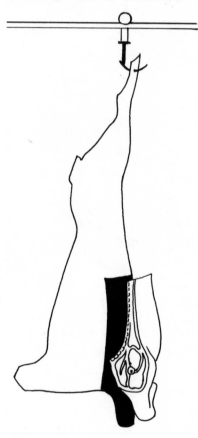

These are two separate and distinct cuts and we'll discuss each individually, but they come off the lamb together from below the Shoulder and Rib.

Breast of Lamb: I would be willing to wager that the cheapest cut of meat in your butcher's meat case is Breast of Lamb. That is *if* your butcher has Breast of Lamb in his meat case. I have worked in markets where all the Breasts of Lamb were ground one time through the coarse plate of the meatgrinder and sold for dog food. With all due respects to dog lovers, what a waste!

The Breast is to the lamb as the Brisket is to the beef, yet there is a

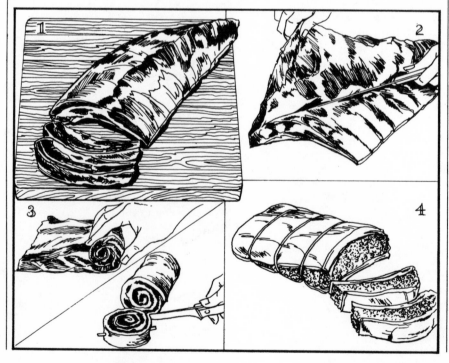

very important difference as far as tenderness is concerned. Beef Brisket is tough and usually requires long slow simmering into submission to keep it from taking hours to chew. Lamb, however, is a younger animal, usually less than six months old, and the Breast—along with the Leg and the Loin and all the rest—is likely to be tender enough to cook with dry heat.

If your butcher doesn't grind it up for dog food, the Breast of Lamb will probably be displayed as "Lamb Spare Ribs" or "Riblets." These are great barbecued over coals with your favorite sauce or simply baked in the oven, perhaps glazed with orange marmalade or apricot jam, and served up with a bowl of steaming rice. But don't stop at that if you can find a good buy on Breast of Lamb, there are other things to be done.

Buy a bunch—three or four—when you see Breast of Lamb at a good price. Take them home, get out the cutting board and your trusty boning knife and do a little creative cutting-up. Here are a couple of ideas.

First bone them out. Your butcher will probably have trimmed most of the outside fat away and all you have to do is run your knife along the top of the rib bones and lift off the top meat in one piece. Save all the rib bones, there is still enough meat on and between the bones for a meal of Barbecued Lamb Ribs.

Now trim the boneless Breasts of any excess fat and roll them up jelly-roll fashion. Cut the roll into ¾ or one-inch thick slices, secure them with toothpicks and pretend they are Lamb Chops. Another possibility is to make what used to be called a "Scotch Roast" when butchers took

the time to make them. I haven't seen one in a meat market in years, but you can easily make one in your kitchen.

When you're boning out your bunch of Lamb Breasts, save one. Don't lift off the top meat completely, leave it attached along one side. Grind the top meat from the other breasts and use the ground lamb as stuffing to fill in between the rib bones and the top meat of the one Breast you saved. Tie the "Scotch Roast" together with string and roast just as you would a meat loaf. Or, cut it between the ribs to make "Scotch Chops" for broiling.

Once you begin to get creative with Breast of Lamb you'll come up with all kinds of possibilities.

Shanks: The term "Lamb Shank" usually applies to the Fore Shank or front leg of the lamb. However, in some markets the Hind Shank, below the stifle joint, is also sold as a "Lamb Shank."

Recipes for Lamb Shanks usually recommend moist heat and I won't argue with that. They, like Beef Shanks, have a lot of connective tissue which makes a great gravy. But again, it needs to be pointed out that lamb is a young animal and the rules can be bent a bit when it comes to cooking. I have had Lamb Shanks barbecued over coals and served to be eaten in the manner of King Henry VIII. They were delicious and surprisingly tender.

Since there is a fair amount of bone in each, count on at least one Shank per serving no matter how you cook them.

PORK

Chapter 6

You *could* raise a pig. That's what my Grandmother did to save money when I was a boy.

Every year, in early spring, she would select two of the cutest, plumpest, potentially most delectable porkers in the litter and bring them into the house. For weeks they would be housed in a box behind the wood stove in the kitchen, away from every hazard except the excessive attention of two small boys (my brother and myself).

When the piglets were old enough, they would be transferred to a pen outside the house. Close enough so that after supper, while Grandfather was "sloppin' the hogs" down by the barn, my brother and I could feed our pigs scraps from the table mixed with cracked corn and warm water to make a mash.

They got nothing but the best all summer long. Then, sometime after school started in September, when my brother and I weren't around to see, they would be sent off to the locker plant in town. For the rest of the year they fed us. Bacon, hams, roasts, chops, head cheese, pig's feet, sausage and scrapple—the only thing that wasn't used was . . . Oh, you've heard that before.

But raising your own pig isn't the only way to save money on pork. In today's marketplace you can save considerably, just as with beef *if* 1) you know a little basic animal anatomy and 2) you do a little cutting-up in the kitchen.

Pork Primal Cuts

Unlike beef, pork never comes into the market in any form that remotely resembles the whole animal. Rather the various parts are purchased "boxed." The butcher buys only the primal cuts of the pig that he can sell easily.

The cuts of fresh pork you are likely to find in the meat case of today's supermarket are not nearly so many nor so varied as those of the beef. Most of the pork that we encounter at the meat counter today is "cured" or "processed" in one form or another. What Granddad used to do with the greatest portion of the pig, in the smokehouse and the pickling barrel, is now done for us. We find pre-packaged and most often pre-cooked such cuts as pigs' feet, bacon, sausage and hams—boiled, baked and honey-glazed; canned, "Cryovac" or "E-Z-pack"; "just heat and eat."

Short of building your own smokehouse and raising that pig, there is little we can do to realize any great saving on "processed" pork products.

Fresh pork is another story. For the most part, the fresh pork available in today's meat case comes from one of two of the primal cuts of the pig—the Loin and the Boston Butt, or Shoulder. A little basic knowledge of these two cuts can add all kinds of variety to your menu and save you a buck or two along the way.

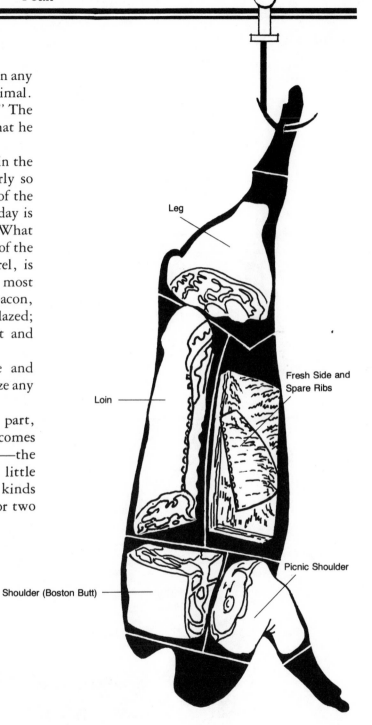

Leg

Fresh Side and Spare Ribs

Loin

Picnic Shoulder

Shoulder (Boston Butt)

The Pork Loin

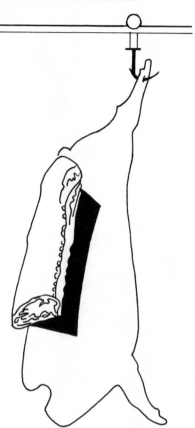

The Loin is to the pig as the Rib, Short Loin and Sirloin combined are to the beef. From the Loin comes the most tender morsels the pig has to offer. The Tenderloin comes from the Loin, Center-Cut Pork Chops come from the Loin, Crown Roasts, Butterfly Chops, Country-style Spare Ribs, and dozens of other cuts are made from the Pork Loin.

The Loin is usually merchandised in three separate portions 1) the Blade End—the end of the Loin toward the front of the pig—is removed and sold as a roast or cut for Country-style Ribs; 2) the Sirloin End—on the other end next to Ham is also most often sold as a roast; 3) between the two is the portion called the Center Loin. This section of the Loin is usually cut into pork chops of one kind or another, thick or thin, boneless or bone-in and sold at a premium. The "Center" is not the place to look if you are looking to save money —rather look to the ends.

The quality of the meat in a Pork Loin is much the same from one end to the other. The only major difference is the fat and bone content. The Blade End, or "Rib End" as it is sometimes called, has more fat but less bone, while the Sirloin End has more bone and less fat. For the novice the Blade End is the easiest to work with, so let's begin there.

Blade End Roast

The Blade End or "Rib End" Pork Roast is apt to be one of the best pork buys in your butcher's meat case. That's true almost any time of year since Blade Ends have a tradition in the meat business of being "slow movers." But it's even more likely to be the case in the summer when the thought of heating up the kitchen with a pork roast is not what most of us have in mind. Usually in the summer when we think of pork, we think of Spare Ribs. Barbecues and Spare Ribs are almost synonymous. Unfortunately since Spare Ribs are what most of us think of, the old law of supply and demand is apt to elevate the price a bit. Spare Ribs are not usually too good a buy in the summer. At least not nearly as good a buy as Rib End Pork Loin. There is a lot more meat for the money and some great potential for good barbecuing in a Rib End *if* you are willing to spend a little time cutting-up in the kitchen before heading for the back yard. From a couple of good-sized Rib End Roasts it is possible to get not only a nice pile of ribs for barbecuing, but also a beautiful boneless pork roast perfect for the rotisserie.

When selecting Rib Ends to work with, look for the largest ones and try to find two nearly the same length. Butchers vary in their methods of merchandising Pork Loins. Some cut off the Rib End containing only three or four ribs while others leave five or six ribs on the roast. The more ribs there are, the more of the expensive "Center Loin" you're getting for your money. All of the bones are visible in a Rib End Pork Loin, so you needn't be a master butcher with a degree in anatomy to take them out. A few moments of finger-probing contemplation will tell you how to proceed.

Most butchers will already have cracked the backbone in between the ribs to make the Roast easy to carve into chops after roasting. This makes it easier for you to divide the bones into serving size for barbecuing. To bone out a Rib End Roast, first place it on your cutting board with the backbone down and study it for a minute. It has a few ribs along one side that are connected to the back-bone along the bottom. Just above the middle of the meaty portion there is another bone; that's the blade bone of the Pork Roast, so called because it's part of the animal's shoulder blade.

First remove the blade bone. Slip your boning knife under the blade bone of the Pork Roast and follow the bone back until it comes loose. Leave the meat on the top part of the bone to make a meaty piece to go along with the ribs for barbecuing.

Next remove the ribs and back bone. Run the blade of your knife down along the ribs to the backbone, turn it parallel to the cutting board and follow the backbone out until the whole meaty center portion of the Roast is free of the bones.

Divide the bones into serving-sized portions by continuing the cut between each rib started by the butcher. Now do the same thing to the other one. Don't try to be neat, you're boning out a Rib End for

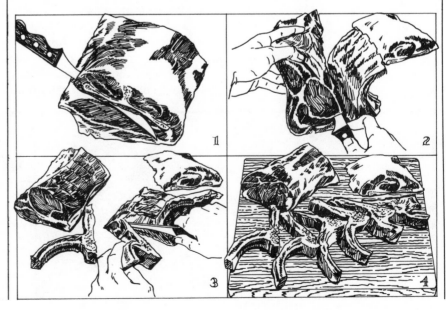

97

barbecuing and you want to leave some meat on the bones. When you're finished you'll have a nice pile of meaty pork bones for barbecuing. They will be every bit as tender and tasty as the best Spare Ribs and, as a real bargain bonus, you'll have two good-sized pieces of Boneless Pork Loin. Have you priced them lately?

What you can do with a couple of Boneless Pork Loins is limited by little but your imagination. It can be sliced thick or thin into Boneless Pork Chops just the thickness you like. Or the two pieces can be tied together with cotton kitchen string to form a uniformly even cylindrical roast ideal for roasting on a rotisserie. Put slices of apples and a few prunes in the center before you tie it up and you have a new-fangled version of a century-old Danish recipe for Stuffed Pork Loin. Just for fun and a bit of good flavor, hide a spicy sausage in the middle—perhaps a Chorinzo or Kielbasa. Put the sausage on one piece of boneless pork, put the second piece on top, tie it tightly, roast in the oven and expect a few "Oh's" and "Ah's" and "Isn't that clever" comments from your guests when you carve it.

Another clever and practical trick with Boneless Pork Loin is Stuffed Butterfly Chops.

Cut double-thick chops from the Boneless Loin piece and "butterfly" them. To accomplish this simple task slice each thick chop part way through the center, leaving the slices hinged along one side. The chop can now be opened out like the wings of a—would you believe—butterfly. Next turn the chop over and cut a pocket in the center of each wing. Fill each pocket with your favorite stuffing. When you open the chop up the stuffing is locked inside.

We've only just begun to count

the ways with Boneless Pork Loin, there are countless other things to be done. Slice strips for Stir-Fry Pork with vegetables, dice cubes for "Chow Mein," "Pork Kabobs" or "Adobu," or grind pork for patties or meatloaf, or make your own sausage. However, you cut it, you can save money and create some imaginative meals with a boning knife and a Blade End Pork Roast.

Country-Style Ribs

Country-Style Ribs are simply Blade Ends of the Pork Loin butterflied. Many markets around the country merchandise Blade Ends this way, particularly in the summer months when barbecuing is the order of the day. More often than not, in most cases, the Country-Style Ribs the butcher cuts up will be selling for more than the Blade End Pork Loin they were made from. So it is very likely that you can save some money by doing it yourself. You'll need a saw—it doesn't have to be a meat saw, although they are nice to have —a hack saw with a clean blade will work.

Buy a Blade End Pork Roast, saw through the rib bones, then cut through the center of the Rib Eye muscle, leaving a hinge along one side. Open it up and it's ready for the barbecue grill.

Pork Sirloin Roast

After you have successfully cut-up a Blade End or two, it's well worth your while to try your blade on a Sirloin End. The Sirloin End of the Pork Loin has a more complicated bone structure than the Blade End and much of the bone (hip bone) is not visible. But it also contains a large portion of the Pork Tenderloin or Pork Filet, the most tender and expensive cut of fresh pork in the pig.

Again, as with the Blade End, you are money ahead to buy the largest Sirloin End Pork Roast the butcher has or will cut for you. The larger the roast, the more "Center" you're getting as well as a larger portion of the tenderloin.

To bone a Sirloin End, put it on the cutting board fat side down and study it for a moment. That little round muscle on top of the bone is the tenderloin. Simply run the blade of your boning knife under the tenderloin and scoop it out.

Now study the bone structure of the piece that is left. Notice the little space between the sections of the vertebrae. Notice, too, the way the bone along one side comes to a point at one end. Just up from that point, where the bone sort of levels off parallel with the cutting board, put the blade of your knife in the little space between the bones and cut through.

The rest of the bone (hip bone) is buried in the meat and must be excavated, so to speak. Start by running the tip of your knife around the portion of the bone that is visible.

Keep the blade edge against the bone and keep on digging. When you get to the bottom on one side, start down on the other. It's really not as complicated as you might think and the nice thing is, each

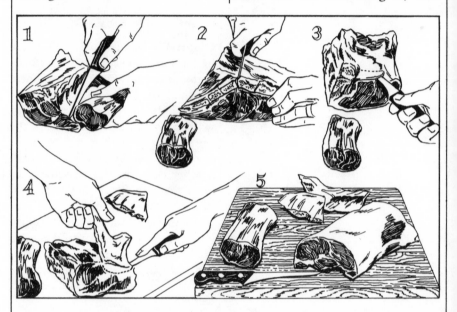

You won't be able to cut completely through but don't panic—all you need do for now is loosen between the bones.

Now slide the blade of your knife under the little finger bones to loosen the meat back to the chine bone. Turn the blade down toward the cutting board and continue along the feather bone until you have loosened the entire section. You have now completed the easy part.

Sirloin End Roast has the same bone structure so the second one you bone-out will seem considerably simpler. When you are finished you'll have: 1) a portion of the Pork Tenderloin; 2) a boneless Top Sirloin of Pork; 3) a pile of bones.

What—you may ask—does one do with all of this stuff. Ah, let me count the ways with it all!

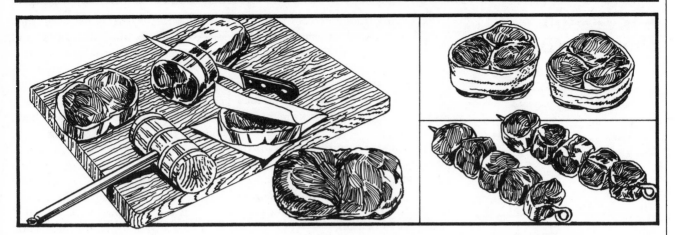

The Tenderloin can be baked, broiled, barbecued, sliced thick or thin or butterflied and fried. Cut 1½ or 2-inch sections and flatten the pieces between two sheets of wax paper for great Pork Cutlets or Sandwich Steaks. Try wrapping two or three thick slices with bacon to make Pork Tournedos for broiling. Thread pieces of Tenderloin on skewers for the most tender Pork Kabobs you've ever tasted.

The boneless Top Sirloin can be sliced in the same ways as the boneless Blade End—thick or thin for stuffing or cutlets or cubed for Kabobs.

Two Top Sirloins can be tied together to make a beautiful Rolled Roast.

1) Bone two Sirloin Ends of about equal length. Use the Tenderloin for a separate meal (see above).

2) Remove the tip of each Top Sirloin piece to make them both the same size. Use the tips to fill the pocket where the hip bone was removed.

3) Put the boneless Sirloins together with large ends opposite each other. Tie with string to make an excellent boneless Rolled Pork Sirloin Roast, beautiful for the rotisserie.

The pile of bones can add flavor to a pot of limas, pintos or sauerkraut—or add them to the stockpot.

101

The Boston Shoulder (Butt)

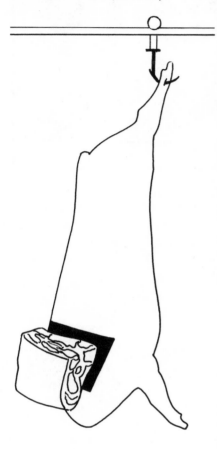

The Boston Shoulder comes off the pig just forward of the Loin. (See Chart.) In most meat markets across the country the Shoulder is merchandised very simply; either sliced into Pork Steaks, left whole and sold for a roast, or some combination of the two.

For those of us willing to do a little cutting-up at home the Boston Shoulder can be a gold mine of goodies. Keep your eye open for Pork Shoulder or Boston Butt on special at a good price and stock up.

lowing around the bone with the blade of your boning knife, you can easily remove the entire bone.

Once the bone has been removed, the possibilities for meal makings are many. The whole Butt can be rolled and tied to make an outstanding roast for the barbecue or the rotisserie. Because it has a fair amount of fat mixed through the lean it will be juicy and flavorful, and being boneless it is easy to balance on the spit. An added advantage is, it presents no

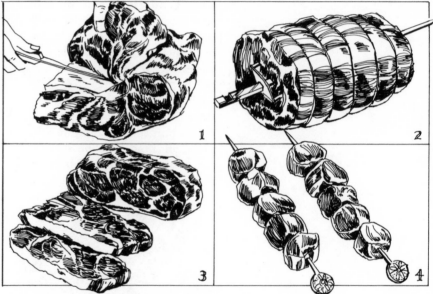

The best buy is usually the whole Shoulder rather than the boneless half, even though you are paying for a bit of bone. Some of the most tender tidbits are around the bone.

Boning out a Boston Butt is a snap. The only bone is a portion of the shoulder blade and you don't have to be a master butcher to take it out, the shape of the bone makes it easy. The bone is flat on one side and only extends approximately half way through the Butt. So, by simply fol-

problems at all when it comes to carving.

A whole Boston Butt will weigh somewhere around six or eight pounds. If that's too big a roast for your family, cut it in half. Use the boneless half for roasting and bone out the other end to make another meal or two.

Slices from the Butt are good fried, braised, baked or barbecued.

Any portion of the Boneless Butt can be cubed for "Pork Kabobs,"

"Adobu" or any other of the millions of recipes from around the world that call for cubes of lean pork.

Any portion on top of the blade bone is excellent for slicing thin into lean strips of pork for any number of Chinese stir-fry recipes, "Chop Suey" or "Chow Mein." Or try threading them on skewers for "Pork Teriyaki" or "Satay."

If you own a tenderizer, boneless slices of Pork Butt can be pounded into excellent Pork Cutlets. They will taste out of this world breaded, fried and served with mushroom gravy and fluffy mashed potatoes.

The Boston Butt has a good ratio of fat to lean, just right for the making of your homemade sausage. So save any scraps and bits of fat in a plastic freezer bag until you get ambitious in the sausage sense, then add them to the fixings for the grinder. Whatever you do with it, the Boston Butt is a good piece of pork to do your own thing with and save money.

Spare Ribs

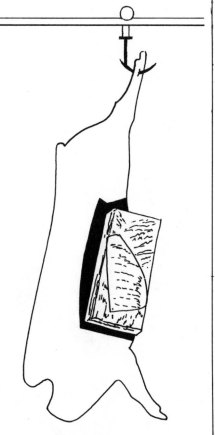

In addition to the various cuts of fresh pork made from the Loin and the Boston Butt, you will almost certainly find fresh Spare Ribs in your supermarket meat case.

Spare Ribs are simply the bones removed from that portion of the pig's side and belly which correspond to the Plate and Brisket of the Beef. What remains after the Spare Ribs are removed is the "Side Pork" which is usually sold cured, either as smoked bacon or salted salt pork.

There is little to be gained in terms of savings with this portion of the pig since there is no "merchandising" involved. Spare Ribs come into the meat market in the same form as they go out. The retail cut and the wholesale cut are the same.

Fresh Side Pork

Side Pork, that which lies on the outside of the Spare Ribs, is seldom available as fresh pork. Most of it is smoked, sliced and sold peeking at you through the window in a plastic package labeled "Bacon." Should you find fresh Side Pork in your butcher's meat case, try it breaded in flour and cornmeal and fried golden brown. For my money it's as good, if not better, than bacon for breakfast.

Side Pork is also available salted. Salt Pork keeps almost forever in the refrigerator and is handy to have on hand for seasoning stews, larding meat that needs a bit more fat and for

all kinds of flavoring. It's even good sliced and fried like fresh Side Pork but it needs to be blanched first to get rid of the excess salt.

Fresh Picnic Shoulder

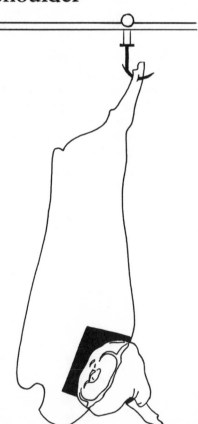

The Picnic Shoulder is the fore leg of the pig and a portion of the Shoulder just below the Boston Butt. Most often the Picnic is smoked and sold as a "Picnic Ham." As such, it can provide some relatively inexpensive and delicious smoked pork. We'll talk about Picnic Hams when we discuss smoked pork later in this chapter.

Occasionally you may see "Fresh Picnics" in the meat case or advertised in the supermarket specials. If the price is right, don't hesitate. There are a number of things and a number of meals you can make with a fresh Picnic and your boning knife.

The Hock can be removed and used for a pot of greens or beans or sauerkraut. Just find the joint and disjoint.

The remainder of the Picnic has only the arm bone to worry about and don't worry about that; just take it out. For a roast tie it back together as you did the Boston Butt. For lean and tender Kabobs, cut into one-inch cubes. Slice it, dice it, mince it or grind it; but whatever you do *save the skin*. "Crisp Fried Pork Skin Squares" make good hors d'oeuvres.

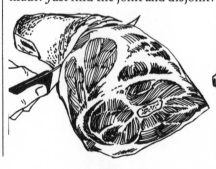

Fresh Leg of Pork

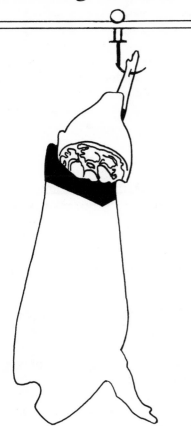

Roast Leg of Fresh Pork with heaping piles of mashed potatoes, gallons of gravy, hot homemade rolls and giant baked apples for dessert. That was standard fare on the farm the Sunday after "threshing." All the aunts, uncles and cousins who were there to help with the harvest early in the week were back on Sunday for a roast pork dinner. It was traditional.

Today we seldom see fresh legs of pork in the meat case. Now, as in Grandma's day, most legs of pork go to the smokehouse. If you want one for a special occasion, ask your butcher to order you one. It won't be inexpensive, but for a change of pace on a holiday or for a great buffet, a Leg of Pork is hard to beat.

Pigs' Feet

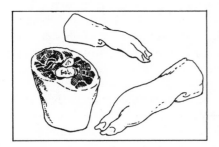

Pigs' Feet & Hocks: Probably the least expensive of all the pieces of fresh pork you'll ever find in any meat case are Pork Hocks and Pigs' Feet. Sometimes they are sold separately, sometimes left together. There isn't a lot of meat on the feet of the pig but what there is can make for some memorable meals when properly prepared. Both the front and hind feet are used and they can be boiled, broiled or baked; sautéed, jellied or simmered in a sweet and sour sauce. But the foot of a pig, in my opinion, can come to no better end than the pickle barrel.

Hams

The first thing that one thinks of when one thinks of smoked pork is Ham.

Country Hams: This country has produced some great and distinctive hams throughout its history. Everyone has heard of, if not tasted, the famous Smithfield Ham of Virginia. This lean hind leg of peanut-fed pork is dry-cured, rubbed with black pepper, slow smoked and then aged for ten or twelve months before being brought into the kitchen, scrubbed and soaked, and simmered and baked to provide what has become an almost legendary delicacy. There are others—the "Country Hams" of Tennessee and Georgia, Kentucky and Maryland; some "dry-salt cured" and "hickory-smoked," others "sweet pickle-cured" in brine and then smoked with fruit wood. There was a time when nearly every country community in America had its own distinctive version of the best way to handle the hind leg of a pig.

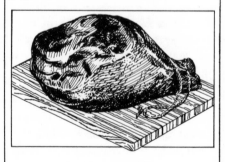

Unfortunately, the hams available in today's average, run-of-the-mill supermarket meat department bear little resemblance to their country cousins of a generation or so ago. They are about as unique, about as distinctive, about as different one from the other as are leaves of grass or needles on a pine tree.

The basic process for converting the pig's hind leg into Ham has remained very much the same almost since the time the first domestic pig was "processed." It involves first "curing"—the addition of salt in some form to retard bacterial action; then "smoking" to give the meat its characteristic flavor. Sometimes the "cure" is applied as a salt mixture which is rubbed into the meat by hand—a "dry cure." Or a brine solution is used and the hams are immersed in the brine—"pickle-cured." But most often today, hams are "pumped." The brine solution is injected into the ham with one or many needles.

"Pumping" has made it possible to save considerable time in the processing of a pig's hind leg. Hams nowadays most often go directly from the pumping room into the smokehouse where they are not only smoked but partially or even fully cooked in less than 24 hours. No more waiting around all winter for great ham, which may account for why there are very few "great" hams to be found anymore. Great hams take time, they just don't happen in 12 or even 24 hours. They also take time in the kitchen. They require more than the "heat-and-eat" treatment most of us feel we have time to give the preparation of a meal.

And so today hams come to the marketplace with little to distinguish one from the other save the shape into which they have been pressed or molded and the degree to which they have been precooked for your convenience. Dry Cured and Country Hams are still around. You can find them in specialty shops. And you can order them by mail from little towns in Kentucky and Virginia and Tennessee, where for some reason they still seem to find the time to take the time. (See page 204.)

But what about what *is* available in the Ham section of most supermarket meat cases? How well-done is "fully cooked?" What's a "Buffet" and a "Gourmet" and a "Tavern" Ham? What are the "natural juices" they add to the can? And what, pray tell, is an "Imitation Ham?"

City Hams: The hams we find in most city supermarkets these days are the well-dressed, mild-mannered, debonair but distant city cousins of the old fashioned hams common a generation ago. "City Hams" have much to commend them, but little to distinguish them one from the other with the exception of the package they come in.

Smoked Hams with the bone left in —are probably the closest kin to the "good old-fashioned country ham." These, like all hams, have been cured in a salt brine and then smoked with *real* smoke (if liquid smoke is used it must be so labeled). The smoking process also includes, to one degree or another, the application of heat. The degree to which the heat has been applied determines which of a variety of phrases like "cook before eating," "fully cooked," "ready to eat," can appear on the label.

Virtually all hams available in today's supermarkets fall under USDA inspection regulations which require that they be heated to an internal temperature of at least 137 degrees in the smoking/cooking process. That degree of heat is sufficient to kill the Trichina parasite but not enough to call the harn "cooked." In order to wear the "fully cooked" or "ready to eat" label the ham must be brought to an internal temperature of at least 148 degrees and most are cooked to 155-160 degrees. If there is no label—and often hams come into the market without wrappers, still wearing the netting in which they hung in the smokehouse—you can pretty well tell how well-done the ham is by checking the *bone*. If the bone is protruding well out of the meat at either end of the ham and if the aitch bone, that flat looking bone about half way up the leg, stands well out from the meat, chances are the ham is quite well-cooked. If the ham is so plump that the bones do not protrude, the ham requires further cooking. As far as flavor is concerned, I think any "City Ham" can be improved by further cooking.

Boneless Hams come in a variety of wondrous and convenient sizes and shapes. Some are formed and molded into uniform ovals, rounds or squares and labeled "Gourmet" or "Buffet" hams. Others—"Tavern Hams"—are simply tied back together in a shape roughly resembling a ham with the bone taken out. Boneless Hams fall under the same USDA regulations with regard to minimum temperature and labels, as do hams with the bone in. The only hams that do not come under those regulations are canned hams.

Canned Hams—those round, pear, or square-shaped cans with the pretty pictures on the front and the "easy" recipes on the back—contain a meat that is (for my money) about as removed from ham as the hind leg of a pig can get. Perhaps that's because the standards they are required to meet are not as strict in some regards as those for other hams. Any ham outside the can may contain no added moisture and still qualify for the name. If the finished product, after curing, smoking, and cooking weighs more than the hind leg of the pig weighed to start with, the product must be labeled "Ham—water added," and if the percentage of extra weight exceeds 10% it must be labeled "Imitation Ham." Canned hams, however may contain as much as 8% added water without letting you know on the label.

All canned hams are "ready to eat" since USDA regulations require that they be cooked to a minimum internal temperature of 150 degrees, and most bear the proud inscription "Fully Cooked" somewhere on their colorful label. Also somewhere there is likely to be the very important but often ignored instruction to "Keep Refrigerated." Some canned hams are "sterilized" and do not require refrigeration but most are not and

they *do*. If the can says do it—DO IT—and don't buy a can from a butcher that doesn't.

Picnic Ham—At this writing, my family has just finished devouring to the last delicious tender morsel, one of the most fantastic hams I have ever tasted. It was meaty and lean with a salty sweet flavor that had some character to it, like an old-fashioned "Country Ham." Nothing like the bland, canned, tasteless things that have come to pass for hams far too often these days.

We picked it up "on special" at 59¢ a pound. It weighed just over seven pounds and came to just under $4.50, which is, you must agree, a very good price for any ham. But I must confess, while it was the best ham I've had in a long time, it really wasn't a ham at all. It was a Smoked Picnic Shoulder; the smoked front leg of a pig, rather than the smoked hind leg which is a true Ham.

Picnics generally tend to have a bit more fat than regular hams, and for that reason they are always far closer to the inexpensive side of the pig. Finding them "on special" at a very good price is not at all uncommon.

Selecting a good Picnic out of a pile is, however, a little more difficult. You can't see a good Picnic, you have to feel it. If it's solid and has a good firm feel to it, chances are it will be fairly lean and, with a little expert carving, will provide a lot more than a good ham dinner.

Cook a Picnic just as you would a regular ham, but be sure to remove the skin first—it makes carving easier. Carving a Picnic is very like carving a ham, once you have figured out where the bone lies. Follow the instructions for "Carving a Leg of Anything" on page 178.

Out of that seven-plus pound Picnic our family of four got the following: 1) One memorable meal of Baked Ham with Mustard-Honey Glaze, the likes of which would make the hind leg of any pig jealous.

2) Ham and Eggs for two mornings from what was left off the solid boneless arm meat. (3) Enough for sliced ham sandwiches for the kids' lunches two more days. 4) Plus, bits and pieces of lean ham which, while too small to slice, were just right to grind one time through Grandma's old meat grinder along with a couple of sweet pickles and mix with mayonnaise to make "Deviled Ham" for another day's lunch. 5) And, on top of all that, a ham bone that—added to 1¼ cups of dry white beans, half an onion, a stalk of finely-chopped celery, and a couple quarts of water —made enough of "Grandma's Good Old-Fashioned Bean Soup" for yet another simple family lunch or supper.

That's a lot of good eating for less than $4.50, without even counting a big bowl of "Cracklin's" made from the skin.

Bacon

Most of what passes for Bacon comes to the market these days in plastic packages and is sold peering at you through little windows with cardboard shutters that say "Lift me and see how lean I am." Like the "City Ham" it is a far cry from the Bacon of a generation ago. It is quick cured, lightly smoked and sliced so thin it almost evaporates in the frying pan. For a real Bacon treat ask your butcher to order you a slab of Bacon, or order one from the old-fashioned firms listed in the Appendix. Slice off a few slices, thick enough so you can at least feel them between your fingers, and then fry them slowly until they just begin to crisp. Don't let the Bacon cook until it's so crisp it disintegrates—you may as well buy the stuff that peeks at you from the package if you're going to do that. Just until it begins to crisp, then pour off and save the fat, drain the Bacon on a paper towel and enjoy!

Not only will you get better Bacon buying it in the slab, you will also get Bacon that lasts longer. Sliced package Bacon tends to go rancid quite fast but slab Bacon will keep for weeks in your refrigerator. Bacon, however, does not freeze well for long periods of time, so don't fill the freezer. Slab Bacon, in most markets, is usually a bit less expensive than sliced Bacon, although that may not be the case if you buy really great old-fashioned, slow-cured Bacon from a mail-order house.

Most Slab Bacon comes with the rind left on and that's an additional treat. Cut the rind into one-inch squares, put them in a baking dish in a hot oven until they snap, crackle and puff up. You've got cracklin's!

Canadian Bacon

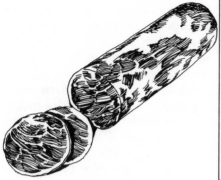

Bacon, as we know it, comes from the belly of the hog, while Canadian style bacon is from the lean, tender "eye" of the Loin, right in the middle of the back. In fact Canadians themselves don't call it "Canadian Bacon," they call it "Back Bacon." It was the English who first started calling it Canadian Bacon, back in the days when they imported most of their bacon from Canada. Now, everybody calls it Canadian Bacon except the Canadians.

Canadian Bacon is often passed up by consumers because the price seems high. It is high compared to regular Bacon but that's an unfair comparison. Canadian Bacon is pre-cooked, so there is little shrinkage; it's almost all lean, so you can get a greater number of servings per pound. Canadian Bacon can be better compared to Boneless Ham. The curing process is quite similar to the needle injection of hams. The Loins are smoked after curing, like hams, and in the process the internal temperature is brought up to a minimum of 152 degrees, which qualifies it as a "Fully Cooked" product according to USDA specifications.

Use Canadian Bacon like Bacon but don't overlook the possibilities of using it like Ham. It can be baked, barbecued and roasted as well as fried.

Cottage Roll— (Smoked Pork Butt)

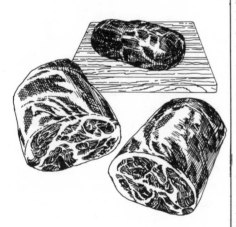

These little goodies make their appearance on the table at my house with more regularity than almost any other type of smoked meat. We have them baked, broiled, barbecued, fried for breakfast and roasted with a honey glaze. They are delicious!

A Cottage Roll is a smoked Boston Butt. It is cured and processed the same way as a Ham or Picnic but, because it is a Butt, it has a bit more fat than either of the others. It has, therefore, as far as I'm concerned, a bit more flavor. They usually weigh between one and four pounds, which makes them a good size for a small family.

Ham Hocks

Ham Hocks used to be the smoked version of the fresh Pork Hocks we mentioned earlier; the upper portion of the lower foreleg, just above the pigs' feet. Those kind are still around and they're great for flavoring a pot of beans or Split Pea Soup, but there is a new kind around.

Since the advent of the Boneless Rolled Tavern Ham and "Gourmet Hams," and all those other boneless plastic-packaged "City Hams," a new form of "ham hock" is available. When legs of pork are boned out to make Boneless Hams, the shank bone is left with some meat around it. These are smoked and sold as "Hocks" or Ham Shanks. They have all the flavor of the old-fashioned version, with much more meat.

Dozens of other pieces of the pig that used to be readily available are seldom seen today outside of small meat markets in various ethnic neighborhoods. If you are fortunate enough to live where you can get them, there is a lot of inexpensive good eating in the heads, tails, jowls and ears of "the guy who pays the bills"—that's a quaint Mid-Western saying for *the pig*.

VEAL

Chapter 7

A t least six times each and every week, I am asked "Why can't I ever find that nice, white, milk-fed veal like they have in Europe?"

My answer has always been, "I'll be damned if I know!" We have better beef, by far, and far better pork than any other country in the world. Only a few countries can equal the quality of our lamb. Even the white Peking ducks of China would turn pink with envy at the quality of some of our Long Island ducklings, and probably pure purple if compared to those of the Reichart farm in Petaluma, California. But when it comes to veal, we seem to fall far short, with a few notable exceptions, of the quality available in other countries.

While I can see no really good logical excuse for our second-rate veal, perhaps the nature of the meat itself offers a partial explanation.

Veal is a by-product of the dairy industry. In order to produce milk a cow must be "fresh," or have recently calved.

The breeds of cattle used for milk production in Europe—the Simmentals of Switzerland, the Limousins from France, Red Angus of Great Britain, the Gelbvieh of Germany—all are much larger, "beefier" breeds than the Holsteins and Guernseys used for that purpose here. As a result their calves make larger, meatier veal. Also, in Europe, where pasture land is at a premium, veal is traditionally marketed directly off mother's milk, while American dairy farmers often let calves graze or "feed them out a little" in order to profit from the added weight.

As soon as a calf starts feeding on anything other than milk, it gets iron in its system and the flesh begins to turn red. And there goes that "nice, white, milk-fed veal like they have in Europe."

There may be a bright spot or two on the horizon for those who love good veal and are willing to pay a premium to obtain it. Many of the "exotic" European breeds are finding their way into this country, primarily for their potential contribution to beef production. Perhaps they will also be used to "beef up" the dairy herds, and ultimately make for better veal.

Meanwhile, there is the "Dutch Method." First introduced to this country in 1962, it provides for the systematic and scientific feeding of select calves with milk "replacers," a powdered milk product supplemented with other nutrients, to provide the iron-free diet necessary for "nice, white, milk-fed veal."

Given time and a consumer demand, the dairy industry will probably be able to provide better veal in the years ahead.

Veal Primal Cuts

Veal, according to the United States Department of Agriculture is "an immature bovine animal not over three months of age: the same animal after three months, and after having subsisted for a period of time on feeds other than milk, is classified as calf." The only way the consumer can tell the difference is by color; calf, because of the iron in its diet, will have a more pinkish cast to the flesh.

Veal most often comes into the market in one of two forms. Either it comes in the carcass, usually split into two halves, or it comes in primal cuts, packed in boxes. In either case, the cuts that end up in your butcher's meat case are much the same. In most respects they resemble their counterparts in the beef and lamb. The method of cooking veal, however, is not related to the location of the cut on the carcass as it is with other meat.

Veal, while it is a very young animal and therefore extremely tender, does not do too well when cooked with dry heat. There isn't enough fat on veal for dryheat methods of cooking. Regardless of where they come from on the veal, all cuts need gentle moist-heat cooking to keep from being dry. To enhance the taste, which can be rather bland, a good sauce is also recommended.

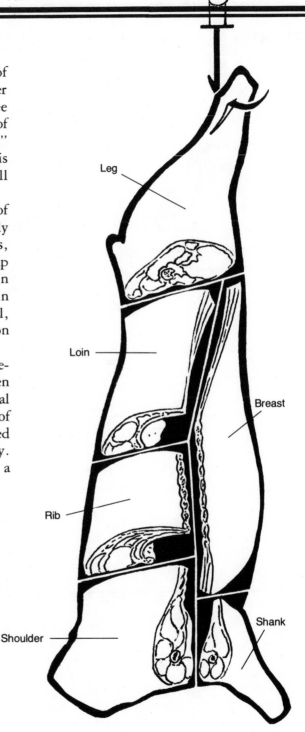

115

Veal Loin

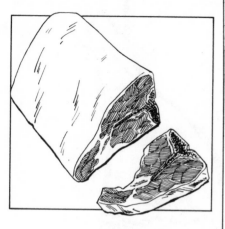

The Loin of Veal is the same as that of beef, lamb, or buffalo as far as the location on the carcass is concerned; it lies between the Rib and the Sirloin. Most markets that handle veal merchandise the Loin simply as Veal Chops. Slices are cut from one to 1½ inches thick and sold for braising. A classic dish from days gone by was Veal Kidney Chops.

The kidney with its surrounding fat was left in the Loin when it was cut into chops. The resulting chops each contained a portion of the kidney. These are almost impossible to find anymore since most USDA inspectors open the kidney "clod" in the process of inspecting the carcass. This destroys the Kidney Chop. You can make a modern version of this classic, simply by wrapping the "tail" of a Veal Chop around a slice of Veal Kidney.

The Loin can also be used for an excellent and elegant roast, but buying one will likely cost you a fortune. If that kind of elegance appeals to you, you can probably save at least a half a fortune if you make your own. Follow the instruction given for making a Rolled Loin of Lamb given on page 79. You can use either one Loin or two Loins rolled together, depending upon the number of people you plan to serve and the size of your fortune. The top loin muscle of the Loin also makes magnificent but expensive Veal Cutlets (see page 117).

Veal Rib

The Rib or "Rack of Veal," like the Rib of Beef usually contains seven rib bones. The most common method of merchandising the Rack of Veal is simply to cut it into Rib Chops. These will probably sell for less than chops cut from the Loin since they do contain more bone and waste, but even at best they will be expensive. All veal is, at best, expensive.

The Rack of Veal can be used as a roast, or two or three can be tied together to make a "Crown." It can be boned and rolled like the Rack of Lamb (see page 84), but unlike the Rack of Lamb, will not roast too well without a little moisture. Veal needs moist heat.

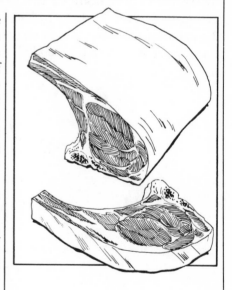

Veal Sirloin

The Sirloin of Veal corresponds to the Sirloin of Beef. It has the same bone structure containing the hip bone, but it is seldom sold with the bone in. Most often the entire Sirloin portion is boned out and the separate muscles—the tenderloin, top loin and Sirloin tip—are sliced thin and labeled "Scallops."

The Sirloin is more often left attached to and merchandised as part of the leg.

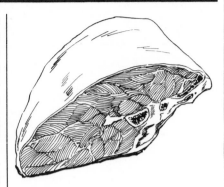

Veal Leg

The Leg of Veal including the Sirloin, is called the Hind Saddle. From this section come the most sought after and expensive cuts of the veal: Veal Cutlets or Scaloppini, Schnitzel or Escalopes depending on whether your veal or your butcher is Italian, German or French. The Leg is usually boned out and the separate muscles divided along the natural seams. Cutlets are then made by slicing thin slices from those separate muscles.

The Top Round, Bottom Round, Eye of the Round, Sirloin Tip, Top Sirloin and Tenderloin cuts all make excellent Cutlets. So for that matter, does any muscle of the veal that is solid and contains little or no sinew or fibers. It is often possible to cut your own cutlets from other parts of the carcass and save some money. The shoulder, for example, has cutlet potential at a possible saving, so for that matter has the leg if you buy it by the roast and slice it yourself.

Many markets merchandise all or part of the leg as Veal Roast. From the whole Hind Saddle the roast possibilities are:

Sirloin Roast: The whole Sirloin section sold with the bone in, a good roast, but a "bear" to carve.

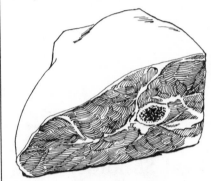

The Rump: The "Standing" or bone-in Rump is an excellent roast, but it does contain a good deal of bone. The aitch bone and the knuckle where the leg joins the hip make up a large amount of the weight of the Rump.

Center Cut Leg: This roast contains only the small arm bone. It is a great one to slice up for cutlets. Just separate the muscles along the seams, slice them thin and pound them. Or use one muscle for cutlets and tie the rest back together to make a rolled roast.

Shank Half of Leg: This portion of the Leg contains lot of the less tender connective tissue present in the Shank. It has a good flavor but will not be as tender as the Rump or Center Cut.

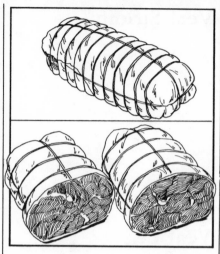

Rolled Leg Roast: Any and all of the cuts of the leg are often sold as boneless rolled roasts. These can often provide some relatively inexpensive Veal Cutlets. Simply untie the roll, separate out the solid muscle for slicing into cutlets, and use what's left for Veal Stew or grinding.

Veal Shoulder

The Shoulder of Veal is, as far as location on the carcass, bone structure and methods of merchandising are concerned, comparable to the Shoulder of Lamb and the Beef Chuck. Like Lamb Shoulder, it is often cut into Arm Steaks and Blade Steaks with the bone left in. Or, like Beef Chuck, it is cut into Pot Roasts from both the arm and blade sides of the Square Cut Chuck.

But most often the Shoulder of Veal is boned and rolled.

This is often the least expensive boneless cut of veal you will find. It can be a gold mine of goodies for a kitchen cut-up, just like its counterpart on the beef or lamb. Of course, you can save even more if you can find a butcher who will sell you a whole Square-Cut Shoulder and you bone it out yourself. See page 88 on boning a Shoulder of Lamb.

Veal Shank

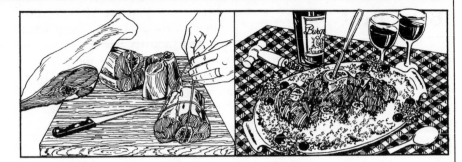

The front leg and the lower portion of the hind leg of veal are both merchandised as Veal Shank. Like the Shank of Beef this cut contains a great amount of connective tissue and is an excellent addition to the stockpot. It gives a pot of stock that rich, thick gelatinous quality that makes for great soups and sauces.

Veal Shanks are at their best and most magnificent when served as "Osso Buco." That's Italian for "hollow bone," but the bone is not hollow. It's filled with marrow and to any Osso Buco enthusiast, that's the best part.

Veal Breast

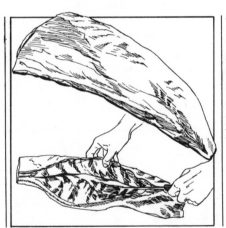

The Breast of Veal, like that of lamb can be used for all sorts of good and relatively inexpensive dishes. It can be stuffed, rolled, simmered, braised, cut into Riblets or boned out and ground. See all of the instructions for Breast of Lamb, on page 90.

Ground Veal

Save any and all trimmings from any cutting-up you do with veal. Add them to your beef trimmings and toss in a bit of pork and you have the makings for the best meat loaf mix you can imagine. Use two parts beef to one part each of veal and pork for great results.

119

Baby Beef

There is nothing at all *new*, (all claims to the contrary), about what the Beef Industry has chosen to put on the market during the past few years as Baby Beef. It has been around since the first cow had the first calf, and will likely be around until a few months after the last cow does the same thing. The difference is that in these past few years "Baby Beef" has been offered for sale and promoted heavily for the first time in a long time.

Actually, it's happened many times before—oh, it may not have been called "Baby Beef"—if my memory serves me correctly, we used to call it "Kip" or "Kipper Calf." It usually made its appearance, (without quite as much promotion), in the fall following a bad summer.

To illustrate, let me tell you about Uncle Virgil, who'd been raising cattle for years. When he had a bad year—when hail ruined the corn crop, the wind blew the roof off the silo and the rain rotted the grain—when things just seemed to go to hell all year, he might drop by the house and talk to my Dad. They'd sit around the big table in the kitchen sipping coffee and the sad story would go something like this:

"Mike, you know things haven't gone too well this year— with the hail and all . . . I've got a couple of real nice "Kipper" calves, been on good grass all summer . . . I was plannin' on feedin' 'em out, but with things bein' how they are, losin' the grain in the silo and all, I just don't think I can afford to finish 'em out. They're awful nice. They won't eat like beef, but they'll be nice and tender. If you've got any room in your locker and if you can see fit, I sure would be obliged if you'd take 'em off my hands. I'll give 'em to you at a good price. Then maybe next year, when things look a little better, I'll feed a good calf out for you like you like and give you a good price on him too. Sure would

120

appreciate it if you could help me out this year. . . ."

In a very real sense, that is exactly what the beef industry has been saying to us the past year or so. Of course now they have Public Relations departments and "Beef Councils" and we don't sit down together around the kitchen table, but the story's the same. The cattlemen of this country have had a whole lot of young calves on grass that—"things bein' how they are" —they just can't afford to feed on out to the quality finished beef we have come to expect of the "Uncle Virgils" of the cattle industry. So, they need help if they are going to be able to stay in business and, maybe in a year or two, get back to providing the kind of quality we have come to expect.

Meanwhile, "if you can see fit" and if you can get it at a good price, you'd be doing the beef industry a big favor by taking a little Baby Beef off their hands. You might like it. It's lean, with hardly any fat, and that should make some of you happy. It should be tender, it hasn't lived long enough (only 7 to 10 months) to get tough. As far as flavor is concerned, however, it may need a little help.

You can cook Baby Beef in all the same ways that you would normally cook beef but it may, to quote an industry press release, ". . . enhance the flavor if you brush the steaks with melted fat before broiling." And, also, "because Baby Beef is similar to veal, in some respects, marinating or breading will enhance the flavor."

POULTRY

Chapter 8

Chicken is one of the most versatile, most nourishing, used to be one of the most inexpensive, and is still one of the most fun foods you can find. It has been for a long time; since sometime around 1000 B.C., in fact, when one of our primitive ancestral gourmets, somewhere in the jungles of India, first plucked and then impaled on a stick and then roasted over hot coals, the forefather of the bird we find in today's supermarket with no plumage to pluck save a cardboard tag on his wing.

It used to be, you could tell a lot about a bird by its plumage. You could easily tell a him from a her by the color or by the shape of the tail. You could tell how old a rooster was by the size of his comb and the spurs on his feet. You could tell if he was still a rooster or had been turned into a capon, not only by his behavior in the henhouse, but also by the size and shape of his head. To some folks the color of the feathers was a sure sign of quality, to others the most important thing was the color of the feet.

These days the only plumage you're likely to find on any bird is some clear plastic wrap and that small paper tag on the wing. No longer is it necessary to scald and pluck and singe to rid the bird of his plumage. Simply peel off the plastic, pull off the tag and he's plucked.

There is, none the less, a good bit you can tell about the quality of the bird if you learn to read the useful information available on that paper and plastic plumage. It can tell you every bit as much, perhaps even more, than its prettier but less legible counterpart of the past. It can give you some assurance as to the "wholesomeness" of the bird. Virtually all poultry offered for sale in this country is inspected for wholesomeness by the U.S. Department of Agriculture. Trained government inspectors keep constant check on poultry farms and processing plants to make sure that birds are raised and processed under sanitary conditions. They also inspect each bird to make sure it is not diseased before it is offered for consumption.

Assurance of wholesomeness   Assurance of quality

Our assurance that a bird has received all of that attention and passed all of the tests, appears as a little round stamp somewhere on the paper plumage. The tag can also tell you better than a cock's comb the approximate age of the bird, which in turn tells you how it should be cooked. Young birds are naturally more tender than old birds and qualify for dry-heat cooking: barbecuing, frying, broiling or roasting. The age of the bird is indicated on the label in terms approved by the USDA.

Young chickens may be labeled young chicken, broiler, roaster, fryer, capon or Rock Cornish game hen.

Young turkeys may be labeled young turkeys, fryer/roaster, young hen or young tom.

Young ducks may be labeled duckling, young duckling, broiler duckling, fryer duckling or roaster duckling.

Tough old birds that require long slow, moist-heat cooking are referred to most often as "mature."

Mature chickens may be labeled mature chicken, old chicken, hen, stewing chicken or fowl.

Mature turkeys may be labeled mature turkey, yearling turkey or old turkey.

Mature ducks, *geese and guinea hens* may be labeled mature or old.

Another bit of useful information that may appear on a bird's paper plumage is the USDA Grade stamp. The Department of Agriculture provides a grading service on a voluntary basis to poultry processors and others who request and pay the fee for it. U.S. grades apply to five kinds of poultry: chicken, turkey, duck, goose and guinea. There are three grades—designated A, B and C, although you will seldom see grade B or C printed on a poultry label.

Poultry must be federally inspected for wholesomeness before it can be graded for quality. When it is graded it will carry the shieldlike mark of class A distinction. Often the shield and the inspection mark are proudly displayed together on one piece of "paper plumage."

Perhaps the most subtle, but I think significant, bit of information on many birds' "plumage" is the point of origin. It doesn't apply so much to frozen birds, but it seems logical to assume that a "fresh" fryer processed and sold in California will be a bit fresher than a bird raised and processed in Arkansas, then shipped to California to be eaten.

Learning to understand the markings on the modern bird's "plumage" is no guarantee that you won't sometimes get a tough turkey or a less than fresh fryer, but it can help. Grandma goofed on occasion, even when the young red rooster did have yellow feet.

High price of parsley

One thing you need to do if you're concerned with saving money on chicken is stay awake when you pick it, and I don't mean pluck it. Doze off for just an instant and you may do something dumb, like paying $104.00 a pound for parsley! I saw people doing just that not long ago at the supermarket in my neighborhood. Let me tell you how I figured out the cost of that parsley.

Frying chickens were on special at 48¢ per pound and, as is so often the case when something is on sale, the display was not the neatest. The chickens were stuffed into plastic bags and unappetizingly dumped into the display case with little regard for aesthetics. They were nice birds; "three and ups," which in the jargon of the trade means between three and three-and-one-half pounds each. And though it was hard to see through the foggy plastic bag into which they had been so unceremoniously stuffed, they did have a good color and they were nice and plump. I bought one: 3.35 lbs. @ 48¢ per, came to $1.61—not a bad buy!

Right next to this pile of dumped-in fryers was a row of "Roasting Chickens." They were beautiful! Each one with its wings carefully folded behind it, the legs tucked up along the side, the skin smooth and sparkling under tight plastic wrap, each in its own clean white styrofoam tray with a piece of green parsley perched between its legs. They were beautiful. Of course they were a bit more expensive; they were 79¢ a pound. I picked one up and looked at the tag. It weighed 3.36 pounds and came to $2.65. I said *"You've got to be kidding!"* so loud I made a baby cry in the cart ahead of me and woke at least three other shoppers out of their supermarket-induced daze.

A roasting chicken at 79¢ per pound, weighing

3.36 lbs., cost $2.65; the fryer I had just put in my shopping cart "on special" at 48¢ per pound weighed 3.35 lbs. and cost $1.61. That's a difference, as far as weight is concerned, of one one-hundreth of a pound —and a difference in price of $1.04. Since it is illegal to charge for packaging material, I can only assume the difference in price was the cost of that parsley!

The only real difference between one young chicken and another is weight, but usually the difference is a bit more than .01 of a pound. Normally young chickens under two or two-and-one-half pounds are classed "Broilers." Between two-and-one-half and four pounds, they fall into the "Fryer" category. Usually "Roasters" are over four pounds. There is, however, no definite division among the classes either in the marketplace or in the kitchen. You can fry a "Broiler," broil a "Fryer," fry a "Roaster" or roast a "Fryer." So if you are asked to pay a premium for one over the other, make sure you're getting more than a pretty package with a piece of parsley.

Chicken is not as inexpensive as it once was but perhaps it is compensation that its preparation is neither as time consuming or as messy. A Sunday chicken dinner at Grandma's house used to start just after breakfast when Gramp, hatchet in hand, headed for the henhouse. That done, there was still the long and tedious process of scalding, plucking, dressing and disjointing before the bird was ready for the pan.

Today all of that is done for us and I really doubt that any of us would have it any other way. For the most part it's worth the money to let somebody else do it. There is one step in the process, however, that we would do well to perform ourselves if we are really concerned about saving money.

As has always been the case, you cut food costs with chicken best when *you* cut the chicken.

Cutting Up a Chicken

The first step in cutting up a chicken is one of contemplation. As with the Ox, you must begin to see "the distinctions." You must look for the "spaces in the joints."

Buy a fryer or, better yet, keep your eyes open for a sale and when the price is right, buy several. Put one on the cutting board and just look at it for a while. Study it. Touch it (feels gickey, doesn't it?). That's all right, get used to it—remember you are saving money. Try to figure out where the component parts seem to be attached. Okay, ready now—cut it up!

1) Turn the chicken so that it is lying on its side with the wings on the left. Take your boning knife firmly in your right hand and the chicken's wing in your left hand. Move the wing up and down a time or two to find the target area. Now place the tip of the knife on what looks like the joint and disjoint. If you hit something hard, you missed. But don't panic. Just wriggle the knife blade around a little, there's a joint there somewhere and it's worth your effort to find it.

2) When you have successfully disengaged the wing, turn the bird so the leg is on the left. Lift the leg with your left hand so that the skin on the forward side is stretched tight. Raise and lower the leg a couple of times to get the feel of it. Notice, as you are lifting, the spot on the back where the thing seems to be attached; that's your next target. Make a little cut with the tip of your knife to mark the spot.

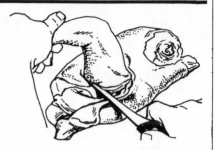

Holding the leg out from the chicken, cut through the tight skin and on down to the joint, first on one side of the leg and then the other. If you zeroed-in on the target correctly, the leg should now come off. If it doesn't, just help it along with the blade of the knife—it will.

Now that wasn't so bad was it? You're doing fine. If you ran into a tough joint or missed a target don't worry about it; just turn the bird over and try it again, first the wing and then the leg.

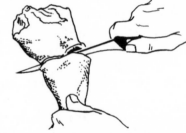

If you want the leg and thigh separated, do that now before proceeding with the rest of the bird. Lay the leg on the cutting board—skin side down. Hold the leg with the left hand and with the right move the thigh back and forth to find the joint. Then slip the knife between the joint. (There is a space, you'll find it.) While you're at it, you may as well remove the tips of the wings. There's not enough meat on them to mess with, so cut them off—*but*—don't throw them away. Set them aside, we'll get to them later.

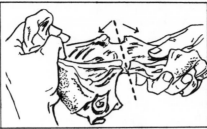

3) Turn what's left so that it is lying on its back with the breast on the left. Hold it steady with your left hand and cut through the skin at the rear to the center of the back. Put your knife down and with your right hand bend the back back until it breaks in half. Cut off the bottom half.

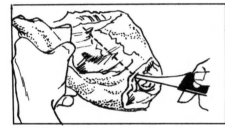

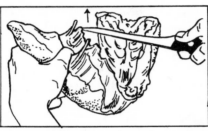

4) Hold the breast in your left hand with the broad end on the cutting board and the pointed end pointing up. Notice the white cartilage where the wing was removed. Just above that cartilage there is an open space. Insert the knife blade through that opening and out the corresponding opening on the other side. Now look on the inside of the bird. Up from where your knife blade is, there is a row of little white dots of cartilage where the ribs are connected to the breast. Lift your knife up, cutting through each of the little dots. It's a little like the dot-drawings you did when you were a kid—only the dots aren't numbered. Again put down your knife and with your right hand bend back the back until it separates from the breast.

Learning this basic kitchen skill is well-worth the effort from an economic point of view and there are tremendous gastronomic advantages as well. You would be hard-pressed to find a friendly butcher anywhere who would bone and stuff chicken breasts for you, or prepare chicken wings Chinese-style, or bone out an entire bird. But you can do it yourself once

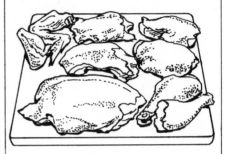

you've mastered the basic art of cutting-up a chicken.

Over the years I have developed what I think is a good system for cutting, packaging and freezing chicken at home to take advantage of good buys without getting sick to death of chicken. With some regularity fresh fryers are an advertised special at one of the neighborhood markets in almost every neighborhood. Sometimes fryers are "loss leader" specials, which means that you can buy them for little if any more than your butcher paid for them. That's the time to buy!

When I find good fryers on sale at the right price, I buy four—that's a good number for my family of four—take them home and get out the cutting board, a good sharp knife, and go to it. Take the little paper tags off the wings and throw them away. Remove the packets of giblets from the inside of the birds, open them, empty their contents on the cutting board and throw the paper away. That's all you get to throw away because, if you really want to save money, the rest gets used.

I love sautéed chicken livers on toast for breakfast, so I separate out the livers and freeze them for a future breakfast treat or to be used for "Rumaki" should a party be in order. The hearts, gizzards and necks go into a separate pile and are set aside.

Now take one of the fryers (the largest), wrap it in foil or some type of freezer wrap and freeze. This will be roasted, stuffed with a good dressing, or perhaps if we feel posh, simply basted with butter and brandy and garnished with artichoke hearts and new potatoes—"á la Mascotte."

The remaining chickens I cut up and pile in separate stacks. All the leg pieces go in one stack, the thighs in another. That's six pieces each, enough for our family of four for two meals of country fried chicken, chicken in orange sauce or any one of the millions of chicken recipes that fill cookbooks in every language from "Poulet" to "Pollo;" "Muraha" to "Gai."

The breasts get boned, and now that you've mastered cutting up a chicken; don't sweat boning a breast. Luckily, since there are so many beautiful and delicious dishes that can be made from boneless chicken breasts, it's a snap.

Boning the Breast

Put a whole breast skin-side down on the cutting board and look at it for a minute. It's almost heart-shaped, right?

Turn the breast so that the point of the heart is away from you. With your boning knife cut through the white cartilage right in the center of the cleavage. Now, if you'll pick it up and bend it back, the keel bone will pop loose.

board, point away from you and look at it again. See the two long bones that extend back toward the point, one on each side?

Slip the point of your knife under the one on the left and loosen it to make yourself a little handle. Hold the little handle in your left hand and lift. The meat will cling to the cutting board and the rib cage will almost come off in your hand if you help it along with your knife. Wasn't that easy? Now do the other side the same way and all you have left is the "wishbone."

Work your fingers down the sides to loosen the meat, then pull out the entire bone including the cartilage at the pointed end.

Put the breast back on the cutting

You know where that is, take it out. There, wasn't that easy and aren't you proud?

From our three fryers we now have a stack of six boneless pieces of breast meat. Each breast can be cut in half to make two servings, so we have more than enough for the family. If we serve it in any one of a million good sauces and accompany it with a rice pilaf, we can even invite guests for dinner.

In another stack are six wings with the tips removed. Not enough for a meal but if they are frozen until next time when six more materialize, then there will be enough for a generous serving for the four of us, Chinese-style perhaps.

What about what's left—the backs, the wing tips, the gizzards and the necks? These become the basis for the best the chicken has to offer, that which science has confirmed to be the most effective medication for the common cold—good old-fashioned *Chicken Soup.* See page 148.

Now that you've mastered cutting up a chicken and boning out the breast, there is no end to the wild and wonderful things you can do with the various parts of the bird.

Stuffed Breasts

There are dozens of classic recipes for various forms of stuffed chicken breasts but they all fall into only two categories as far as "cutting up" is concerned. Either they call for whole breasts or half-breasts, most often the latter.

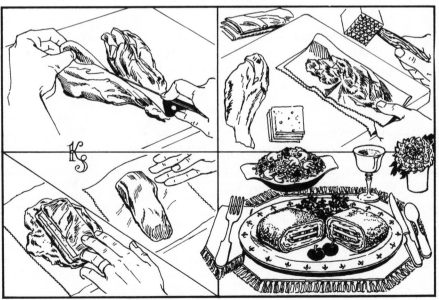

To stuff a half chicken breast simply cut a boneless breast in half along the mark where the keel bone came out. Remove the skin by running your fingers under it and gently pulling it away. Place each half between pieces of waxed paper and flatten them slightly with a mallet, the side of your meat cleaver or the bottom of a heavy frying pan. Then put a bit of stuffing in the center of each (ham and cheese for "Cordon Bleu," butter for "Chicken Kiev," whatever) and fold it over. Depending on what the breast is being stuffed with, it may or may not be necessary to secure the two sides with toothpicks and/or string. Most often it is enough to simply fold the breast over whatever is inside. The breast will firm up during cooking and hold everything in.

Stuffing a whole breast is a little more trouble but it can make a very attractive little individual "bird" for a special dinner party.

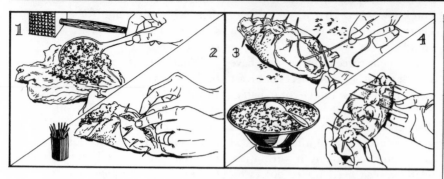

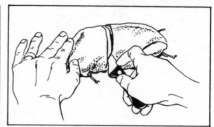

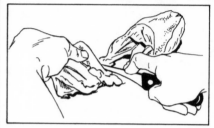

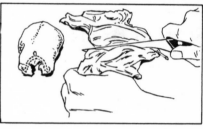

This time don't split the breast, but do flatten the whole piece lightly between two sheets of waxed paper. Put some of your favorite stuffing in the middle—it could be a brown rice or a bread stuffing, I have even had it stuffed with tiny cooked shrimp, sautéed in butter and served with a white wine sauce. Use your imagination.

Now hold the two sides together and secure with toothpicks at about one-inch intervals. Using a piece of cotton string, lace around the toothpicks, the way you would an old-fashioned pair of high top shoes, and you've got it—Stuffed Chicken Breasts. These make elegant individual servings for a special dinner party and they can be made at a very reasonable price.

Saving the wishbone

If the "little ones" around your table outnumber the gourmets, you may want to cut the breast so that the wishbone is left intact, for the kids to wish with. That used to be an important part of Sunday dinner at Grandma's house when I was growing up.

To save the wishbone, put the whole breast on the cutting board skinside up and find the point of the breast bone. Cut down next to the breast bone as far as you can, then turn the blade of your knife and follow the bone down to the joint where the wing came off. Cut through the joints on either side and lift off the meaty wishbone piece. The rest of the breast can be divided into two pieces by removing the keel bone just as in boning the breast. Then cut along the mark where the keel bone came out.

Stuffing the Leg

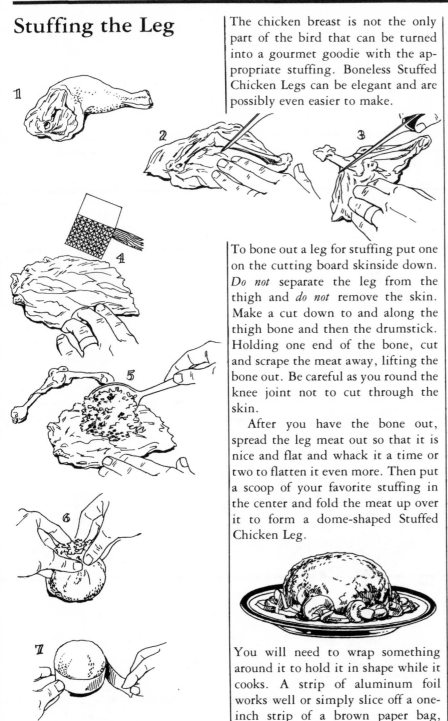

The chicken breast is not the only part of the bird that can be turned into a gourmet goodie with the appropriate stuffing. Boneless Stuffed Chicken Legs can be elegant and are possibly even easier to make.

To bone out a leg for stuffing put one on the cutting board skinside down. *Do not* separate the leg from the thigh and *do not* remove the skin. Make a cut down to and along the thigh bone and then the drumstick. Holding one end of the bone, cut and scrape the meat away, lifting the bone out. Be careful as you round the knee joint not to cut through the skin.

After you have the bone out, spread the leg meat out so that it is nice and flat and whack it a time or two to flatten it even more. Then put a scoop of your favorite stuffing in the center and fold the meat up over it to form a dome-shaped Stuffed Chicken Leg.

You will need to wrap something around it to hold it in shape while it cooks. A strip of aluminum foil works well or simply slice off a one-inch strip of a brown paper bag,

moisten it and use it to wrap around the dome.

These little goodies, as well as the Stuffed Chicken Breasts, can be made ahead of time and frozen for a quick meal later. There are purists who will tell you that you should not freeze anything with stuffing in it, but look through your supermarket frozen food case, you'll find all kinds of stuffed things frozen.

Speaking of "stuffed things," one day while browsing through one of Aunt Gert's old cookbooks, I ran across a recipe for "Stuffed Goose Necks." Now, I knew that Aunt Gert used to make good use of every part of the goose and gander but "Stuffed Goose Necks?"

I probably wouldn't have given that part of the goose or that recipe another thought if, a few days later, I hadn't seen Chicken Necks on special at the local supermarket for 19¢ a pound. That's inexpensive meat, however you slice it, and I couldn't help thinking: "What's good for the goose . . ." and for Aunt Gert might work out for me with the chicken. I bought two pounds—10 necks, or 38¢ worth—and determined to see if it was possible, with Aunt Gert's help, to feed my family of four a complete well-balanced meal and get change back from my dollar.

In keeping with economic aspects of the entire undertaking, I served the stuffed chicken goodies with a barley casserole; barley being one of the least expensive, most delicious, and often overlooked cereal grains available. A one-pound package of pearl barley was 29¢ and I used only half of it for this meal, 15¢ worth! Kentucky

Wonder beans were the "hot special" in the produce department and one pound at 39¢ filled out the menu.

So give or take an onion, a pinch of salt or two and a few slices of day old bread, the whole meal came in for 92¢—or 23¢ per person—it was fantastic! Although I must confess I got some very strange looks from wife and family when they asked, "What's for dinner?" and I said, "Stuffed Chicken Necks."

Stuffed Chicken Necks

Remove the skins from 2 lbs. of chicken necks. Try not to tear the skins anymore than they already are; set them aside. Put the now nude necks in a saucepan, cover with water, add a few slices of onion, a bay leaf and a few peppercorns; bring to a boil, then reduce heat, cover and simmer for an hour or so, until tender.

Meanwhile, turn the skins inside out and rinse under running water. Pull off and discard any loose bits of fat, etc. Turn them right-side out again and pat them dry with paper towels. Tie one end of each skin tightly with clean string.

Remove the necks from the heat, drain off and reserve the broth. Allow the necks to cool, then pick off every little morsel of meat. You'll be surprised at how much there is.

Make your favorite simple bread stuffing, adding the neck meat and moistening with a bit of the broth. Stuff the skins and tie off the other end. Place in a baking pan and bake in a moderate 325 degree oven 1½ hours until brown and crisp, basting occasionally with melted butter.

Serve with a good gravy made from the pan drippings and whatever is left of the broth.

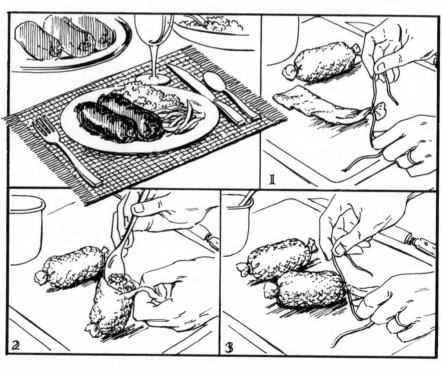

Chinese Chicken Wings

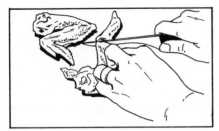

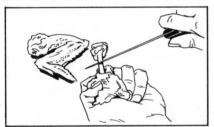

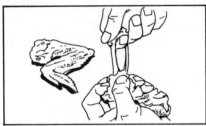

This is, to say the least, a tedious and time-consuming task, so don't tackle it unless you have some time to spend. It is, however, a neat little trick for turning a pile of chicken wings into a delightful meal.

To prepare each wing, cut off the tip at the first joint. Remove the two small bones in the middle section by first cutting through the skin around the small end and then, with your fingers, pulling the meat inside out down over the small bones and over the larger section of the wing. With your knife, scrape and push all of the meat to the opposite end of the large bone until it resembles a small drumstick. Hold the meat in place, if needed, with a toothpick. Once the wing is cooked the meat will firm up and the toothpick can be removed before serving.

These are great simmered in a sauce or simply sautéed. But for a real treat try them dipped in a batter and fried in deep fat. The skin and fat, and with them the flavor, are on the inside; as they cook that flavor seeps all through the meat. When you bite into one it almost spurts good juices like a "Kiev" filled with butter.

You can make smaller versions of this little treat to impress guests at a cocktail party.

After removing the tip, separate the two remaining sections at the joint. Make two tiny drumsticks by turning the meat inside out from the smaller to the larger end of each. The smaller of the two bones in the middle section can be pulled out with your fingers, leaving the larger bone for a drumstick.

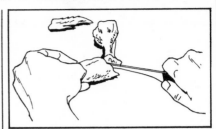

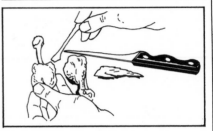

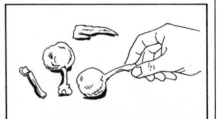

Split and Quartered

There will be times when you don't want your chickens cut up in a lot of little pieces, or boned out, or stuffed. There are times when all you want is a fryer or two split in half or perhaps quartered for the barbecue.

I must warn you: as far as most butchers are concerned "Whole" means whole and "Split" or "Quartered" is the same as cut up. If you are going to take advantage of the best price on chicken you're going to have to do the same thing you have always had to do. . . . Cut it up yourself!

If that means "Splitting" or "Quartering," don't panic. It's easy! And remember you're saving money, as much as 10¢ a pound on every pound you throw on the barbecue grill or under the broiler. That can add up if you have a large family or entertain a lot. There is another advantage to doing it yourself. As is so often the case, "If you do it yourself, you'll get it done right." You'll see what I mean after you've done a couple.

To split a fryer in half, hold it firmly by the legs so that the back is toward you. Put the breast side against the cutting board, and with a good sharp knife with a fairly stiff blade, make a cut from just to the right of the tail straight down the back to just to the right of the neck. Then repeat the process from the left side of the tail to the left side of the neck. Remove the narrow strip of backbone and save it for the stockpot.

Now relax your grip on the legs, lay the bird on the cutting board breast-down, put down your knife and relax for a moment. The rough part is over but the next step will require some study. Examine the inside of the bird. Notice the dark bone in the center of the breast? That in the jargon of the trade is called the keel bone. At the front, or neck end, of the bird, the keel bone is rounded; adjacent to that rounded end is a piece of white gristle or cartilage. That's your next target.

With the tip of your knife cut through that gristle. Also with just the tip of your knife, and very gently, trace a line straight down the keel bone from the rounded end to the tip. Don't try to cut through any more than the thin membrane that covers the bone. That done, lay aside your knife and run your hand up under the breast. By pushing against the keel

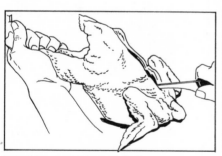

bone from the underneath, you will easily pop the rounded end loose. Then just run your thumb and index finger down the side of the keel bone and lift it out. Cut through the breast along the mark left by the keel bone and Presto! You've split it! And you've done a better job of it than most butchers would.

In the market, where the butcher is spliting dozens or maybe hundreds of fryers, he will very likely do this job on his electric saw to make the job go a lot faster. One zip and it's split. He won't bother taking out the backbone or the keel bone, and as a result the fryers he splits won't lie nice and flat on the grill like yours will. Doesn't that make you feel good? If a whole half-fryer is too large for a single serving, simply cut each half in half again following the natural contour of the breast.

Boning the Bird

The element of surprise has been used since the beginning of time to win honors on the field of battle. It can be used as well to win honors in the form of "oh's" and "ah's" at the dinner table.

Once you have mastered cutting up a chicken and you've practiced boning out a breast or two, you're ready to tackle the task that is almost guaranteed to bring that kind of response. Imagine the reaction when you put a roasted chicken on the table and start to carve it, and it turns out to be a Boneless Roasted Chicken stuffed with another Boneless Roasted Chicken!

Now that you have a working knowledge of the anatomy of the bird and have practiced up on boning a breast, boning out a whole chicken should present no major problem. First place the bird on your cutting board breast down and, with the point of your knife, make a slit along the backbone from the neck to the tail. Now, lift the skin around the neck with one hand and using just the point of your knife and making small cuts, free the meat from the backbone. Cut as close to the bone as you can and take your time. Try not to cut through the skin. When you reach the thigh joints cut through them carefully and proceed on.

Once the entire backbone has been loosened and is free of the leg and wing joints, it simplifies the process to remove it. Cut through the carti-

135

lage between the ribs and the breast on both sides and lift the backbone out. With the backbone gone, the rest is just like boning out the breast. Remove the keel bone, find the little handles and lift out both sides of the rib cage cutting through the joint where the wing is attached. Leave the wing on the bird. Then remove the wishbone.

Lastly, carefully cut through the joint between the leg and the thigh and remove the thigh bone. *Do not* cut through the skin underneath. Leave the drumstick and the wing intact. *Save all* the bones for the stockpot. What you now have is a slab of boneless chicken with the legs and wings attached. You're well over halfway home.

Chicken-Stuffed Chicken

For this surprise filled treat you will need, in addition to the bird you've just boned out, one boneless, skinned chicken breast, flattened slightly, one hard boiled egg and one recipe of your favorite stuffing.

Lay the boneless chicken on the cutting board skin-side down. Spread a layer of stuffing on top of the meat, lay the boneless chicken breast on top of the stuffing, and spread a layer of stuffing on top of that. Place a peeled hard-boiled egg right in the middle of the stuffing. Bring the two sides of the chicken together, fasten them at one-inch intervals with toothpicks or metal skewers and then lace it up with string. Turn the whole thing over and mold it back into something resembling the original shape.

After your Boneless Bird is roasted, and the skewers and the string are removed, it is ready to be presented and rather simply carved —much to the surprise of the assembled guests.

To Carve: Place the bird before the carver just as you would a more conventional model. First remove the wings then slice crosswise into ½-inch thick slices. Each will be a pinwheel pattern of meat, dressing, meat, dressing and in the middle—an egg—Beautiful!

Stewing Hens

One of the family favorites in my family when I was a kid was "Old-Fashioned Stewed Chicken with Dumplings." I can remember looking forward to hearing Grandma come in from gathering the eggs to announce, "That old red hen ain't been layin' lately." Whenever she said that, it was only a matter of time, perhaps a Sunday or two, before "Stewed Chicken with Dumplings" or "Chicken Fricassee" with homemade noodles and hot buttered biscuits would be the featured dish on the dinner table.

Old stewing hens are not as common these days as they were back in the days when almost everybody "kept a few hens for the eggs," but they are available. You can find them in most markets, occasionally fresh, but more often frozen in plastic. They will very likely *not* be a bargain. As a matter of fact they are often expensive, more expensive by far than their younger cousins, the frying chickens. So expensive, in fact, that you may be tempted to cross "Stewed Chicken and Dumplings" off your menu, even if it is a favorite in your family. You needn't. You can make a great stew or fricassee from a couple of those inexpensive and often "on special" fryers, if you treat them right.

Cut the fryers up in the usual fashion. Set the meaty parts (the breasts, legs and large part of the wings) aside in the refrigerator. Put the bony parts (the back, neck, wing tips and the giblets) in a good-sized stockpot and cover them with cold water. Add a small whole onion, a stalk of celery and a teaspoon of salt. Bring to a boil, reduce heat, and remove any scum that comes to the top. Cover and simmer for 1½ to 2 hours.

What you are doing is making a good rich broth in which you will later cook the meaty pieces. If you simmered the whole bird long enough to produce the broth, the meat would be falling off the bone and not nearly as appealing on the plate.

When the meat in the stockpot is "falling off the bone," strain the broth and set aside the cooked chicken. You can pick the small bits and pieces from the bones later for Chicken Salad

or something. Don't throw it away! Don't throw anything away until you've gotten the last ounce out of it. There's a lot of goodness left on those bones and that's how you save money.

Melt 3 tablespoons of butter in a good sized skillet, add the meaty parts of the fryer and sauté gently until golden brown. Remove from heat and transfer the chicken into the strained broth. Simmer gently only until the chicken is tender (about 30 minutes). Meanwhile add three tablespoons of flour to the skillet and blend with the butter.

When the chicken is tender, remove the pieces to a warm platter and keep warm. Reduce the stock over high heat until about two cups remain in the pot. Add the stock to the flour-butter mixture in the skillet and stir over moderate heat until the sauce is the desired consistency. For a richer, more "old-fashioned" sauce you can at this point add the yolks of 2 eggs mixed with 1 cup of heavy cream (what's called Half 'n Half is about as close as we can come in today's supermarket). Combine the egg yolks with the cream, then mix in a tablespoon or so of the hot sauce to temper the cream mixture. Stir the cream mixture back into the sauce until nicely blended and thickened.

Serve some of the sauce over the chicken; the rest separately. Buttered noodles (they don't have to be homemade) or rice or mashed potatoes are good with this dish. But I still prefer dumplings. Serve it with something like succotash or corn on the cob for a good old-fashioned Sunday dinner. It will be almost as cheap as if you had an "old red hen who hadn't been layin' lately."

Turkeys

One of the best buys you're apt to find in your butcher's frozen food case, most times, is that big old bird you don't usually think much about except at holiday times: Turkey.

Recently, turkey production has been such that (with the exception of a month of two around Thanksgiving and Christmas, when the demand and the price goes up) turkey is about as inexpensive a meat as you are likely to find. And you can find it, these days, in a wide variety of new and different forms, many of which you won't even recognize.

The Turkey Industry, in its attempts to sell ever more turkey, has come up with all manner of new "merchandising" ideas. Now, in addition to buying the whole (I-wonder-if-it-will-fit-in-my-oven) bird you can buy Turkey parts, Turkey Rolls, and Ground Turkey to be used in any of those money-saving ways you now use Hamburger. Turkey Steaks are available. They have even come out with Turkey Hot Dogs, Turkey Sausage and Turkey "Kabobs."

But of all the new turkey things available, the best turkey buy is still likely to be the whole bird, all 12 or 16 pounds of him or her. You needn't pass up a good money-saving special on whole turkeys, simply because Roast Turkey with bread stuffing, cranberry sauce and candied yams wasn't what you had in mind or on your menu this week. Take one home, take it apart and then take a tip or two from the turkey industry on what to do with all that meat.

Don't worry about whether it's a Tom or a Hen, there is very little, if any, difference in quality anymore, but if there is a difference in price, go for the cheap one.

It may sound like an awesome task but, with a little "Cutting-up in the Kitchen," you can turn a turkey into all manner of good and different meals. And without a lot of leftovers that require eating turkey eight days in a row. If the turkey industry can do it, so can you.

Cutting up a turkey is very like cutting up a chicken except for the obvious difference in the size of the bird. And because the average turkey is a bit older than the average chicken, there is not quite as much space in the joints for the knife to slide through. It will undoubtedly, therefore, take a little longer. It is, however, a feat easily accomplished, particularly if you already have practiced on a chicken or two.

It is important to remember that —if the bird is frozen when you buy it, and most often it will be—it should be thawed out in your refrigerator, *not* on the kitchen counter. Cut it up while it's still a little frosty and get the component parts back in the freezer as quickly as possible; that means, *before they reach room temperature!* As long as the meat is cold it is unlikely that any bacterial growth will have started, and nothing is lost by refreezing.

To cut up a turkey, first put the bird on the cutting board and examine it for a moment. Wiggle a wing, tug at a leg; try to determine where the parts are attached. Now— take it apart.

1) Remove the wing where it joins the body.

2) Then disjoint the leg and thigh. Turn the bird over and do it again on the other side. Separate the legs (drumsticks) from the thighs. Wrap

up all the wings and legs together for a single meal. But wrap each thigh separately, there's enough meat on each for all kinds of different things.

3) Separate the breast· from the back and remove the meaty little "tenderloins" on either side of the backbone. These can be added to one of the other packages; they are much too tasty and tender to go in the stockpot with the rest of the back.

4) Bone out the breast. The two halves of the breast make up a large percentage of the weight of the bird and there are dozens of different things you can do with the meat they yield.

Turkey Breast Roll—the two halves of the breast can easily be tied together to make a great roast for a small family at a fraction of what the same thing would cost you if you bought it already rolled. Boneless Turkey Breast Roll is selling in the neighborhood of $2.00 a pound in my neighborhood, so it is obvious that the two breast halves of a 49¢ turkey will furnish your own five to eight pound Roll for a lot less than $10 to $16. The difference will very likely be more than enough to buy the whole bird.

To make a Breast Roll place one half of the turkey breast on your cutting board, skin-side down. Put the other half on top of it with the skin-side up. Place them so that the large end of one is on top of the small pointed end of the other. Tie two or three strings around the length of the breasts and tighten only enough to pull the Roll into shape. Then make ties around the Roll at about one-inch intervals to hold it firm. If you want a really professional-looking Roll—one that holds together when you slice it, as if it were a solid piece of meat—try this:

Before rolling, dust each of the inside surfaces lightly with dehydrated egg white, available at a bakery or bakers supply store. The egg white is odorless, tasteless and you can't even see it after the Turkey Roll is roasted, but it holds the two sides together. It's handy to have on hand whenever you're "home rolling" any kind of meat. Be sure to leave the skin on the Breast when you make Turkey Rolls. The fat is right under the skin and if you remove it, your Turkey Roll won't have much Turkey flavor. At times that is a desirable characteristic. Turkey Breast, without the skin, has a very mild flavor and can very effectively be substituted for Veal.

Considering the difference in price between Turkey and Veal, you'll have to admit that it's worth a try. Remove the skin from a Breast half and lay it on the cutting board with what was the skin side down. Lift out the Breast filet (or "tender"). This can be sliced separately and it leaves the main portion of the Breast in one solid piece. Slice the Breast across the grain into ¼-inch slices. Pound them lightly if you want them thinner and try them in place of Veal in your favorite recipe for Scallopini, or Picatta, or Wiener Schnitzel. You'll be surprised.

Legs and Wings—Unfortunately the turkey industry has not figured out a way to pull the tendons out of the drumsticks. Grandpa used to manage it but modern industry can't. So rather than fight trying to eat them as they are, put them in a pot along with the wings (there isn't enough on two of those to go very far) add a small onion, sliced; a small carrot, sliced; a stalk of celery, chopped; salt and pepper to taste. Add just enough water to barely cover, put on a lid and simmer for about three hours. When the meat is tender, remove from heat and allow to cool in its cooking liquid. Then strip the meat from the bones and use it for salads, casseroles, and so forth. Save the cooking liquid; just strain it and put it in a couple of paper cups or a securely sealed plastic bag and pop it back in the freezer for the next time you're making a sauce, soup or gravy to go with your Turkey Roll.

Thighs—The thighs can be used for all kinds of interesting dishes. Remove the bone and the skin, then forget that it's a turkey. Cut it in cubes and use it for Kabobs; slice it thin and use it in your favorite stir-fry recipe. Or, while it's still a little frosty, fresh from the freezer, run it one time through Grandma's old-fashioned meat grinder and call it Turkey Burger.

Next time you see the big bird at a bargain price in your butcher's frozen food case, don't think of cranberry sauce and all that stuff—use your imagination and you'll save money.

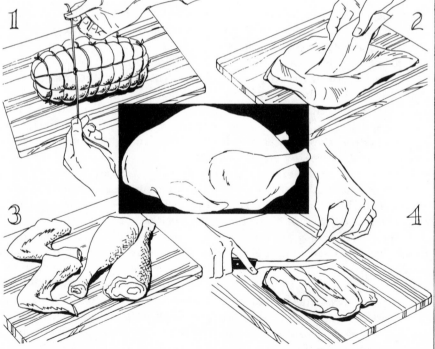

Capons

This "eunuch of the barnyard" is for my money the tastiest of all the barnyard birds. It is meatier and more delicate in flavor by far than its more muscular cousin, the young roastable rooster. Something happens as a result of surgery that allows the capon to fatten from within, depositing "marbling" throughout the meat rather than only between the flesh and the skin as with other birds. The result is delicious.

Capons are expensive and *real* ones are hard to find. "Real" capons (the quotes are mine) are surgical capons; young roosters that have been castrated by the time they are a few weeks old and have grown fat and juicy as a result of that surgery. There are two impostors.

(1) "Artificial" capons (again the quotes are mine) are chemical capons; young roosters that have been shot full of hormones in an effort to get them to develop the qualities of "real" capons in less time. It doesn't work. They may develop the size but not the flavor of the "real" capon.

(2) The "false" capon is even less successful. "False" capons, by my definition, are those birds I have seen in meat markets occasionally with a sign on them reading "Capons" and a price that seems right, perhaps even cheap, but no other qualifications. It seems difficult for some butchers to resist the temptation of selling you a nice plump roasting chicken for a premium price, by taking advantage of the reputation for quality rightly attributed to "real" capons. Don't be misled by a quality name, look at the tag.

A "real" or "artificial" capon will say so very officially on the tag on his wing or on the plastic package somewhere. A "false" capon will very likely say *nothing*.

Rock Cornish Game Hens

These delicious little birds didn't even exist back in the days when Grandma was a girl. Their ancestors did, the Plymouth Rock hen and the Cornish game cock, but they hadn't gotten together yet in those days. That event in gastronomic history didn't happen until around 1950 and since then Rock Cornish Game Hens have become almost commonplace. Almost every supermarket in America has them in stock, often at a very reasonable price. They are not quite as inexpensive as fryers yet—and they may never be—but they are often very reasonable and they are delicious.

Rock Cornish Game Hens are all white meat, weigh usually around one pound each and make elegant company fare. Plan on serving a whole bird to each guest. Keep your eye open for them and when the price is right put a few in your freezer.

Ducks and Geese

Duck to most people means Long Island Duck, since most of the ducks available in markets across the country are born, bred, processed, frozen and shipped from there. Long Island Ducks are a strain of white-feathered ducks descended from the Peking ducks of China. They're delicious prepared a million ways but, no matter how you prepare them, ducks are expensive. The average weight is between 3½ and 5 pounds which is barely enough to feed four people. So the cost per serving is likely to be out of sight. The only way to save money on duck is to raise your own. The same is true of geese.

The goose was once the traditional holiday bird and every barnyard had at least one fattening up for the occasion. Keeping a few geese in the yard used to be more than just holiday tradition, it was very practical as well. Grease from the pan in which they were roasted was saved for cooking another day or, if need be, mixed with a bit of camphor and rubbed generously on the chest of any kid with the slightest hint of a cold. Goose down was used for pillows and quilts and feather beds. But practicality and tradition have lost out, the goose is just about gone from the holiday table these days. You can still find them in the butcher case, and not just at holiday times, but they will seldom be fresh, always frozen and always expensive. They're already plucked so you can't use the down. They are fat, but nobody would spread goose grease on their chest these days— it's not mentholated, not even lemon-scented. By the time you pour off the fat the cost of a goose is almost prohibitive for all but the most affluent traditionalist. They are delicious but I'm afraid they just aren't practical. That is, unless you've got your own gaggle.

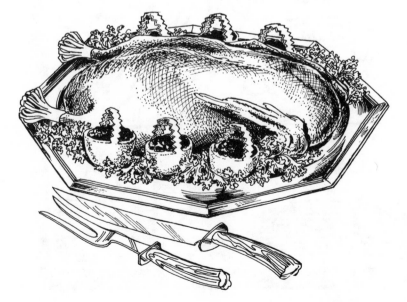

STOCKPOT

Chapter 9

There was a time, when I was a boy, when I thought it was magic, that huge ever-present pot on the back of my Grandmother's wood-burning stove. It seemed that every time she dipped into it, some new and different and delicious food would come out. For breakfast she would mix a few things together, ladle in some of that magic stuff and presto! Creamed Chipped Beef on Toast. I found out later, in the Army, that it had another name, but at Grandma's house it was Creamed Chipped Beef on Toast. By noon the "magic pot" was offering up Barley Soup to go with peanut butter sandwiches on homemade bread. And by the time it was time for supper, that pot had put together the best damned Stew any kid in Allen, Nebraska ever ate.

It wasn't until long after those summer days at Grandma's house that I discovered every kitchen worth its salt had a stockpot on the back of the stove, much, if not most of the time. And they are magic, they really are! They are also an absolute necessity in the kitchen of any cook concerned with saving money. You certainly won't find any kitchen concerned with *making* money without one. They are as much a part of any restaurant or hotel kitchen as they were a part of Grandma's. At least one should be a part of yours, too.

Out of a stockpot come all of the great soups and sauces the world has to offer. And if the stockpot they come from is on the back of the stove in your kitchen, those soups and sauces will cost you a whole lot less than if they came from somebody else's stockpot by way of a can on the supermarket shelf.

Now I'm not suggesting that you do as Grandma did, and keep a stockpot on the stove all of the time. Your stove is likely not as easy to do that with as Grandma's was. Her old wood-burner was going all of the time just to keep the chill off the kitchen and, with a stove like that in a cold kitchen, you might as well keep something cooking. Also, you probably don't, and don't want to, spend as much time in the kitchen as she used to—"Keepin' an eye on the stove." That doesn't mean you can't take advantage of a good stockpot and all you can save with it. Make a practice of *always* saving every scrap of meat and bone that results from your kitchen cutting-up. Put them in plastic bags and store them in your freezer. Have a bag for chicken bones and scraps, another for beef bones, and another for pork, and so forth.

When you have an accumulation sufficient to warrant it, as well as some time to spend "keepin' an eye on the pot," take out a bag of bones and make a big pot of stock. Then re-freeze the stock in one-cup containers and you're set. Next time a sauce recipe calls for a cup of stock or you want a bowl of soup to go with a luncheon sandwich, simply dip one out of the freezer like Grandma used to dip one out of the stockpot. Every time you take a cup of your own stock out of the freezer rather than open a can of bouillon or chicken soup, you're saving 25¢ or 30¢. That adds up fast!

147

Chicken Bones

Making your own stock from your stock of accumulated bones is an extremely easy task. While it does take time, it's not time spent laboriously but rather time spent doing little more than enjoying the great aroma that emanates from a pot of simmering stock. It literally fills the kitchen with the smell of good cooking.

There are different kinds of stocks to match the different kinds of bones you have in your freezer.

Chicken Stock is the basis for countless soups and sauces, ranging from simple to super-elegant. It is the very foundation of Vichyssoise; it's virtually indispensable in Veloute; makes a magnificent Minestrone; and is hard to beat as a cure for the common cold. Ask my Grandmother or yours.

Chicken Stock

One plastic bag of chicken necks, backs, wing tips, gizzards, skin, miscellaneous bones, etc. from fryers you have carefully cut up yourself.
  One onion stuck with a couple of cloves
    Six or eight peppercorns
    One carrot
    One stalk of celery
    One bay leaf
    Water to cover
    1 T. salt
    Parsley & thyme

Put the chicken parts in your big old stockpot. Add the onion, peppercorns, carrot, celery and bay leaf. Cover with cold water and bring to a boil over medium heat.

Skim off the scum that comes to the top. Reduce heat, season to taste with salt, add a bit of parsley and thyme, cover and simmer for 3 or 4 hours, or overnight on low heat, if you like (although you won't get full benefit of the fragrance that way). When the stock has cooked long enough to develop a full rich chicken flavor, or when you get tired of smelling it—whichever comes first—remove from the heat and allow it to cool. Strain and then refrigerate for a few hours or overnight. All the fat will rise to the top and turn hard. You can peel it off the way you used to peel chocolate off an ice cream bar when you were a kid. Save the chicken fat, it's great for frying all kinds of things and it keeps well in the refrigerator for weeks.

You now have a rich delicious Chicken Stock, the beginning of at least six-thousand, four-hundred and seventy-three different and delicious soups and sauces, from the extremely simple to the rather complex. With nothing more than a little patience and a handful of barley or rice you can turn a few cups of your chicken stock into a great "Chicken Barley" or "Chicken Rice Soup," as good and a whole lot cheaper than any you'll find in a can. Simply pick the bits and pieces of meat from the chicken bones left in the stockpot, add a couple of handsful of pearl barley or rice and four or five cups of Chicken Stock. Simmer until the grain is tender. Then enjoy.

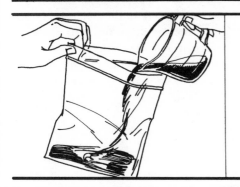  

Package up the rest of your stock in one or two-cup containers and freeze for later use. A good way to store stock in the freezer is to put it in sealable plastic sandwich bags. Just measure out a cup or two of stock, put it in the plastic bag and zip up the top. If you use a plastic drinking straw to draw the air out of each bag as you zip it up, they will lay nice and flat and take up very little room in the corner of your freezer.

Now, when your recipe calls for a couple of cups of stock, simply dip one out of the freezer, hold it under warm running water for a second to loosen it, then zip open the top and slip it—still frozen—into the sauce or the stew.

There is no end to the uses for chicken stock. It is a basic ingredient in some of the greatest soups and sauces the world's gourmets have ever come up with. But, when I find myself with a couple of quarts of the stuff and need to feed a small army, or want to fill a corner of the freezer with a half-dozen quick, easy and absolutely delicious meals for the family, there is but one thing to do with chicken stock: make Minestrone. It is not an easy job. It is tedious but worth it. Good Minestrone is a meal in itself, served with nothing more than a basket of French bread with lots of butter and a glass of red wine. It doesn't even have to be good red wine because good Minestrone has a way of making even bad red wine better. Also Minestrone is one of those dishes that is even better a day or so after it's made, so don't hesitate to spend the time and the chicken stock. And, in addition, it keeps well and freezes beautifully.

Minestrone

½ cup dry white beans

4 T. butter

1 cup each of any *four* of the following: fresh green peas, zucchini-diced, carrots-diced, *potatoes-diced, turnip-diced, cabbage-shredded, green peppers-diced, summer squash-diced

¼ lb. salt pork, diced

⅓ cup thinly sliced celery

2 T. finely chopped leeks and 2 T. finely chopped onions

2 cups canned whole-pack tomatoes, drained and coarsely chopped

1 bay leaf

1 T. parsley flakes

1 tsp. salt

fresh ground pepper

½ cup of *one* of the following: rice, *barley, Ala, wheat, macaroni (almost any shape) or a combination. (*For a thicker soup use potatoes and barley)

Cook the beans according to package directions until just barely tender. Drain and set aside. (You have just successfully completed Step One. You may take a break if you like, you may need it.)

Melt butter over moderate heat in a 10 or 12-inch frying pan. Add one cup each of any four of the vegetables selected. Cook 2 or 3 minutes, tossing constantly until the vegetables are lightly covered with butter. Remove from heat and set aside. (If you need another break, take it now, you may never get another chance.)

Put the diced salt pork in a 6 or 8-quart stockpot and fry, stirring frequently, over moderate heat until crisp and brown. With a slotted spoon remove the salt pork. Into the fat remaining stir the celery, onions and leeks (if leeks are not available, forget them). Cook, stirring constantly for 5 minutes until the vegetables are soft and browned.

Stir in tomatoes, vegetables from the frying pan, chicken stock, bay leaf, parsley flakes, salt and pepper. Bring to a boil over high heat, reduce heat and simmer for 30 minutes.

Add all remaining ingredients—grain, (rice, barley, etc.) cooked white beans and the salt pork. Cook for 15 or 20 minutes until the grain is tender.

Adjust seasoning and serve sprinkled with the following garnish:

1 tsp. sweet basil, crumbled

1 T. parsley, chopped or dry flakes

½ tsp. finely chopped garlic

Pass a bowl of grated fresh Parmesan cheese. This makes enough for at least a dozen hearty eaters; but Minestrone can be very successfully frozen so don't worry about having leftovers.

Beef Bones

The basics for making Beef Stock, more often referred to in recipe books as "Brown Stock," are almost the same as for making Chicken Stock. The only major difference is in the coloring. You want your Brown Stock to have that rich beefy caramel color you get when you open a can of beef broth, so that all of the soups and sauces you use it in will have a good rich color as well.

Brown Stock

To assure a good brown color, put your beef bones along with any scraps of meat you've collected in a 400 degree oven and brown them well. Then, before you put them in the stockpot, pour off any excess

fat that has accumulated in the bottom of the pan. Pour a cup or so of water in the pan to dissolve any of the coagulated juices. Add these to the stockpot. Proceed just as with Chicken Stock.

Cover the bones with cold water, add an onion stuck with a couple of cloves, six or eight peppercorns, a carrot, a stalk of celery and a bay leaf or two. Bring the pot gently to a boil. Skim off the scum that accumulates. Reduce heat, add one tablespoon of salt and a sprig or two of parsley and thyme. Cover and simmer for 3 or 4 hours.

When you have succeeded in cooking all of the good rich beefy flavor out of the bones, remove the stock from the heat, cool and strain. Then refrigerate overnight or long enough to let the fat come to the top and harden so that you can peel it off. Save the beef fat in a container separate from your chicken fat—but do save it. You can use it for all kinds of frying. And, who knows, you might even want to make some soap someday.

If even after browning the bones, your Beef Stock doesn't have that nice rich caramel color you get from a can of beef broth, do what the canners do to get that nice rich caramel coloring—add some caramel coloring. Yes, they do! Read the label on the can. Better yet, add a tablespoon or two of liquid beef extract to your stock. You can buy it in the spice section of your supermarket. Not only does that improve the color but it will add strength and flavor to your Beef Stock.

Package up your Beef Stock just as you did your Chicken Stock, in one or two-cup packages to put in the freezer. They'll be ready to add to a sauce or make into a soup whenever a recipe calls for Beef Stock. Save out a couple of pints or so to make a good beef-and-vegetable or beef-and-noodle or beef-and-almost-anything soup with the bits of beef left in the stockpot.

Veal Bones

Veal bones are the magic of the saucemaker's skill. They impart to any stock a wonderfully gelatinous quality that makes any sauce better and is an absolute necessity in some. Veal bones can be added to beef bones in making Brown Stock. You can put a couple in with your chicken bones to give Chicken Stock a bit more body. But for the classic White Stock called for in hundreds of fancy recipes for fancy French sauces, use veal bones.

White Stock

White Stock is made exactly the same way as Chicken Stock, using veal bones instead of chicken bones. (See Chicken Stock) If you can find one, a calf's foot will do wonders for the gelatinous quality of your White Stock.

Pork Bones

Pork bones, either fresh or smoked (ham bones), are seldom used in making stock, although you can add a fresh pork bone or two to your beef bones in making Brown Stock if you have some you'd like to get rid of. Too many tend to give the stock an undesirably sweet flavor. That's not to say there aren't all kinds of uses for that bag of pork bones you have in the freezer.

If there is any meat left on the bones at all, consider the possibilities of Barbecued Pork Bones. That is after all what Spare Ribs are. Or cook some pork bones in a pot of sauerkraut, or beans or greens. Check through any old cookbook for a recipe for Pork Neck Bones.

Lamb Bones

Lamb bones are never used in making basic White or Brown Stocks to be served with other meats, but you'll not be sorry for saving them. Lamb Stock can be used in the preparation of any sauce to be served with lamb, or as the basis for several delicious soups, the most notable of which is simple, rich and delicious "Scotch Broth."

Lamb Stock

One bag of frozen lamb bones
3½ quarts water (or enough to cover)
1½ tsp. salt
½ tsp. pepper
2 onions, sliced

Put the lamb bones in a good sized pot, cover with water, add salt, pepper and sliced onions. Bring slowly to the boil, reduce heat and simmer 3 to 4 hours. Strain, cool and chill the stock. Save any meat that you can pick from the bones for a great pot of "Scotch Broth." When your stock is chilled the fat will have congealed on top and you can lift it off, before packaging the stock for freezing or making a pot of soup.

Scotch Broth

One of the simplest and most delicious uses for any pot of Lamb Stock is a big pot of that classic soup "Scotch Broth."

> 2 quarts Lamb Stock
> ½ cup barley
> 1 T. butter
> 2 or 3 cups cooked lamb meat, diced
> ½ cup onions, chopped
> ½ cup celery, sliced
> ½ cup carrot, diced
> ½ cup, turnip, diced
> 1 T. parsley, chopped
> salt and pepper

Rinse the barley. Bring Lamb Stock to a boil, add barley. Cover, reduce heat and simmer for one hour. Melt butter in a skillet, add bits of lamb, onions, celery, carrot and turnip, and sauté gently for 10 minutes, stirring frequently. Add to the soup pot and continue simmering another hour. Season to taste, add parsley and serve.

Clarifying Stock

For most of the soups and sauces you will be making from your frozen stock, there is no need to clarify it. Just use it as it comes from the stockpot or the freezer. But for those beautifully clear, sparkling aspics and consommés like the ones you can get in the can, you'll want to clarify your stock. To accomplish this, put a quart or two of the stock in a saucepan over medium heat. For each quart of stock allow one egg white along with its crumpled shell. Beat the egg white and shell together slightly and stir into the stock. Bring slowly to simmer, without stirring. Allow to simmer for 10 minutes, then gently remove the pan from heat and let it set for 10 or 20 minutes. Skim off any scum that forms on top and then strain the stock through a couple of layers of cheesecloth.

Once you have turned your plastic bag accumulation of bones into a variety of frozen stocks there is no end to the magic you can perform in the kitchen. All of the gastronomic treats Grandma used to come up with by dipping into the stockpot you can make by dipping into your frozen stock. Not the least of which is an almost endless list of sauces to accompany any meat dish. And you can make your own for far less than you would spend on those little packages of sauce mix at the supermarket.

Sauces

Sauces, for some reason, seem to scare people. Cooks who have all the confidence in the world when it comes to cookies and cakes come unglued when faced with making a sauce. Perhaps it's all those fancy French names—"Sauce Bechamel," "Sauce á l'Ail á La Provençale," "Sauce Veloute," "Sauce Soubise"—there are hundreds, enough to frighten any lover of good food who is not a linguist.

There is really nothing frightening about sauces, particularly those sauces that are served with meat. Most of them, in spite of their fancy names, are little more than what's left in the pan after cooking some meat, mixed with a dab of imagination and a dipper of what's in the stockpot.

Basically there are three different methods of making a sauce. The one you choose will depend on what's left in the pan after you've cooked the meat—nothing, a little bit, or lots.

Nothing-Left Sauces

First there are those that begin with *nothing*. Most of the French classics are in this group, their main ingredient is imagination. When you have nothing to do it with, what do you do? Make a Roux. A Roux is simply flour cooked in some type of fat, usually butter, for some period of time and used to thicken whatever liquid you put with it.

Two tablespoons of flour cooked in two tablespoons of butter will thicken one cup of liquid to the medium-thick consistency desired for most sauces. So if you'll keep the number "221" in mind, it will help you know how to begin.

Depending on what you plan to serve the sauce with, you may want to make a "White Roux," a "Blond Roux" or a "Brown Roux." These are all essentially the same except for their color, which is a result of the length of time they are allowed to cook.

White Roux

White Roux is the beginning of dozens of "white sauces" to be served with light meats like chicken, veal, sweetbreads and brains, as well as with fish and eggs. It's also the beginning of most cream soups and almost all soufflés.

To make White Roux, melt two tablespoons of butter in a saucepan over very low heat. Or, better yet, use a double boiler. Add two tablespoons of flour and let the mixture cook very slowly, stirring constantly, for about five minutes. The flour should cook but *not* color. For a basic White Sauce, simply add one cup of milk, stir until it thickens and season with salt and pepper. If you need a fancy name, call it Bechamel.

To turn White Sauce into just the right sauce for whatever you're serving it with, add a bit of your own imagination.

- Substitute one cup of Chicken Stock for the milk if you're serving it with chicken.
- Use Veal Stock and call it "Veloute."
- Sauté a chopped onion in the butter before adding the flour and presto—"Sauce Soubise."
- Add whatever flavorings are appropriate. Here's a sample:

tablespoon of chopped dill—Dill Sauce

cup of grated cheese—Cheese Sauce

tablespoon of curry powder—Curry Sauce

tablespoon of mustard—Mustard Sauce

hard boiled egg, chopped—Egg Sauce

tablespoon or two of chopped parsley—Parsley Sauce

Blond Roux

Blond Roux is the same as White Roux except that it is cooked longer and allowed to turn to a light golden-brown color before the liquid is added. The liquid can be anything from the stockpot—Chicken Stock for chicken dishes, Veal Stock for veal dishes, Beef Stock when it's to accompany a rich beef dish. Or almost any combination to suit your taste. Remember "221"; two tablespoons of flour and two of butter or other fat will thicken one cup of liquid. Be sure to add the liquid slowly and keep stirring as you add it, otherwise your sauce might get lumpy.

Turning Blond Roux into any one of dozens of great sauces usually requires a second pan. Oh, you can come up with all kinds of variations by simply tossing in a tablespoon of this or that, just as with the variations on the basic White Sauce. But with another pan—*voilà!* While your Roux is cooking to a golden brown in one pan, let your imagination run wild in another. Sauté a little bit of almost anything in a dab of butter, add herbs and spices to suit your taste and your nose, and perhaps a dash of wine "for thy stomach's sake" then mix the one pan with the other before you add something from the stockpot.

Sauté a few chopped green onions and a couple of sliced mushrooms in a tablespoon of butter. Add ½-cup white wine and a tablespoon of tomato paste. Cook it down to about half the amount you started with, mix it with the roux and add some stock. Call it "Hunter's Sauce" or "Sauce Chasseur."

Skip the mushrooms, use about ¼-cup brandy instead of the wine, substitute one teaspoon of Worcestershire Sauce for the tomato paste. Call it "Sauce Diable"—perhaps not "classic" but close.

Don't be afraid to experiment! Use anything in your sauce that you would eat and drink with the meat. If you like mustard, sweet pickles and a glass of beer along *with* your Baked Ham, chances are you can make a successful sauce to go *on* it from the same basic ingredients.

Brown Roux

Brown Roux is like White and Blond Roux—a mixture of flour and fat, this time cooked together until the flour turns a rich nutty brown color before the liquid is added. To achieve the proper color some cooks brown the flour first by putting it in a baking pan or dry skillet and browning it in a slow 350 degree oven for about 30 minutes. If you do this be sure to keep your eye on it and stir it frequently, so that it doesn't scorch. Nothing tastes worse than a scorched sauce.

Since sauces are most often the finishing touch to a dish, and since making Brown Roux takes a bit of time (browning the flour and all), it's a good idea to make Brown Roux ahead of time. It keeps well in the refrigerator and will be ready and waiting when you need it. Brown Roux is also convenient to have on hand to thicken the sauces made by the two methods described later in this chapter. (See pages 156 and 157.)

Brown Sauce

A really conscientious gourmet cook will prepare basic Brown Sauce ahead and have it on hand for all the hundreds of compound and complex recipes in which it is a basic ingredient. But most of us don't do that kind of thing much, even though we probably should. That's all right, even without basic Brown Sauce it is possible to come up with a few sauces that come close to the classics with little more than a little Brown Roux.

The Butcher's Bordelaise Sauce

This is a two pan sauce unless you are one of those rare individuals who actually does what we all should do —prepare Brown Sauce ahead. If you're like me, most sauces start from scratch—in which case, this will be a two pan sauce.

3 T. butter
3 T. flour
1½ cup Beef Stock or canned Beef Bouillon or 2 bouillon cubes disolved in 1½ cups water
1 cup dry red wine
¼-cup onion, finely chopped
1 tsp. thyme
1 T. brandy
1 T. lemon juice
1 T. chopped parsley
salt and pepper

Melt butter in a heavy saucepan over low heat, add flour, blend well and simmer for several minutes. Stir in Beef Stock and continue simmering, stirring often, until the sauce thickens. In a second saucepan combine wine, onions and thyme. Reduce over high heat to ⅓ cup. Strain into first pan; add brandy and lemon juice, blend well and simmer for 4 to 5 minutes. Season with salt and pepper and stir in chopped parsley. Serve over steak.

That covers the first group of sauces, those that have as their basic ingredient a Roux mixed with imagination and used to thicken something from the stockpot.

A-Little-Bit-Left Sauces

The second group of sauces have as their beginning whatever is left in the pan after you've cooked some meat with dry heat, by roasting, broiling or frying. Usually in dry-heat cooking there isn't much left in the pan when you're finished—a little more than the "nothing" we started with in the first group of sauces, but not very much. But at least we have something more to work with than imagination; we have "pan drippings." These are more than just fat to be thrown away, they are good flavorful juices that have cooked from the meat. They can be used as the basis for delicious sauces and gravies to be served with the meat they came from.

There are two methods for turning pan drippings into a sauce. One is a variation on the previous method—make a Roux. Pour off all of the fat that has dripped from the meat, then put back just enough to make as much Blond or Brown Roux as you need. Remember "221." Stir in the appropriate amount of flour and cook it to the desired shade of Blond or Brown. Then add the necessary amount of the appropriate stock and whatever else your imagination dictates.

The second method for turning what's left in the pan into a delicious sauce is called "deglazing." The procedure is different here. No more complicated, but different in that it does not involve flour. Instead, much to the delight of many a sauce lover, it involves "booze."

Deglazing

To make a sauce by deglazing, first pour off almost all of the fat that's left in the pan after you've roasted or fried or sautéed some meat. Then put the pan back on the stove over medium-low heat and add about ¼-cup of the appropriate "booze." Cook, stirring to loosen and dissolve all of the good meat juices that have coagulated in the bottom of the pan. Continue cooking until the sauce has reduced in volume and thickened slightly. Stir in a dab of butter and you have a sauce perfectly suited to the meat it is to accompany; made with the drippings from the meat itself mixed with a bit of whatever you plan to drink with it. If the meat you have cooked is chicken and you're serving white wine with it, use the same wine to deglaze the pan. If your meat is "Roulade of Beef" stuffed with pickles and onions and you plan to serve it with beer—use beer. You can deglaze a pan with the appropriate stock, or for that matter even with plain water, but without a "bit of booze" your sauce will suffer.

Lots-Left Sauces

The third group of sauces have their beginning in what is left in the pan after you have cooked some meat with moist heat. After you have stewed a Stew, or braised a Brisket of Beef in beer, or simmered a chicken in wine with mushrooms and onions; what you have left in the pan after the meat is cooked is a quantity of rich delicious broth. All that is required to turn the broth in which the meat was cooked into a sauce to serve with it, is to thicken it slightly.

There are several ways to thicken a soup and make it a sauce. We have already discussed the use of a Roux in the previous groups of sauces, and the Roux can be used with this group as well, but there are other ways:

Beurre Manie: Mix 2 tablespoons of flour with 1 tablespoon of butter. Knead them together until they form little balls. Then sprinkle a few of these at a time on the surface of the soup, gently simmering *not* boiling. Stir them in to thicken a sauce to the desired consistency.

Cornstarch: The Chinese in most of their stir-fry recipes call for thickening with cornstarch. It gives a sauce a beautifully translucent quality that adds a great deal to its appearance. Mix a tablespoon or two of cornstarch with enough *cold* water to dissolve it, then stir slowly into the hot liquid. Add the cornstarch slowly and allow to cook for a minute or two to eliminate any starchy taste. Keep adding cornstarch until the desired consistency is reached.

Potato Starch (Potato Flour)*:* Scan-dinavian cooks often prefer "Potatis Mjol" for thickening. It also adds a nice translucent quality to the sauce but requires less cooking to eliminate the starchy flavor. It requires a bit more potato starch than cornstarch to thicken the same amount of liquid; figure about one tablespoon per cup of liquid. Mix the potato starch with cold water before adding to the hot stock. Again, add it slowly, you can always add more if you need it.

Flour Paste: Unfortunately for the sauces of far too many American cooks, and for those who have to eat them, one of the most common thickening agents used in this country is flour mixed with cold water.

If you must use flour paste, at least make sure that you simmer the sauce for at least 5 minutes after you've added the flour-water mixture to minimize the pasty taste.

Arrowroot: For my money, this is the best and simplest thickener to use in almost any sauce. It is virtually tasteless, so you don't have to worry about any "raw" flour or starchy taste. It thickens quickly and at a fairly low temperature, which makes it perfect for delicate sauces that should not boil. It gives a sauce that glossy appearance and smooth velvety texture that is often hard to achieve. A little arrowroot goes a long way. One teaspoon mixed with a little cold water will do the work of one tablespoon of flour. You will find arrowroot in the spice section of your supermarket. One thing to keep in mind when using arrowroot, however, is—*don't overcook it!*—make your sauce just before serving and don't let it sit very long.

VARIETY MEATS

Chapter 10

Brains, hearts, kidneys, liver, sweetbreads, tripe and other miscellaneous stuff that falls off the carcass as it is dressed are listed in most American cookbooks as "variety meats." The English call them offal, literally meaning "off-fall."

Don't be put off, the various variety meats of beef, lamb, veal, and pork are delicious, nutritious and, in many cases, relatively cheap. Conscientious would-be-gourmets should spend at least as much time learning to appreciate this "offal" stuff as they do acquiring a taste for $60 a pound fish eggs called "Caviare" and fancy French snails labeled "Escargot." The cost will be considerably less and the gastronomic gains at least as great. If French helps, call them "Abats de Boucherie," somehow that doesn't sound so awful.

Brains

It is, I think, something of a paradox that the most difficult of all the variety meats for most people to get past their minds and into their mouths are Brains. It's a shame because Brains have delicious texture and flavor. They are extremely tender and have a delicate flavor very similiar to that of Sweetbreads. As with Sweetbreads, consumer preference is usually for Veal Brains, but beef, lamb and pork develop equally good brains that, due to the law of supply and demand, are probably quite a bit cheaper.

Brains are extremely perishable and should be cooked and enjoyed as soon after purchase as possible. If you plan on keeping them much more than 24 hours, freeze them. Brains freeze well and lose little in terms of texture or flavor in the process. But they don't freeze well too many times, so if they were frozen when you bought them (or before you bought them), don't plan on freezing them again.

As soon as you get them home from the market, Brains of any kind should be soaked for an hour or so in enough cold acidulated water to cover. Acidulated means water to which you have added a little acid—lemon juice, vinegar, wine, etc. Then rinse under cold water and peel off the outer membrane. Peeling off the membrane is more traditional than practical. It's not really necessary but most cooks do it. If it makes you feel better, do it.

Next blanch them in acidulated water, using a dash of lemon juice or vinegar (don't waste the wine), for 20 minutes or so. Be sure not to let the water boil, that will toughen the brains. Simmer them gently, very gently. Blanching helps hold the shape and it also eliminates any trace of blood. Most people appreciate that. After the Brains are blanched, let them cool in their liquid. Then refrigerate until you are ready to proceed; do proceed soon, they won't keep more than a couple of days.

Here is a recipe for Brains that was my first success in getting past the minds of my family in my ongoing effort to broaden their gastronomic horizons.

Scrambled Eggs & Brains

1 pound or so of Brains, precooked as above. (They can be calf, beef or lamb.)

3 T. butter or margarine

¼ cup minced parsley or chives, or a combination of both

6 eggs, beaten—with just a splash of milk added

salt and pepper

Dice the cooked Brains and brown them gently in butter over medium heat along with the parsley and/or chives. Add the eggs and cook slowly until just set; don't let the eggs get dry.

Sweetbreads

The most sought-after, scarcest and, therefore, most expensive of all the offal are Sweetbreads. A large portion of those available go to the hotel and restaurant trade, leaving few for the home kitchen by way of the butcher's meat case.

There are two kinds of Sweetbreads found in beef, veal and lamb. The first are Throat Sweetbreads, the elongated thymus gland, found in the neck of young animals such as veal and lamb. These shrink as the animal matures, becoming almost non-existent in beef or mutton. The second, the Heart or Belly Sweetbreads, are rounded in shape and do not shrink as the animal matures. Rather, they grow larger and tougher. The small, round belly sweetbreads of the calf are the most cherished by lovers of sweetbreads, with those of the lamb running a close second.

Most of the Sweetbreads that find their way into the market arrive frozen, either packed in five-pound boxes or in one-pound packages, often with each pair of sweetbreads individually wrapped. Freezing has little effect on their flavor or quality, so don't hesitate to take advantage of a good buy on Sweetbreads, even if they are frozen. Another thing that has little effect on the tenderness or flavor—but often has a big effect on the price—is whether or not the sweetbreads are paired. Those matching sets, with the two lobes of the Sweetbreads attached, are apt to sell at a considerable premium over those that are not paired.

Like Brains, Sweetbreads are extremely perishable and should be cooked as soon after purchase as possible. Also, like Brains, they require preliminary soaking, parboiling and peeling before they are ready for any finished preparation. As soon as you get them home from the market, soak the Sweetbreads in several changes of cold water for about an hour. Then blanch them, put them in a pan, cover with cold water, add a dash of salt and a bit of vinegar or lemon juice. Bring to a gentle boil, reduce heat and simmer for five to fifteen minutes depending on how you plan to prepare them. If the recipe you plan to use calls for long simmering in some kind of sauce, five minutes of blanching is plenty. That is enough to firm them up a bit and make them easier to handle and peel. If they are to be sauced and served without further simmering, blanch for fifteen minutes. After blanching, drain and plunge into cold water to help make peeling the membrane a less tedious task. Once the membrane is peeled, they are ready to be fried, braised, broiled or sautéed and served up with any one of a hundred sauces.

Many cooks use Brains and Sweetbreads interchangeably since they are somewhat similiar in texture as well as taste. I think it is safe to say that anyone who enjoys Brains will love Sweetbreads. The reverse, however, is not necessarily true.

Tongue

Tongue is one of the easiest of all the variety meats to get past the mind and into the mouth. If it has been properly prepared, sliced and sauced up a bit, it will pass for meat. The response you're likely to get is more apt to be a raised eyebrow than a wrinkled nose, once you have gotten any reluctant gourmets around your house to taste it. The secret is to identify it only *after* they've tasted it.

The tongues of beef, veal, pork and lamb are all available and can all be used interchangeably in almost any recipe, but beef or veal tongue is likely to be more expensive. I think it's because of larger size and easier slicing.

Tongues are merchandised fresh, smoked and corned. They can be served either hot or cold, plain or with any one of a dozen-and-one sauces to enhance or disguise them. But no matter how you plan to serve tongues the basic preparation is always the same.

Basic Boiled Tongue

Rinse the tongue (or tongues) in cold water. Put in a large pot and cover with cold water. Add: one onion, peeled and stuck with a couple of cloves, a carrot, a stalk of celery, a bay leaf, six or eight peppercorns and a teaspoon of salt.

Bring to a boil, then reduce heat. Add a tablespoon of vinegar to help make it easier to peel off the skin later, cover and simmer until tender. Two and a half or three hours for Beef Tongue, only about 1½ hours for veal, pork or lamb. Remove the cooked Tongue from the pot and plunge it into cold water to help loosen the skin. Peel the Tongue and trim the root end, removing any small bones and fat. Strain the cooking liquid, discarding the vegetables but reserving the stock. Put the Tongue back in the strained stock and refrigerate until you decide how you want to serve it. If you want to keep it longer than a day or two before serving, freeze it. Tongue freezes well, but be sure to freeze it in the stock. Not only does it keep the Tongue moist, but you'll need some of the stock for sauce in almost any recipe you choose.

Simple boiled Tongue is excellent served hot or cold, just as it comes from the pot. But to make it a memorable meal, serve it with a sauce. Make a rich Brown Sauce using the stock from the cooked Tongue as your base and then let your imagination go wild in a second pan. (See Stockpot Chapter.)

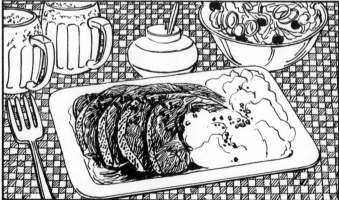

162

Hearts

Gastronomic legend has it that the heart of the animal was the trophy awarded the warrior who brought home the beast. Or maybe saved for the Chief, since the heart was considered to be the source of strength, courage and wisdom, and everybody knows that any big chief or even small brave warrior needs all of that kind of stuff he can get. But legends and myths are made of fragile stuff and the heart no longer holds the place of honor it once enjoyed in the minds of chiefs and warriors. I have a hard time getting the young warriors around my house to try it at all. Heart has become probably the least sought-after and therefore the least expensive of any of that offal stuff. It is obviously, therefore, one kind of variety meat that deserves careful consideration by any cook concerned with saving money. In other words, it's cheap.

The Hearts of beef, veal, lamb and pork are all good food if you treat them right. The procedure most often recommended in recipe books is some type of moist-heat cooking, but Hearts, particularly those of young animals—veal, lamb, even small beef—are tender enough to be cooked with dry heat. Try trimming up a few Lamb Hearts, cutting them into cubes and using them in place of more expensive lamb meat in your favorite recipe for "Shish Kabob." If you don't let them cook past the point of medium rare, you'll be surprised at how tender and full of flavor they will be.

The family favorite Heart recipe from down on the farm, back in the days when my Grandma was a girl, was for Stuffed Beef Heart. It is to this day a favorite in our family.

Stuffed Beef Heart

1 beef heart (or 2 veal hearts, or 6 lamb hearts)
1 tsp. salt
½ tsp. pepper
2 T. fat
½ cup water
2 cups of your favorite stuffing mix. (The favorite in our family is "Onion Stuffing," right out of Aunt Gert's old cookbook—see below)

Wash the Heart (or Hearts), trim away the hard arteries and ligaments inside the cavity and any excess fat from the outside. Fill the Heart with the stuffing mix. Brown all sides in the hot fat, add water, cover and simmer slowly for 3 hours or until tender. Remove and slice the Heart, arrange the slices on a warm serving platter. Turn what's left in the pan into a delicious sauce by adding a splash of brandy to "deglaze" the pan and then thickening with a tablespoon of arrowroot mixed with a tablespoon of cold water. Serve the sliced, stuffed Heart covered with just a glaze of sauce. Serve the rest of the sauce in a gravy boat.

Aunt Gert's Onion Stuffing

½ onion, minced
¼ cup melted fat
2 cups soft bread cubes
1 tsp. salt
¼ tsp. pepper

Sauté onion in hot fat until limp and transparent. Add remaining ingredients and stuff lightly into meat. Don't pack too tightly, the dressing will expand.

Liver

When I was a boy serving my apprenticeship in the Amalgamated Meatcutters and Butchers Workmen of North America, I worked for a while at a very exclusive and therefore very expensive (or vice versa) gourmet market in Sioux City, Iowa. The man in charge of the meat department—we called him the "meat head"—had his entire clientele convinced that Calf's Liver was the *only* liver. It was, after all, considerably more expensive than any other so-called liver and since, "we get what we pay for" and "the best always costs more," Calf's Liver must be the best. What it was, however, was not liver from a calf at all. For years that meat head sold Lamb's Liver for Calf's Liver to people who couldn't tell the difference. I doubt very much if you could either.

Liver, particularly Calf's Liver and Lamb's Liver, varies only slightly in flavor. Pork Liver has a coarser texture and somewhat stronger flavor, but the livers of beef, lamb and calf can be used interchangeably in almost any recipe and—if you don't tell, I won't—no one will ever know.

The major difference between one liver and another is price. Calf's Liver is "out of sight," Beef Liver is high, Lamb's Liver is a real bargain.

There is also another Liver that seems to be gaining in popularity with consumers, it's called "Baby Beef Liver." It's a little more expensive than plain Beef Liver, but still less than Calf's Liver. One thing bothers me, however; I see a great deal more "Baby Beef Liver" on the market than I see Baby Beef. And since each animal—beef, calf, lamb or buffalo—has only one liver, I am led to assume that much of what is termed "Baby Beef Liver" is in fact "bull."

The classic recipe for Liver, which consists of a combination of Liver with Onions or Bacon or both, needs little explanation. Except to say: *Don't overcook it*! Nothing tastes more like the sole of an old shoe than a slab of well-done liver. And since that's the way most people have always been served liver, it's probably why most people think they don't like it. All liver should be cooked slowly and not much past medium-rare. You can use any kind of liver in almost any liver recipe. But to give your budget a break, try Lamb Liver at least once. You're in for a money-saving surprise.

Tripe

Tripe as we know it in this country is the wall of the first and second stomachs of the beef. Before it leaves the packing house, tripe is thoroughly washed, scraped, soaked in lime water and then partially cooked. None the less, it will require long, slow simmering in the kitchen to make it tender enough to eat. Stomach muscles work hard and get tough. Tripe is also available in some markets pickled; this will very likely cost a bit more, but it will cook quicker. The most tender and therefore the most desirable is the second stomach called "Honeycomb Tripe." It gets its name from the fact that it looks like a honeycomb, unlike the less tender Tripe which is smooth.

Throughout recorded history Tripe has found its way into literature, from Homer to Shakespeare. It is even credited by some historians, undoubtedly Tripe-lovers, as being the dish that saved the troops at Valley Forge. When Washington's forces were on the verge of starvation, so gastronomic history has it, the company cook created a concoction from a few scraps in the "mess," plus a hundred pounds of Tripe, which were a gift from the local butcher. The dish—Philadelphia Pepper Pot—is said to have brought not only full stomachs but new hope and ultimate victory to the ragged troops at Valley Forge.

Cookbooks are filled with great recipes for Tripe. They range from the classic "Tripe à la mode de Caen" to simple "Broiled Tripe" like that offered Kate in Shakespeare's *Taming of the Shrew*. But no matter what recipe you use, Tripe will require pre-cooking. Simmer the Tripe for two hours in enough water to cover. Add one teaspoon of salt for each quart of water used. The favorite Tripe recipe for the hungry forces around my house comes from Aunt Gert's old cookbook.

Aunt Gert's Fried Tripe

Pre-cook the Tripe, then cut it into pieces the size of an oyster. Combine 1 egg, 1 cup of milk, 1 teaspoon salt, and 1¼ cups flour to make a smooth batter. Dip Tripe in the batter and brown in fat in a skillet.

Kidneys

Fortunately or unfortunately, depending on how you look at it, good Kidneys have become increasingly difficult to find. The reason being that USDA inspectors in the process of checking each carcass for wholesomeness, open the clod of fat surrounding the Kidney so that it can be examined. This exposes the Kidneys to the air and, as a result, they often arrive at the market dried-out and useless for all but cat food. Lucky cats; Kidneys can be delicious.

Beef, veal and lamb kidneys usually find their way into the market still attached to the carcass. Pork Kidneys must be ordered from the packer since pork seldom comes in carcass form. All are good food if properly prepared. Beef and pork are the least tender and have the strongest flavor. They are, therefore, usually soaked before cooking and cooked with moist heat. Veal and Lamb Kidneys, on the other hand, are milder in flavor and very tender. These need nothing more than quick cooking with dry heat to provide extremely good eating.

In selecting Kidneys, look for those that have a fresh glossy appearance. Avoid any that look dried-out. They should not only *look* fresh, they should *smell* fresh, with at most only the slightest hint of the odor of ammonia.

All Kidneys have a thin membrane surrounding them. This should be peeled off before cooking. So should the little button of fat on the underside. Veal and Lamb Kidneys can be used interchangeably in any recipe. Consult your favorite cookbook.

SAUSAGE AND STUFF

Chapter 11

Sausage-making used to be a tradition when I was a boy growing up on a farm in Nebraska. My grandfather had a recipe for Country-Style Pork Sausage that he treasured and guarded like Grandma did the family Bible; even more so—I sometimes got to look at the family Bible. He would no more tell you what went into that sausage, before it was packed in a poke and lightly smoked, than he would light his pipe in the hay loft. It was *his* and it was good, and if you wanted sausage: "Drop on by, I'll give you some." But not the recipe; that was going to stay his, and it did.

My father made his own sausage in the little meat market where I began to learn the trade. It had something of the flavor of Gramp's but it wasn't smoked and it wasn't packed in cloth pokes. Instead, Dad stuffed hog casings and twisted them into links. He was, however, like his father before him—damn secretive about what went into them.

So, a while back, when Dinah Shore asked me to come on her show to demonstrate how to make sausage, I said, "Sure, I'd love to. Why my Grandfather used to . . . and my father used to . . . I'd be happy to, too." It was only after hanging up the phone that the realization hit me—I had never made sausage in my life. I learned fast! And it's a ball experimenting with different stuffing methods.

First select the right cut of meat. You'll need about 2 pounds for a good test batch. There are two cuts of pork that I have found work best for home sausage-stuffing makings: Pork Butt, sometimes called "Boston Butt" and the Rib End of the Pork Loin. Both of these relatively inexpensive cuts are readily available in today's meat markets and both have a good ration of fat to lean. Also, it is fairly easy to remove what bone there is from either, even without a degree in animal anatomy. (See pages 97 and 102.)

After removing the bones (and don't throw those away, they are great flavoring for a pot of beans or sauerkraut) cut the meat into small cubes and put into a large mixing bowl.

Now you have to decide what kind of sausage you want to make.

Is it **Country Style with Sage?**
for every 2 lbs. of pork add:
   2 tsp. salt
   1 tsp. pepper
   1 or 2 tsp. sage
   (If you like it hot, add a dash of cayenne)

Is it **Polish Style (Kielbasa)?**
for every 2 lbs. of pork add:
   1 lb. Ground Beef
   2 tsp. salt
   1 tsp. pepper
   4 cloves garlic, crushed
   (You'll also need hog casings for stuffing)

Is it **Italian Style?**
for every 2 lbs. of pork add:
   2 tsp. salt
   1 tsp. pepper
   ½ tsp. crushed anise seed
   1 T. paprika
   pinch of cayenne (if you like it hot)
   1 or 2 T. of Sauterne wine

Or perhaps what you have a taste for had its origin in Czechoslovakia, Germany, Holland or France; or in China or Spain or your Grandmother's kitchen in Pennsylvania. Let your imagination be your guide to seasoning your sausage.

Mix the seasonings over the cubes of meat and toss well. Set in refrigerator to chill well before grinding. The meat grinds better if it is very cold.

Now to the stuffing

Country-Style Sausage meat can be formed into patties, partially cooked and kept for months covered with lard in a crock in the cold-cellar. That's how Grandmother used to do it. A more appealing way from Grandma's day is to pack it in a "poke." You've probably heard the expression "pig in a poke," without knowing what a poke was. It's a sack. To make your own, sew little bags out of unbleached muslin or sack cloth, about 3″ × 12″, leaving the top open. Fill the bags with sausage meat and tie the open end securely. Grandma used to dip her pokes in paraffin, to seal out the air and preserve them, but you can wrap yours in foil and put them in the freezer. They will keep frozen for months.

The real fun in sausage-making comes in the stuffing. Pork casings are the most often used, although the familiar little "breakfast sausage" is traditionally stuffed into sheep casings. Casings come thoroughly cleaned and packed in salt. They are available from butcher supply companies in bundles selling for as little as one dollar. And a dollar's worth is enough to make a lot of "links."

To make links you will need some type of "stuffer." There are several inexpensive attachments for meat grinders (either hand or electric) which make the job a snap. Or, for little more than the price of the casings, you can get a "hand stuffer." With either the process is about the same.

Rinse the casings in cool running water to remove the salt. Then soak them for a half-hour or so in clear water with a little vinegar added. To stuff: tie one end of the casings securely, then fit the open end over the nozzle of the stuffer and pull the casings over the nozzle until you have reached the tied end. With the grinder-stuffer the meat is ground and stuffed at the same time; with the hand stuffer the meat must be ground first then stuffed into the casing. Either way, the process is easy and the results are delicious and gratifying. It's fun to stuff your own sausage and you have the advantage of knowing what went into them.

Other Stuff

Speaking of stuffing things, when you ask your friendly butcher for assistance in stretching your food dollar, you must understand that despite being bitched at, boycotted and generally bombarded with abuse with some regularity since about 1973, he is probably *not* being impertinent when he hands you a piece of meat and says, "Here take this and stuff it." What he is offering is an almost magic method of making all manner of meat go much, much further. There are dozens of cuts of meat that can be effectively stuffed with an appropriate dressing and appropriately dressed with an effective sauce, much to the benefit of both palate and pocket.

Of all the stuffable possibilities available in your butcher's meat case, and the possibilities are almost endless, the most money-saving potential is likely to be Bottom Round or Rump Roast. Both the Rump and Bottom Round are solid muscle and both are by nature a little on the tough side. Now normally that would be a disadvantage, but when you're planning on stuffing, those qualities are definitely desirable.

The end result, after stuffing and rolling slices of this meat, will be beef rolls. There are hundreds of good recipes, which may be called "Roulades" or "Oiseaux sans Têtes" (Birds without Heads), depending on the language you speak. Here are a few that have become favorites in my family:

Beef Rolls in Beer

6 thin (¼-inch) slices of Beef Rump
6 tsp. mustard
1 onion, peeled and cut into 6 wedges
3 slices of bacon, cut in half
3 small dill pickles, cut in half or one big one cut in 6 wedges
1 carrot, chopped
½ cup flour
salt and pepper to taste
3 T. cooking oil
1 12-oz. bottle of beer
Arrowroot

Trim any excess fat from the meat. With a mallet, a heavy frying pan or a rolling pin, give each piece of meat a few good whacks to pound it good and thin.

Spread each piece with one teaspoon of mustard. Near one edge of each piece, place a strip of bacon, a wedge of onion, and one of pickle.

Roll up jelly-roll fashion, secure with toothpicks, and lace with string.

Put flour, salt and pepper in a bag. Add meat rolls, two or three at a time and shake, coating well.

In a heavy skillet or frying pan, heat the oil over moderate heat until it begins to sputter. Add the floured meat rolls and brown well on all sides. Reduce the heat to low, add celery, carrots and half of the beer. Cover and simmer for about 1½ hours until tender. Turn the rolls once or twice during cooking and add more beer if needed.

Remove rolls to warm platter. Remove the toothpicks and string. Strain the cooking liquid and return to the pan over high heat. Thicken with arrowroot that has been dissolved in water. Pour sauce over meat rolls and serve.

This dish is good with simple boiled potatoes and perhaps a dish of sautéed red cabbage.

Oiseaux Sans Têtes

1 lb. pork sausage meat
2 onions, finely chopped
1 clove garlic, crushed
½ lb. mushrooms, chopped
½ cup bread crumbs
8 thin slices of beef rump
4 slices of bacon, cut in half
Seasoned flour
2 T. butter and/or oil
2 carrots, peeled
1 onion, stuck with 2 cloves
1 bay leaf
1 cup beef stock
1 cup red wine
½ cup cream
Arrowroot

Combine the pork, onion, garlic, mushrooms and bread crumbs, and mix well. Pound beef slices between two sheets of waxed paper to make them nice and thin. Spread each slice with ⅛ of the stuffing mix, roll up, wrap with bacon and tie with string. Coat the rolls in seasoned flour and brown them in butter or oil. Arrange in a casserole with carrots, onion and bay leaf. Add stock and wine, cover and simmer gently for 1½ hours, adding more wine or stock if needed. Remove the strings and arrange rolls on serving platter. Keep warm. Strain the sauce and add the cream, return to heat and thicken to the desired consistency with the arrowroot dissolved in water. Pour sauce over rolls and serve. Serves four.

Beef Roulades

8 slices of beef rump
1 recipe of Neva's All-Purpose Stuffing or any bread stuffing
3 T. butter
8 or 10 small white onions
⅓ cup flour
1 T. tomato paste
1 cup beef stock or 1 10-oz. can beef bouillon
2 cups red wine
1½ lbs. mushrooms
½ cup whole blanched almonds.

Place rump slices between two sheets of wax paper and flatten. Trim any excess fat. Spread on the stuffing mix, roll up and tie with string. Heat the butter in a heavy skillet, add the roulades, and brown well on all sides. Remove the meat and add the onions to the pan. Sauté until limp.

Mix the flour and cook, stirring until nicely brown. Add tomato paste, beef stock and wine. When the sauce has blended well and begun to bubble, add the roulades. Cover and cook in a 350 degree oven for 1½ hours.

To serve: remove strings and arrange the roulades on a serving platter, correct seasonings and consistency of sauce, if necessary, and pour over roulades. Serve with buttered noodles and a crisp green salad.

Neva's Quick All Purpose Stuffing

4 T. butter
1 onion, chopped fine
6 mushrooms, chopped
2 cloves garlic, crushed
½ tsp. thyme
¼ tsp. each of caraway and celery seed
1 T. parsley flakes
1 cup bread crumbs
1 egg beaten
3 T. milk
salt and pepper to taste.

Sauté onion, mushrooms and garlic in butter until soft. Remove from heat and add all remaining ingredients, mix well.

This is a good stuffing for beef, veal, chicken breasts, or pork chops. Or, you can add one pound of ground meat (lamb, pork, sausage or hamburger) and use it to stuff vegetables such as green peppers, zucchini or tomatoes.

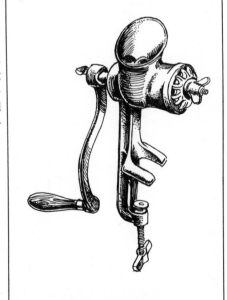

CARVING

Chapter 12

One of the best and simplest ways to get more meat, as well as more tender meat, out of your meat-buying dollar is to learn a few of the basic rules of proper carving.

Don't panic! I'm not talking about the artistic display of knife-wielding wizardry required for a suckling pig or even the Thanksgiving turkey. Those are "special." What I'm talking about is the day-in and day-out slicing of meat you put on your table so that it looks good, is easier to eat, and provides more slices per pound.

The first basic rule of proper carving has to do with proper cooking. Any meat that is overdone or cooked at too high a temperature will crumble when you try to slice it. While it will probably be tender and easy to eat, I can think of few things less appealing than a pile of meat crumbs trying to pass for a slice of roast beef.

After it is cooked, most meat that is to be carved should be allowed to "rest" for a few moments before carving. Ten or fifteen minutes out of the oven will allow the meat to "firm up" and make it much easier to slice when you bring it to the table. The exception to this rule is steak, which should be served "sizzling," of course.

The most important rule of meat carving sounds like it came from a carpenter's manual: "Cut across the grain." Like wood, meat has a grain, and by carving across that grain you cut the muscle fibers shorter. While that doesn't technically make the meat more tender it does make it easier to eat.

Carving in the Kitchen

Most of the day-in, day-out carving of meat is done in the kitchen, and that's a good place to learn the basics before you attempt a performance (and it is a performance) at the dining room table before an audience of assembled guests. In the kitchen you don't need all of the props—the fancy carving set, silver platters, and other accoutrements—that are part of the "on stage performance" at the dining room table. Here the same good sharp knife and your trusty cutting board are all the accessories you'll need. You don't even need a carving fork, you can secure a rocking roast unceremoniously with your fingers. If you've let it rest for a while it won't be too hot to hold.

When you do the carving in the kitchen and the finished product makes its appearance at the table all sliced and ready to serve, one of the most important considerations is how it looks. A whole turkey or a Standing Rib Roast carried proudly to the dining room table to be carved needs little more than a piece of parsley here and there to make an elegant presentation, unlike meat carved in the kitchen, which all too often makes its appearance at the table as an unaesthetic heap of meat piled on a platter. Even a piece of parsley doesn't help in such circumstances.

A little care with the arranging of kitchen-carved meat can make a great deal of difference in its appearance. All meat has something of a pattern to it, in the grain and in the relationship of the fatty parts to the lean. If you will take this natural pattern into account when you place kitchen-carved meat on the platter, you will serve some much more attractive platters.

When you are carving a roast, for example, carve the whole roast first, before you start piling it on the platter. Save out the prettiest center slices and set them aside. Arrange the less attractive end pieces on the platter first and then cover them with the pretty ones, using the natural pattern in the meat to its most appealing advantage.

This way, not only are the best slices offered first, with the less attractive saved for seconds or for

another family meal on another day but, in addition, the platter makes its appearance looking grand—with or without a piece of parsley.

The same principle of appealing presentation applies when you are pre-carving poultry in the kitchen. Take the Thanksgiving turkey, for example. Carve the whole bird before you start arranging it on the platter. Set aside the drumsticks, the bony first two sections of the wing, even the tail. Carve the meaty parts—the breast, thighs and the large section of the wing—into slices as uniform as possible and again set aside the best slices to put on top.

When you have the whole bird carved, start arranging it on the platter. Put the smallest, tough-

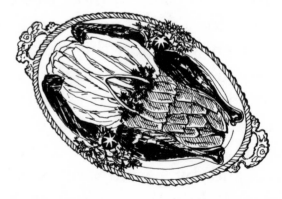

est, least appealing slices of white meat at one end of the serving platter and cover them with a careful arrangement of the nicer breast slices. Do the same with the dark meat at the other end of the platter, covering them with the larger slices of thigh meat. Then prop the wings up on either side of the pile of white meat, place the drumsticks along each side of the pile of dark, and put the tail in its appropriate place. Add a piece of parsley, if you wish, and your kitchen-carved turkey is ready to make its appearance at the table looking like more than a pile of meat; looking as a matter of fact, very much indeed like the turkey it is.

Directions for Carving

There are three basic directions for carving any meat: horizontal, vertical and diagonal. Which one you use depends on the cut of meat, its shape, the direction of the grain, and its natural tenderness (or lack of it).

To carve meat horizontally means that you carve parallel to the platter. The knife never touches the serving platter so there is no need for any kind of wooden cutting surface under the meat.

To carve vertically you will need either a wooden carving board or a wooden insert for your carving platter, since you will be cutting vertically through the meat to the surface underneath.

Diagonal carving is a cross between the previous two and again you will require some type of wooden surface under the meat, since each cut ends with the edge of your knife against whatever is under the meat.

Carving at the Table

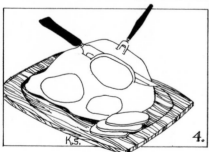

What follows are some basic instructions for the most commonly carved cuts of meat. They should enable you to carve with enough flare and showmanship to make you and the meat you're carving co-stars at the dining room table. You may want to rehearse a time or two in the kitchen before you perform "on stage" but the basics are the same, except that you can't use your fingers when you carve at the table.

In most homes one of the first carving performances held at the table is either a duel or a duet with the Thanksgiving turkey. So let's begin there.

Carving a Turkey

It is a rather dubious distinction but, since distinctions of any kind are rather hard to come by, I'll count it—dubious or not. I have, I believe, the distinction of being the only butcher (certainly one of the few) who has ever cut his finger carving a turkey on national television.

I was once invited down to Los Angeles to demonstrate the proud and proper art of carving a turkey on the Dinah Shore Show. I was fantastic! At least I was fantastic up to the point when Dinah said, "Merle, you're fantastic! You make it look so easy, but you go so fast I'm always afraid you'll cut yourself!"

At just that point, I did! It was just a nick. I doubt that most of the millions who watched "Dinah's Place" even noticed. True to the tradition of show-biz, I tucked the wounded thumb under a wing and continued on unflinchingly. "The show must go on"—and carving at the table is a show.

You will get off to a much better start if you let the turkey rest for about 20 minutes after it comes from the oven before carrying it "on stage." You will need, in addition to the platter or carving board upon which the turkey makes its grand entrance, a smaller platter or carving board and a serving platter. You will also need plenty of room. So clear away anything that might get in the way of any broad theatrical gestures. It is impossible to play a great scene without the proper staging.

You will need, for this and for all "on stage" carving, a carving set. It doesn't have to be a fancy one; it doesn't even have to have stag horn handles. But the knife does need to be *sharp*. If the fancy set you got for a wedding present doesn't have a sharp knife, just use the fancy fork and steel and substitute a good sharp knife from the kitchen. Remember "the play's the thing," not the props.

Position the turkey in front of you so that the legs are pointing to your right. Now before you begin, run the blade of the knife a few times deftly across the steel. It probably doesn't need it, and the traditionalists of the art of carving frown on it, but it is a great way to begin the act—a little like a drum roll or a fanfare.

Always carve the side nearest the audience first. Remember this is "show biz" and the people want to see what you're doing. 1) First remove the drumstick. Cut down between the thigh and the body and, with the fork, push the leg outward so that you can find and sever the joint that connects the thigh to the back bone.

2) Remove the drumstick to the

smaller platter and separate the leg from the thigh. Carve both into slices as uniform as possible parallel to the bone.

3) Next make a horizontal "base cut" deep into the breast at the point where the wing is attached. Press down on the wing tip to find the joint and sever the wing. Remove it to the smaller platter and divide into smaller portions at the joints.

4) Now comes the finale—carving the breast. Before beginning you might want to give yourself another fanfare; so sharpen your already sharp knife one more time, just for effect. Then, with the fork firmly planted to steady the bird, start carving the breast into thin slices, beginning about halfway up and carving down to the base cut made when you removed the wing. If you have your act together, the slices should fall neatly away from the bird.

Arrange both light and dark meat along with some of the stuffing, if there is any, on the serving platter for passing to your guests. Carve enough for—but only enough for—a single generous serving for each of your guests. Nothing is drier than dry turkey and it keeps much better on the carcass. When more is needed, you'll be called on for an encore.

Carving a Rib Roast of Beef

Carving a Standing Rib Roast is much easier and therefore more effective on stage if you solicit the assistance of your backstage crew—in this case, the butcher. Make sure that he removes or at least loosens the backbone so that you can remove it before bringing the roast to the table.

Standing Ribs are traditionally carved horizontally, meaning that you carve across the meat parallel to the serving platter. You therefore need no wooden cutting board under the meat. Place the roast on the serving platter with the larger end on the bottom. Set the platter on the table so that the rib bones are to the carver's left. Anchor the carving fork firmly between two ribs and proceed to cut off nice uniform slices at least

¼-inch thick from the outer edge into the rib bones. Free each slice by cutting along the edge of the rib with the point of your knife, lifting each away to the serving platter before starting the next slice. After you have sliced to below the first rib, cut the bone off and set it aside before continuing on to the next rib bone. Arrange the slices neatly and serve to the assembled guests.

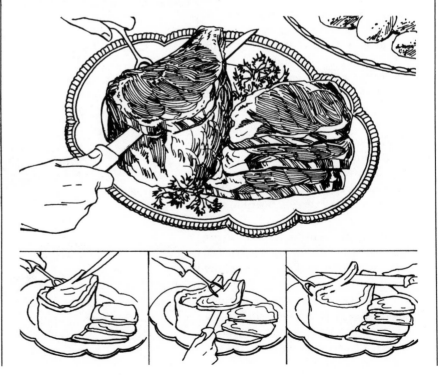

Other Rib Roasts

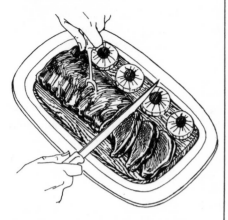

Rib Roasts from other than beef are usually carved vertically down between each rib to the serving platter. Whether it's a Rib Roast of Pork, a Rack of Lamb or several rib sections formed into a Crown Roast, the procedure is basically the same. Since these are carved vertically, you will need some type of cutting board or wooden insert for your serving platter to keep from dulling your knife when you cut through the meat. Nothing will do in a sharp edge faster than cutting across the surface of a china or metal serving platter.

Again, as with the Beef Rib Roast, you will look better carving at the dining room table if you have the butcher loosen or remove the backbone before you get home. Place the roast on the carving board so that the ribs are toward the carver. (This is automatic with a Crown Roast since all the ribs are on the outside anyway.) To carve, simply secure the roast with your carving fork and carve between the ribs. For thick chops slice between each rib leaving one bone in each chop; for thinner chops cut one chop with the rib and the next between the ribs.

Carving a Leg of Anything

As we have seen, there is more than a basic similarity between the bone structure of one type of meat animal and another. This similarity makes carving a lot easier. Once you've become proficient at carving the leg of one, you can carve a leg of almost anything.

Here for purposes of illustration we show a Leg of Lamb, but the procedure is essentially the same for any leg. Whether it is a whole Leg of Pork or a Ham, a Leg of Mutton, Veal, Venison or Bear, all can be carved with ease and with flare if you'll follow these simple steps.

Place the leg on the carving platter with the shank bone to your right. Cut off a slice or two from along the bony side close to the knee joint. This provides a flat surface upon which to rest the leg for the re-

mainder of the job. Turn the leg up so that it sets firmly on the flat surface you have just created and cut a little wedge-shaped piece from just above the knuckle at the shank end. Now make as many slices as you need, starting where the wedge was removed, cutting down through the meat to the bone. When you have carved as many slices as you need, cut along the top of the bone freeing all of the slices at once. Remove them to a serving platter.

Carving Boneless Roasts

There are two methods of carving boneless roasts. The one you choose will be determined by the diameter of the roast and the direction of the grain. Large roasts—Rolled Ribs, Cross Ribs, Hotel Rounds, and so forth—are usually carved horizontally.

Place the roast on a platter with the largest surface down. Insert the fork into the left side and proceed to slice off slices across the grain from right to left. Remove any strings as you come to them.

Boneless roasts of a lesser physical stature, such as Sirloin Tip Roasts, Rolled Veal, and Lamb Roasts, can better be carved vertically. Place the roast on the carving board or on a wooden insert in the carving platter. Anchor it firmly with the carving fork and simply carve off slices.

Carving Pot Roasts

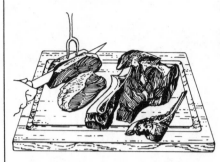

Because of the method of cooking—long and slow in moist heat—Pot Roasts often present a problem for the carver. It is, in most cases, a totally frustrating waste of time to try to carve nice thin slices across the entire roast. Unless the roast is one solid muscle, like a Rump or Bottom Round, it will more than likely come out of the pot tending to fall apart at the seams. Let it. To carve, separate each muscle along the natural seams, remove any bone, and then slice each muscle vertically as if it were a tiny boneless roast. Be sure always to slice across the grain. That can be tricky; in a Chuck Pot Roast, for example, the grain goes every which way.

Carving Steaks

If a steak is really tender and juicy, like a good thick **Prime** Porterhouse or T-Bone or Top Sirloin, it doesn't have to be carved. Just cut it, you can't hurt it. Nothing can hurt a great steak except cooking it too long. You can cut off sections from any angle and the results will be tender and juicy. It is tradition, however, when carving a Porterhouse to try to give a little portion of the tenderloin to each person by re-

moving the bone and then cutting off hunks across both the tenderloin and the top loin so that each person gets a bit of both, and for seconds perhaps a little piece of the tail.

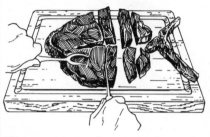

There are steaks, however, that benefit tremendously in the tender department by a bit of careful carving. The classic example is Flank Steak when it is broiled and served as "London Broil." Arrange the steak on a carving board so that the end you plan to start slicing, with Flank Steak this should be the small end, is angled slightly away from you. Secure the meat with a carving fork and, with the blade of your knife almost parallel to the surface of the steak, make very thin slices diagonally across the grain of the meat.

You can use the same principle to shorten the grain of any potentially tough steak: Top Round, Bottom Round, Rump, etc.

PRESERVING AND FREEZING

Chapter 13

Since the beginning of time it has been a necessity of life to store up food in times of plenty. No matter how bountiful the harvest or abundant the feast, it has always been a good idea to save some, for there always seems to follow, for one reason or another, less plentiful times.

Over the years man has developed all manner of methods to preserve meat. He has dried it in the sun, salted it, smoked it, cured it in brines, canned it and pickled it. But, of all the methods man has devised for making today's meat edible tomorrow, by far the best and most widely used in today's kitchens are refrigeration and freezing. What Grandma used to accomplish in a crock in the cold-cellar we now do in a refrigerator-freezer in the kitchen. Drying, smoking, corning and pickling are still used by some cooks in some kitchens, but more for fun and good old-fashioned flavor than out of necessity.

Keeping Meat in the Refrigerator

Keeping meat in your refrigerator doesn't require the precautions that were required to keep meat in a crock in the cold-cellar, but it does require a bit more care than most people give it. It also helps to use a little common sense.

Don't, for example, buy your meat and leave it in the car for an hour or so while you get your hair done. Some meat can be well on its way to "gone" in an hour or so without refrigeration. And, even with refrigeration, some meats hold up better than others. A **Prime** grade Standing Rib, for example, would very probably keep a week or more under refrigeration without any problems, while a pound of Veal Stew would—to say the least—smell bad, long before the week was out.

Meat should be stored in the coldest part of your refrigerator. Many refrigerators mark the spot with a sign, such as "meat keeper." If yours isn't marked, check around with a thermometer to find the spot. It will probably be someplace close to the ice-cube compartment or on a lower shelf.

As a general rule, fresh meat should not be stored in the package in which it came from the market. Some wraps are okay for a day or so, but most are not. So, you'll be better off in the long run if you unwrap everything as soon as you get it home from the store. Fresh meat keeps better if air is allowed to reach its surface. This causes some drying of the surface area which helps protect the meat.

Wrap meat loosely in waxed paper and set it on a plate in the refrigerator. Don't stack too many pieces one on top of the other, as this is apt to force good meat juices out of the ones on the bottom. When you lose juices, you're losing both flavor and food value.

Don't try to keep any fresh meat more than a day or two under refrigeration. If you plan to keep it longer, very likely less quality will be lost by freezing it in the first place, rather than letting it sit in the refrigerator for a longer period.

Variety meats, ground meats, chicken and fish should be used within twenty four hours or frozen. On the other hand, meats that keep well, such as cured and smoked meats, hot dogs, bacon or ham, can be stored in the refrigerator for up to a week with no problem. But these, too, will keep better if loosely wrapped so they can "breathe."

Cooked meat (leftovers) should be cooled to room temperature and refrigerated as soon as possible. Unlike fresh meat, cooked meat should be tightly wrapped to prevent further drying. Plastic wrap or aluminum foil work well.

Keeping Meat in the Freezer

Common sense and a few precautions are all that are needed to assure that the meat you put in your freezer will come out as good as it went in.

The first precaution is selecting the proper meat in the first place. Don't put something in the freezer to keep it from "going bad." It won't work! It will be just as far "gone" when you take it out. Decide what you're going to freeze ahead of time and get it into the freezer as soon as you bring it home from the market.

The second precaution is proper wrapping. The package you pick up at the meat market, whether it is wrapped in old-fashioned "butcher paper" or clear plastic wrap is *not* wrapped for freezing. It needs to be rewrapped in some airtight, moisture-proof freezer wrap. Unlike meat wrapped for refrigeration, where you want the air to reach the surface of the meat, when wrapping for the freezer it is important to keep air away from the meat. Air draws the moisture out of the meat and causes what is known in the trade as "freezer burn." There are a number of good wraps available: aluminum foil, polyethylene plastic bags, freezer paper with a wax coating on one side, etc. One very inexpensive freezer wrap that I've found works well for short-term freezing is a combination of waxed paper and those plastic bags that are free for the taking in the produce section of your supermarket for bagging lettuce or peas. Save them, rinse them out, check to make sure they will still hold water, and use them as an outer wrap over waxed paper. They work well and are certainly the most inexpensive freezer wrap you'll find.

When preparing meat for the freezer, it is a good idea to trim away as much fat and bone as you can. There is no sense wasting freezer space on non-edibles and, in addition, the bones tend to tear the wrapping, leaving the meat exposed to "freezer burn." I suggest using the bones to make stock and then freezing the stock.

Whenever possible, wrap steaks and chops in single layers rather than in stacks. They will freeze better and thaw easier. When you do put more than one layer to a package, put a double layer of waxed paper between layers. If possible, don't stack meat in the freezer for its initial freezing. Spread it out over a broad area of your freezer, so that the freezing process is accelerated by contact with previously frozen meat.

"Rotate your stock." That's retail jargon for "use the old stuff first." It applies to your freezer as well. Develop some kind of labeling system (with dates, color codes or whatever), so that you know what you have in your freezer and at least approximately how long it's been there.

Refreezing Meat

Occasionally I get an urgent call from a somewhat frantic customer that goes something like this, "The cat pulled the plug on the freezer. It's been off for a couple of days. Do I throw it all out? Can I cook it and freeze it again? There's over a hundred pounds of meat in there. . . . What'll I do?" Relax! Don't panic, don't kill the cat; just plug the freezer in again.

There has grown up over the years something of an "old butcher's tale" with regard to refreezing meat once it has been thawed. Every cookbook I have ever read, without exception, says, "Never refreeze meat." Obviously they don't take into account clumsy cats or the possibility that after you have taken a steak out of the freezer to thaw, somebody says, "Let's go out for dinner." I shudder to think how much good meat has been fed to the dog because somebody said, "Let's go out to dinner."

There is basically nothing wrong with refreezing meat that has thawed, provided that you take a few simple precautions, and use a little common sense. The first precaution is proper freezing in the first place. If the meat was fresh when you froze it, and if you have wrapped it properly in good freezer wrap, you have greatly reduced the possibility of it going bad, even if the cat should pull out the plug.

The most important factor in determining whether or not a piece of meat can be or should be refrozen is the degree to which it has thawed. If, for example, you take a steak out of the freezer and put it on the drainboard of the sink to thaw, the surface temperature of that steak will very quickly reach a degree sufficient for bacterial growth to begin. Once that happens, your only option is to cook it. If, on the other hand, you had put that steak in the refrigerator to thaw, it could be left for a day or two and then be refrozen, with no worry and, at most, only a little loss of quality.

My advice is, therefore, always thaw meat in the refrigerator still wrapped in its freezer wrap. That way you have some time to change your mind.

Are you still worried about that plug-pulling cat? Don't be. Unless he has also managed to open the freezer door, the meat will stay cold for several days—so, as long as it's good and cold, refreeze it.

Stocking the Freezer

"Can I save any money buying a side of beef?"

I think I am asked that question with more regularity than any other by customers concerned with saving money. I wish there were an easy "Yes" or "No" answer—but there isn't.

There are numerous "ifs" to consider before buying a side or a quarter of beef for the freezer. If you live over fifty miles from any selection of supermarkets, and if there is a good possibility that you may be snowed in for the winter, and if you have a large hunk of cash kicking around in the kitty, and if you are willing to gamble on the price of beef today being lower than the price of beef tomorrow; then, perhaps, you should consider buying a side or quarter of beef. Not so much for the saving, but for the convenience of not having to plow through the snow for the fifty miles to get to the nearest supermarket.

For most of us, in my opinion, buying a side or quarter of beef is not apt to be a saving. We would likely do better taking advantage of the weekly "specials" in the local supermarket or keeping an eye open for good seasonal buys.

Buying Carcass Beef

It's a little like fixing your own TV set. If you know what you're doing, you're fine and you may even save a few bucks. If you don't, be very, very careful, or you could get a shock!

Aside from being on the alert for the "bait and switch" bunko operators offering bulk meat "bargains," there is much to be aware of, even when dealing with an honest repu-table butcher. Don't, for example, assume that because T-Bone Steak is $2.59 per pound and you can buy a whole hindquarter for a dollar fifty a pound, that you are saving money.

Carcass beef is sold by "hanging weight." What that means is, "What you see is what you get," including all that fat and all that bone. The cutting loss on a side of beef (meaning how much waste goes into the "bone barrel") may be 20% to 30%, or even as much as 50%, of the "hanging weight." The only measure of what the percentage of waste might be on any given carcass is the USDA *yield grade*. Yield grade, like quality grading (**prime**, **choice**, etc.) is a voluntary service provided by the United States Department of Agriculture. If you only buy meat in retail cuts from your supermarket meat case, yield grades need not concern you. The meat has already been trimmed of excess fat and bone, and the price you pay takes that into account. When you buy carcass beef in sides or quarters, however, awareness of yield grades is a necessity.

According to the USDA, yield grades measure the amount of "boneless, closely trimmed retail cuts from the high value parts of the carcass; the Round, Loin, Rib and Chuck." There are five USDA yield grades numbered 1 through 5. Yield Grade 1 carcasses have the highest yields of retail cuts; Yield Grade 5, the lowest. A carcass which is typical of its yield grade would be expected to contain about 4.6% more edible meat than the next lower grade. Granted that's a lot of figures for the non-professional to deal with, particularly when you're standing in the cold cooler trying to decide which of many identical-looking carcasses is the best buy. To simplify the whole "yield grade" dilemma, just remember that 1 is better than 2, 2 is better than 3, 3 is better than 4, and so forth. Just be sure you know the yield grade before you buy.

Yield grading is relatively new to the meat industry, dating back to only June of 1965, but it is becoming a strong force in relating consumer preferences for lean beef back to the producer. Nobody wants to pay good money for a lot of excess fat that ends up being thrown away. And yet, if you are concerned at all with quality, you must remember that some fat is necessary because "Fat makes meat taste good."

If, in spite of my warnings and reservations, you are determined to invest in a side of beef, here are a few tips that may help you get the most for your money:

1) Buy your quarter of beef from the market where you normally shop. You are obviously satisfied with the quality of meat you get there or you wouldn't be a regular customer. In addition, you are familiar with the cuts of meat normally available there. You would be surprised at what strange-looking cuts you could come up with from a "strange" market.

2) If you are at all concerned with the quality, as contrasted to an out-and-out bargain hunt, you would do well to select **Prime** or **Choice** beef and (if at all possible) have it "hung" for a week or two or six before having it cut and wrapped for freezing. "Aging" is one of the major contributors to quality in beef but you'll lose some weight in the process. Two or three percent can be lost in shrinkage alone and considerably more in trimming. If you like good beef, however, it's a must.

3) Don't make the transaction over the telephone or even over the meat counter. You wouldn't buy a car without kicking the tires, so don't buy a side of beef without at least slapping a flank. Get into the cooler with the butcher—it can be a very educational experience.

Seasonal Purchasing

Meat is not as seasonal as strawberries but there are best buy times at the meat counter, just as there are in the produce department. During the summer, for example, you may see Ox Tails priced as low as 39¢ a pound; they'll be twice that in the winter when it's soup season. On the other hand, steaks are usually less expensive in the winter than in the summer, when the barbecue grills come out of the garages all over the country.

Professional buyers in the hotel and restaurant trade have long taken advantage of seasonal purchasing. They stock up their freezers with Full Loins and Strip Loins during January and February, knowing from experience that these wholesale cuts will almost certainly be considerably higher priced during the summer months. You can do the same thing if you have a little extra freezer space. There are two ways to take advantage of good steak prices in the winter. One way is to keep your eyes open for "specials" at your local supermarket. When your favorite steak is "on special" at a good price or when you see some that look especially appealing to you, don't hesitate to buy a bunch. Wrap them well in the appropriate freezer wrap, file them away in a corner of your freezer, then sit back and wait for spring. You'll save money!

Another way is to do just what the hotel or restaurant buyer does: buy a whole trimmed Loin. The Loin is the site of all of the most tender and delicious steaks the beef has to offer. A trimmed Loin is one which has had the greatest percentage of waste removed. The kidney and all of the fat surrounding it, as well as the Flank with all of its waste, have been removed from the trimmed Loin. What remains are steaks, lots of steaks. An average trimmed Loin from a **choice** carcass will weigh in at around 50 pounds. From that, if you have it sliced up with the bone in, 30.6% will be Porterhouse and T-Bones, 49.8% will be Sirloin Steak. 6.4% will be "lean trim" (steak tails which make the best Ground Beef in the world), leaving somewhere in the vicinity of 13.2% (or just over 6½ pounds) of waste in the form of fat and bones.

Just how good a buy you can make on a steak during any given winter depends on a lot of very variable factors. I can tell you, however, that January and February are good months to be thinking about stocking up on steaks for the summer, whether you buy a whole trimmed Loin or individually cut steaks.

Bringing Back the "Good Old Days"

Crocks! They were standard equipment in the kitchen, as well as in meat market, back in Grandma's day, when butchers wore flat straw hats and supposedly put their thumbs on the scales. You hardly ever see real old-fashioned crocks anymore, the kind that used to line the shelves of cold-cellars and "meat coolers." They were filled with all manner of good things to eat: pickled pigs' feet, corned beef, sauerkraut, sauerbraten. But, most of all, at a certain time of year — every year—mincemeat, the kind with meat in it, smelling strong of brandy.

Crocks are still available. They're more expensive than they once were, but they are also every bit as practical as they ever were for making all kinds of good old-fashioned goodies. And when it comes to making mincemeat, they are practically indispensable.

Old-Fashioned Crock Mincemeat

2 or 3 pounds of Beef Rump or Bottom Round
1 fresh Beef Tongue (about three pounds)
1 pound of Beef Kidney suet
4 cups seedless raisins
4 cups golden seedless raisins
2 cups currants
1 cup citron, diced
Rind of two large oranges, diced
Rind of one good-sized lemon, diced
1 cup dried figs, chopped
3 cups sugar
1 tsp. ground cloves
2 tsp. *each* of salt, cinnamon, allspice and nutmeg
1 quart *each* of brandy and sherry

Simmer the beef and tongue in enough water to cover until tender, approximately two hours. Remove from the heat and allow to cool. Remove any fat from the beef, and skin and trim the tongue. Cut both into cubes and run them, along with the uncooked suet, through the coarse plate of a meat grinder. Add all the remaining ingredients except the brandy and sherry, and mix well. Then add enough brandy to make a nice gooshy mixture.

Cover and let stand for at least a month—two months is better—and it will keep almost forever. Refrigeration is not necessary, just stick it in some cool corner of the kitchen. Check after a week or so. If the mixture has absorbed most of the brandy, add enough sherry to moisten again.

Lift the lid every week or two just to keep check on things and to let the wonderful fragrance fill the kitchen. Add a little brandy and sherry alternately as needed to keep the mixture moist.

When you're ready for mincemeat pies sometime around Thanksgiving or Christmas, add one cup of chopped tart apples to each 1¼ cup of drained mincemeat before using.

For many years, a one-pint "Mason" or "Kerr" jar filled with mincemeat, tied up with a bit of red yarn and bearing a simple "Season's Greetings" (along with the information about adding the apples), has been a kind of special holiday gift from our family to very special friends. If you have any left in the crock come Christmas, give some to a friend. I can guarantee it will be well received.

Corned Beef

"Put about four gallons of water in the crock, then add enough salt to make a brine that will float an egg." These, basically, were the instructions Dad gave me when he sent me into the back room years ago, during my apprenticeship in the meat business, to make Corned Beef. Seasonings, of course, were added to the brine. Every butcher had his own special mixture of spices. My father's included, among others, juniper berries and bay leaves.

These days, along with almost everything else in the meat market, Corned Beef comes in plastic packages. It's usually a very mild product, guaranteed not to offend anyone with a too robust old-fashioned flavor. It is convenient. It seldom needs to be soaked. And often it can even be cooked in the plastic pouch it comes packed in. What more could you ask for in the way of convenience? Perhaps a bit more flavor, and possibly a little better price.

The only way to get Corned Beef that is everything you want it to be, is to make your own. It's easy, fun, and you can vary the seasoning to suit yourself.

In the following basic recipe you can use your own combination of spices in place of the pickling spice; you can even vary the meat you use. Try corning a Beef Tongue or a Shoulder of Pork. The only thing that should not be changed is the strength of the brine. If less salt is used, the whole corning procedure will need to be kept under refrigeration, not to mention that the egg won't float.

Corned Beef Recipe

4 to 6 lbs. of fresh Beef Brisket (or you can use Rump, Bottom Round or Eye of the Round)
4 quarts of cold water
1½ cups salt
1 T. brown sugar
2 T. pickling spice
6 bay leaves
½ ounce saltpeter*
6 cloves of garlic, sliced
1 onion, sliced

*Saltpeter—it's an interesting, if somewhat sad, commentary on our times that saltpeter (Sodium Nitrate or Potassium Nitrate), once available in any drugstore in the country, is now a little hard to find. Any druggist can, and probably will, order it for you but few are apt to have it on hand. "I don't like to carry it," my local druggist told me, "It's one of the things people use to make explosives."

In making Corned Beef, saltpeter is responsible for the beautiful pink color most people look for. In some parts of the country however, people prefer a grey color to their corned beef. More and more people these days want to avoid the use of nitrates altogether. If such is the case, the saltpeter can be omitted. A fairly good color can be achieved by substituting cream of tartar in place of saltpeter.

Combine all the ingredients except the Brisket, garlic and onion in a large sauce pan. Bring to a boil, reduce heat and simmer for 5 minutes. Remove from heat and allow to cool. Place the beef in a crock (actually, you can use any container as long as it is *not* unlined metal). Add the pickling liquid, the sliced garlic and onion. Weight the meat down with a board and some kind of non-metal weight like a sterilized boiled brick. Do not allow any meat to project above the liquid, not only will it not cure properly, it may spoil.

Cover the crock or container and store in a cool corner of the kitchen for 12 to 14 days—refrigeration is not necessary. If a thick cut of meat like Rump or Bottom Round is used it may take a bit longer. The meat should cure until the saltpeter has given it a nice pink color throughout. Cut through a piece after 12 days or so to check. A mold of sorts will very likely develop on the brine. Don't panic, that's a normal part of the curing process. Simply rinse it off before cooking.

To cook: Rinse Corned Beef thoroughly. Place in a large kettle and cover with cold water. Bring to a boil, reduce heat and simmer for 2 to 2½ hours. Most recipes for a "Boiled Corned Beef New England-Style Dinner" call for adding vegetables—cabbage, carrots, potatoes, etc.—the last 30 or 45 minutes of cooking. I prefer to boil the vegetables separately, not only do they maintain more of their own distinct individual flavor, but they keep a much nicer color.

Beef Jerky

With the beginning of the Bicentennial Celebration and all, there has come into the marketplace a whole *new* line of real old-fashioned, All-American merchandise, the major ingredient of which (though it's not listed on the label) is nostalgia. You find it everywhere; bread "with that good old-fashioned flavor," jam "just like Grandma used to make," I'm sure you can add to the list.

We just got a shipment in the meat market where I work—Beef Jerky, "just like the Indians used to make," one and one-third ounces for only $1.00. Now you can't get anymore old-fashioned and All-American than "just like the Indians used to make," but you sure can be nostalgic for a lot less if you make your own Beef Jerky. Why pay a premium for a little plastic package? At $1.00 per 1-5/16 oz. package, which figures out to around $12.00 a pound, you're paying half the Indian selling price for Manhattan Island!

Making Jerky the way the American Indians of the Great Plains did is a bit impractical, if not impossible, these days. They used the best meat they could find, usually old bull buffalo. The closest equivalent you can find in the "Great Plains" of today's supermarket is the worst meat you can find. Everything you look for in a good steak—tenderness, marbling, aging—is best avoided. What you want is the leanest, toughest meat you can get. It should be aged like the old bull buffalo, "on the hoof," not like the good steak in your butcher's cooler. Whatever you do, *don't* buy **prime** or even **choice** beef if you can find a lower grade. There's too much marbling in the better grades for a good chewy Jerky and, besides, the fat tends to go rancid. You'll ruin the whole thing if you use high quality meat.

Many markets use frozen boxed bull meat to mix with their own beef trimmings to make Ground Beef. If the market you shop in has it and if the butcher will sell you a hunk, bull meat makes excellent Jerky; almost as good, I'll bet, as buffalo. If you can't get bull meat, get the leanest, toughest beef you can find. Bottom Round or Eye of the Round works well, but perhaps the best alternative to bull or buffalo is Flank Steak. Flank has an elongated grain that makes for good chewy Jerky, if you cut it *with* rather than across the grain.

Here is a simple recipe for turning a pound and a half or so of Flank Steak into Beef Jerky at a cost considerably less than buying those little plastic packages at the supermarket. You can vary the seasonings to suit your own taste, adding a bit of liquid smoke flavoring if you like and eliminating the soy sauce. In the original Indian recipe the only ingredient for seasoning used was sunshine, but my "tribe" likes this recipe:

Beef Jerky Recipe

1½ to 2 lbs. Beef Flank Steak
⅓ cup soy sauce
1 clove garlic, crushed
⅛ tsp. salt
⅛ tsp. pepper

Slice the Flank Steak lengthwise *with the grain* into ¼-inch strips. Combine soy sauce, garlic, salt and pepper. Mix with steak strips and let stand about 15 to 20 minutes. Drain and arrange in a single layer on a rack set in a shallow baking pan. Bake in very slow oven (150 degrees F.) overnight or 12 hours until dried. Cut into 1-inch pieces. Store in a tightly covered container.

Pickled Pigs' Feet

Dad used to keep a 50-gallon barrel at least half full of Pickled Pigs' Feet in the cooler of the little market where he taught me the trade. Every Saturday night about six o'clock or so, he would go over on the grocery side, buy a couple of bottles of beer and drop them into the pigs' feet barrel to cool. Then after the store closed at nine, while we cleaned up the shop, he and Gene (his "second man") would drink a cold beer and have a couple of Pigs' Feet while I had an orange soda. Pigs' Feet don't go very well with orange soda.

Then, one Saturday night, my Dad dropped three bottles in the brine and opened one for me come nine o'clock. I think I felt as big that night as I've ever been and I've loved Pickled Pigs' Feet ever since. Nothing tastes better on a hot summer day than chilled Pickled Pigs' Feet and a cold beer.

You can buy Pickled Pigs' Feet in jars over on the grocery side but I've yet to find a jar that can compare to Pigs' Feet you pickle yourself in a barrel in the cooler or in a big crock in the refrigerator. And while Pickled Pigs' Feet are not the most expensive delicacy on your grocer's shelf, they are almost certainly more expensive than those you can make yourself. Besides, you can't fit a bottle of beer into one of those jars.

Fresh Pigs' Feet are readily available and quite inexpensive in most markets, but if they're not in your butcher's meat case, ring the bell and ask if he can and will order some for you. You may be surprised at what the butcher will do for you if you'll only ask.

Have your butcher split six or eight Pigs' Feet lengthwise. Wash them well and scrape the skin if it needs it. To help keep the feet in shape while you cook them, if that's important to you, wrap them tightly with cheesecloth.

Put the feet in a good size pot, cover them with cold water and add: one stalk of celery, one onion, a carrot, a bay leaf, six or eight peppercorns and a sprig of parsley. Bring the pot to a boil, reduce heat and simmer slowly for 3 or 4 hours, until the feet are tender. Drain well, reserving two cups of the broth. Set the feet aside to cool.

Meanwhile, slice up an onion and a couple of carrots into thin slices and peel a clove or two of garlic. In a second pot put the 2 cups of the broth in which the feet were cooked, 2 cups of vinegar (white wine vinegar is best), a bay leaf, a few peppercorns, 3 or 4 whole cloves and about ¼ teaspoon each of marjoram, mace, and nutmeg. Bring all of that to a boil and simmer it for about 5 minutes.

Now unwrap the Pigs' Feet, put them in the crock; toss in the sliced onion and carrot and pour the vinegar/spice mixture over them; let it cool and then refrigerate for a day or so before you sample any.

APPENDIX

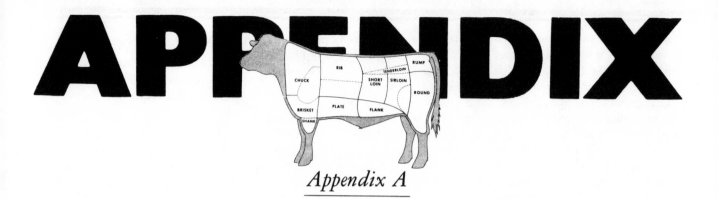

Appendix A

Dictionary of Beef Cuts

The following "Dictionary of Beef Cuts" was compiled in California for California consumers. But merchandising madness knows no state boundaries and this Dictionary can help clear away confusion at the meat counter from California to Connecticut. It is reprinted here through the courtesy of the California Beef Council.

Arm Bone Pot Roast See O-Bone Roast.

Back Ribs RIB Narrow strips of 7 short, flat bones connected with small amount of meat. Cut from Rib section near back bone. Alias *Riblets.*

Barbecue Ribs (*BBQ Ribs*)RIB Suitable for cooking on barbecue. Long meaty rib bones with one irregular, knobby end. Cut when rib section is used for boneless steaks and ribs. Alias *Beef Backs, Beef Spareribs, Beef Ribs.*

Barbecue Short Ribs (*BBQ Short Ribs*) Indicates cooking method. See Short Ribs.

Barbecue Roast (*BBQ Roast*) SIRLOIN Retail name for solid side of Sirloin Tip. Cut, rolled and tied to make small diameter roast for spit roasting.

Barbecue Steak (*BBQ Steak*) Bone-in or boneless steak suitable for barbecue grilling or broiling.

Bavet Steak See Filet of Bavet.

Beef Backs See Barbecue Ribs.

Beef Bacon PLATE Cured, thinly sliced with streaks of lean and fat. Alias *Breakfast Beef.*

Beef Bones See Soup Bones.

Beef Filet See Tenderloin.

Beef Jerky Beef cut in strips and dried. Popular snack food.

Beef Links Highly seasoned chopped beef made into sausages.

Beef Ribs See Barbecue Ribs.

Beef Spareribs See Barbecue Ribs.

Blade Cut Pot Roast See Blade Roast. *Pot* indicates cooking with moist heat.

Blade Roast CHUCK Cut 1 ½ to 3-inches thick from Rib end of section. Usually 3 roasts per section, with varying amount of blade bone and sometimes part of back bone and rib bone. Portions of flat iron, chuck tender and inside chuck muscles surround blade bone. Alias *7-Bone Roast, Chuck Blade Roast, Center Cut Blade Roast, Blade Cut Pot Roast.*

Blade Steak CHUCK Cut same way as Blade Roast only thinner. Bone-in or boneless.

Boiling Beef PLATE, SHANK, NECK Less tender, less expensive beef requiring long cooking in water or other liquid.

Bone-In Chuck Steak CHUCK Usually from top part of Chuck next to Rib section containing blade bone. Alias *7-Bone Steak, Blade Steak, Texas Broil.*

Boneless Chuck Steak CHUCK Cut without bone from tender muscles next to Rib section or from outside shoulder clod muscle. Alias *Cross Rib Steak, Shoulder Clod Steak, Fluff Steak, Patio Steak, Family Steak, Barbecue Steak.*

Boneless Rolled Chuck Roast CHUCK Tender rolled and tied roast cut from large, meaty outside shoulder clod muscle weighing 12 to 16 pounds. Usually cut into smaller roasts of 3 pounds and up. Alias *Cross Rib Roast, Shoulder Clod Roast, X-Rib Roast, Diamond Jim Roast.*

Boneless Short Ribs See Rib Lifters.

Bottom Round ROUND Lean, compact, boneless muscle cut for Steaks, Roasts, Stew and Ground Beef. Less tender than Top Round.

Bottom Round Roast See Bottom Round. Alias *Silverside Roast.*

Bottom Round Steak See Bottom Round. Alias *Swiss Steak* when cut ½ to 1½-inches thick. Alias *Minute Steak* or *Cube Steak* when tenderized. Alias *Sandwich Steak* or *Breakfast Steak* when cut ⅛-inch thick.

Brains Organ in cranium made up of nerve tissue weighing less than a pound. Soft consistency, gray color, thin membrane covering. Considered a delicacy.

Braising Beef Less tender beef requiring moist heat cooking. See Rib Lifters.

Braising Ribs See *Short Ribs*. Name indicates cooking with moist heat.

Braising Strips See Rib Lifters.

Breakfast Beef See Beef Bacon.

Breakfast Steak ROUND, SIRLOIN Thin boneless Top Round, Eye of Round or Sirloin Tip Steaks suitable for pan frying.

Brisket Basic forequarter cut from below Chuck section. Contains lower portion of ribs 1 through 5 and breast bone. Less tender muscle.

Butcher Steak See Hanging Tender Steak.

Butterball Steak ROUND Tender ¾ to

1-inch thick First Cut of Top Round.

Buttered Beef Steak ROUND, CHUCK Cube Steak topped with pat of butter.

Cap Meat RIB Separates rib eye muscle from outside fat in Chuck end of Rib section. May be included as part of Standing Rib Roasts or removed and used for Rib Lifters, Ground Beef, Stew. Alias *Rib Cover, Rib Cap.*

Center Cut Blade Roast See Blade Roast. The middle roast when 3 are cut from a Chuck section.

Chateaubriand TENDERLOIN, SIRLOIN Extra thick (2 to 3-inch) multi-serving steak cut from butt end of tenderloin or small end of top sirloin.

Cheeks Jowls. Have gristly texture, require long cooking.

Chicken Fry Steak ROUND Thinly sliced Top Round, Bottom Round or Cube Steak cut for dipping in seasoned flour or crumbs and frying in skillet.

Chili Beef Lean boneless pieces about ½-inch diameter cut by hand or machine for making chili. Alias *Diced Beef.*

Chitterlings *(Chitlins)* Intestines of cattle (or hogs) used in popular ethnic entrees.

Chuck Basic forequarter cut containing ribs 1 to 5 without Neck, Brisket and Fore Shank. About 24% of carcass. Muscles run in different directions and vary in degree of tenderness. Cut to give great selection of retail cuts—Roasts, Steaks, Stew, Ground Beef, Soup Bones, Short Ribs.

Chuck Blade Roast See Blade Roast.

Chuck Filet See Chuck Tender Roast.

Chuck Roasts CHUCK Boneless or bone-in roasts containing one or more muscles. Flavorful and less expensive than Rib, Short Loin and Sirloin cuts. See Boneless Rolled Chuck Roast, O-Bone Roast, 7-Bone Roast, Chuck Tender Roast, Flat Iron Roast, English Roast, Inside Chuck Roll.

Chuck Steaks CHUCK Cut from most tender muscles about ¾ to 1-inch thick. Flavorful but less tender than Rib, Short Loin and Sirloin steaks. See Boneless Chuck Steaks and Bone-in Chuck Steaks.

Chuck Tender Roast CHUCK Lean, tender 2 to 3 pound muscle from top of section near back bone. Alias *Jewish Filet,*

Chuck Filet, Shoulder Filet, Jewish Tenderloin and *Medallion Roast.*

Chuckwagon Roast Retail name. See Inside Chuck Roast.

Clod Roast See Boneless Rolled Chuck Roast. Retail name used more often in Southern than in Northern California.

Clod Steak See Boneless Chuck Steaks.

Club Roast *(Club Style Roast)* See Strip Loin Roast.

Club Steak RIB, SHORT LOIN ¾ to 1-inch steak cut from small end of Rib section or Rib end of Short Loin. Contains strip loin muscle covered with outside layer of fat. May contain part of rib and back bones. Alias *Rib Club Steak.*

Corned Beef BRISKET, ROUND, TONGUE Cured with salt brine.

Cross Rib Chuck Popular retail name for meaty outside shoulder clod muscle.

Cross Rib Roast See Boneless Rolled Chuck Roast. Popular retail name in Northern California.

Cube Steak CHUCK, ROUND, FLANK Thin, lean, boneless single serving scored by passing through tenderizing machine. Alias *Minute Steak.*

Culotte Steak *(Coulotte)* SIRLOIN From small end of top sirloin muscle. Small, irregularly shaped, tender and flavorful. A 1-inch steak weighs about 5 ounces.

Diamond Cut Roast Retail name. See Rump Roast.

Diamond Jim Oven Roast Retail name for deluxe center cut. See Boneless Rolled Chuck Roast.

Diced Beef See Chili Beef.

English Roast *(English Cut Roast)* CHUCK Square meaty piece containing 2 or 3 rib bones. Continuation of Rib section muscles. Alias when boned *Inside Chuck Roll, Chuckwagon Roast.*

English Short Ribs CHUCK, RIB 5 to 6-inch lengths of rib bones with alternating lean and fat layers attached.

Eye of Round ROUND Solid lean bottom round muscle. About 3-inch diameter, 8 to 10 inches long, weighs 4 to 6 pounds. Cut for Steaks and Roasts.

Eye of Round Roast See Eye of Round. Single muscle roast.

Eye of Round Steak See Eye of Round. Thinly cut for pan broiling. Alias *Sandwich Steak, Breakfast Steak.*

False Filet See Filet of Bavet.

Family Steak *(Family Cut Steak)* CHUCK, ROUND, SIRLOIN Steak cut 2 to 3 inches thick, large enough to make 4 or more servings. Weighs about 3 pounds boneless and 3½ to 4 pounds bone-in. May need to be marinated or tenderized before broiling or barbecuing.

Filet *(Fillet)* Lean, boneless piece of beef.

Filet of Bavet LOIN Lean side strip muscle attached to Tenderloin. Sometimes rolled, tied and cut crosswise into steaks. Alias *False Filet, Bavet Steak.*

Filet Mignon Roast *(Filet Mignon by the Strip)* TENDERLOIN 2 to 3-pound boneless piece cut from Head Loin or butt end of tenderloin muscle.

Filet Mignon Steak TENDERLOIN Small steak from tip or smaller end of tenderloin muscle. A 1¼-inch steak weighs about 4 ounces.

Filet Steak TENDERLOIN Cut from middle section of tenderloin muscle. A 1¼-inch steak weighs about 6 ounces. When thinly cut called *Tournedo.*

Filet Tails TENDERLOIN Small pieces of steak cut from butt end of tenderloin muscle in Sirloin section.

Filet Tips See Tenderloin Tips.

First Cut Top Round Steak ROUND Extra thick steak, about 1½ pounds, cut from Top Round next to Sirloin. Alias *London Broil.*

1st-5th Standing Rib Roast RIB Retail description of roast cut from small end of section next to Short Loin. More deluxe than a 6th-7th Standing Rib Roast from Chuck end of section.

Flank Basic hindquarter cut coming from underside next to Short Loin.

Flank Steak FLANK Lean, flat, boneless 1½ to 2½-pound muscle with long coarse fibers. One per side of beef. Alias *London Broil.*

Flat Bone Steak See Sirloin Steak.

Flat Iron Roast CHUCK Tender triangular shoulder muscle. About 3 pounds; covered with layer of outside fat. Has sheath of gristle through center.

Forequarter Front half of beef side. Separated between 12th and 13th ribs from hindquarter. Contains Chuck, Brisket, Shank, Rib and Plate basic cuts.

Fore Shank Basic forequarter cut. Contains upper shank bone of front leg. Flavorful, coarse, less tender meat with much connective tissue. Often crosscut into 1 to 1½-inch slices.

French Roll Roast SIRLOIN Retail name for Sirloin Tip Roast.

Full Cut Round Steak ROUND Large, lean oval steak containing small round leg bone surrounded by 3 muscles—top round, bottom round, eye of round.

Full Cut Sirloin Steak SIRLOIN Large steak with several muscles—eye of sirloin, butt end of tenderloin, culotte, and flank of sirloin. Bone-in or boneless. Seldom found in California markets. Alias *Head Loin Steak.*

Gourmet Cut Steak Thick cut.

Gourmet Pot Roast Retail name for boneless roast requiring moist heat cooking.

Ground Beef Lean beef and trimmings put through grinding machine. By law has no more than 30% fat. May not have water, binders or extenders added.

Hamburger Popular term for Ground Beef.

Hanging Tender Steak Narrow, thick, 1½-pound hindquarter muscle. Attached in part to diaphragm. One per carcass. Alias *Butcher Steak.*

Head Loin Steak See Full Cut Sirloin Steak.

Heart Hollow muscular 4 to 6-pound organ. More readily available halved or sliced than whole. Calf Heart weighs about one pound.

Heel of Round Roast ROUND Least tender Round cut. Contains thick connective tissue and ends of top round, bottom round and eye of round muscles. Boneless, wedge-shaped. Alias *Pikes Peak Roast.*

Hindquater Has one rib bone (13th). Contains Short Loin, Tenderloin, Sirloin, Flank, Round and Rump basic cuts.

Hind Shank Hind leg containing shank bone. About 50% bone surrounded by lean connective tissue. Makes good soup bones.

Inside Chuck Roast *(Roll)* CHUCK Tender boned and rolled roast cut from continuation of rib eye muscle in Chuck section. Alias *Chuckwagon Roast.*

Inside Round Roast See Top Round Roast.

Kabobs CHUCK, SIRLOIN or TOP ROUND Tender beef cut into 1-inch cubes for cooking on skewers.

Kidney Either of a pair of glandular organs in abdominal cavity between the 12th and 13th ribs. Veal Kidney has milder flavor than Beef Kidney. Available whole or sliced.

Knitted Cube Steak Two or more thin slices of boneless beef run through tenderizing machine to make single Cube Steak.

Knuckle Bones See Soup Bones.

Liver Largest glandular organ weighing up to 16 pounds. Has two lobes, one considerably larger than the other. Available sliced or by the piece. "Young steer" and "baby beef" terms to describe liver from young cattle.

Loin Roasts SHORT LOIN, SIRLOIN, TENDERLOIN Tender and flavorful. Short Loin Roasts have only one muscle —the strip loin. Sirloin Roasts have several muscles including top sirloin and butt end of tenderloin. Tenderloin extends through both Short Loin and Sirloin.

London Broil Multi-serving steak for broiling then cutting into thin diagonal slices to serve. Retail name for Flank Steak or thick First Cut of Round Steak.

Manhattan Roast RUMP Retail name for boneless roast.

Manhattan Steak RUMP Retail name for boneless steak.

Marinated Steak Any cut of steak previously marinated in tenderizing liquid.

Marrow Fat contained in interior porous cells of bones.

Medallion Roast See Chuck Tender Roast.

Melon Roast Retail name for Rump Roast.

Melts SPLEEN Large, porous, dark red vascular organ used mostly for pet food.

Menudo Beef Tripe Cut into strips for making spicy Mexican soup. See Tripe.

Minute Steak See Cube Steak.

Neck Bones See Soup Bones.

New York Cut Sirloin Steak SIRLOIN Popular name in Northern California for tender boneless steak cut from top half of sirloin. Alias *New York Top Sirloin.*

New York Steak See Strip Loin Steak. Popular name in retail markets and restaurants.

New York Strip Roast See Strip Loin Roast.

New York Strip Steak See Strip Loin Steak.

New York Tips See Sirloin Tips.

New York Tip Steak SIRLOIN Small muscle from top of section near back bone.

New York Top Sirloin Steak See New York Cut Sirloin Steak.

O-Bone Roast CHUCK Contains cross section of round arm bone surrounded by forearm, brisket and shoulder muscles. Sometimes boned, rolled and tied. Alias *Arm Bone Pot Roast, Round Bone Roast, O-Bone Shoulder Roast.*

O-Bone Shoulder Roast See O-Bone Roast.

O-Bone Swiss Steak CHUCK Steak cut same as O-Bone Roast. Retail name indicates cooking method. See Swiss Steak.

Osso Buco Retail name for beef or veal shanks cut to make Italian entree of same name.

Oven Ready Beef Loaf Retail name for loaf made of ground beef and other ingredients.

Oxtails Beef tail, weighs 1½ to 2 pounds, available whole or disjointed.

Patio Steak CHUCK Retail name for tender steak cut from cross rib (shoulder clod) or inside chuck muscle.

Pikes Peak Roast See Heel of Round Roast.

Plate Basic forequarter cut below Rib section containing ends of rib bones 6 through 12. Less tender cut.

Plate Boiling Beef PLATE Pieces of bone with some meat attached.

Plate Ribs PLATE See Short Ribs. Less expensive than those from Chuck or Rib section. End pieces of rib bone with layers of fat, meat and bone cartilage attached.

Porterhouse Steak SHORT LOIN Cut from Sirloin end of section. Has both strip loin and tenderloin muscles with the T-bone (finger bone) separating them. Looks like but larger than T-Bone Steak. May or may not have tail attached. A

1½-inch steak weighs about 2 pounds. Alias *His and Her Steak.*

Pot Roast Indicates moist heat cooking is required.

Prime Ribs *(Primal Ribs)* Popular retail name for basic forequarter Rib section.

Prime Rib Roast See Standing Rib Roast.

Rib *(Ribs)* Basic forequarter section extending between Chuck and Short Loin sections. Contains 7 ribs (6, 7, 8, 9, 10, 11 and 12). Muscles second only to those of Loin in tenderness. Alias *Prime Ribs, Primal Ribs.*

Rib Cap *(Rib Cover)* See Cap Meat.

Rib Club Steak See Club Steak.

Rib Eye Filet See Rib Eye Steak.

Rib Eye Roast *(Eye of Rib Roast)* RIB Boneless tender eye muscle of Prime Rib section with other muscles, bone, cartilage and fat removed. Entire muscle weighs 10 to 12 pounds. Alias *Market Roast, Spencer Roast.*

Rib Eye Steak RIB Boneless, cut from ribs 6, 7 and 8 in large or Chuck end of section. Contains rib eye muscle and generous streaking of fat. Alias *Market Steak, Spencer Steak, Market Filet, Rib Filet Steak.*

Rib Filet Steak Retail name for boneless Rib Eye Steak.

Riblets See Back Ribs.

Rib Lifters RIB Narrow, boneless elongated pieces of Cap Meat usually 1 to 1½-inches thick. Coarse texture, less tender than rib eye muscle. Alias *Braising Strips, Boneless Short Ribs, Market Tops.*

Rib Loin Steak See Club Steak.

Rib Roast RIB Any bone-in or boneless roast cut from section. 2 to 3 rib roast popular size. See *Rib Eye Roast, Standing Rib Roast.*

Rib Steak RIB Cut to include bone and muscle. May include Rib Lifters if cut from large or Chuck end. Alias *Club Steak* or *Rib Club Steak* when cut from Short Loin end.

Rib Triangle CHUCK Thin triangular piece containing 4 or 5 ribs and attached meat.

Rolled Rib Roast RIB Prime Rib Roast with bones removed, rolled and tied.

Rolled Rump Roast RUMP Lean, boneless cut from tail end of hindquarter. Tied

to form compact, easy-to-carve roast.

Rolled Sirloin Roast SIRLOIN Has several flavorful tender muscles including top sirloin and tenderloin butt. May be boned and rolled, covered with strips of fat and tied.

Rotisserie Roast CHUCK, ROUND, SIRLOIN Tender boneless beef cut and rolled to make small diameter roast suitable for spit roasting.

Roulades ROUND Thinly sliced Top or Bottom Round cut for making roulades.

Round Basic hindquarter section from middle of hind leg. Makes up about 20% of carcass. Has 4 compact muscles with little marbling—top round, bottom round, eye of round, sirloin tip. Cut for Steaks, Roasts, Ground Beef, Stew, Kabobs.

Round Bone Roast See O-Bone Roast.

Round Steak ROUND Less expensive, usually boneless, versatile. Cut thick or thin for specific entrees. Alias *Breakfast Steak, Sandwich Steak, Swiss Steak, London Broil, Chicken Fry Steak, Family Steak, Salisbury Steak, Chili Beef, Barbecue Steak, Roulades, Stroganoff, Sukiyaki, Steak Tartare, Round Steak Country Style.*

Round Steak Country Style ROUND Retail name indicating cooking method (pan fried with milk gravy).

Round Tip Roast Retail name for Rump Roast.

Rump Triangular basic cut from top end of hindquarter. Tail end of carcass between Sirloin and Round, containing ends of muscles from both. Moderate amount of fat, fairly tender. Used for Roasts, Steaks, Stew, Ground Beef.

Rump Roast RUMP Bone-in, semi-boneless or boneless containing several muscles. Alias *Wedge Cut, Melon Roast, Watermelon Roast, Diamond Cut Roast, Round Tip Roast, Manhattan Roast.*

Rump Triangle RUMP Boneless 4 to 6-pound roast.

Salisbury Steak Shaped Ground Beef patties.

Sandwich Steak ROUND, SIRLOIN Thin, boneless steak for pan frying.

Scotch Oven Roast Retail name for Eye of Round Roast.

7-Bone Roast Popular retail name for roast containing blade bone which looks like a 7. See Blade Roast.

7-Bone Steak CHUCK Large steak cut thinner than 7-Bone Roast.

7-Inch Standing Rib Roast RIB Standing Rib Roast with Short ribs removed. Popular California style. Alias *Short Cut Rib Roast.*

Short Cut Rib Roast See 7-Inch Standing Rib Roast.

Short Loin Basic hindquarter section between Rib and Sirloin. Used mainly for steaks. Contains tender strip loin and tenderloin muscles.

Short Loin Steaks SHORT LOIN Tender, flavorful, fine textured, marbled with fat. Include Club, T-Bone, Porterhouse and Strip Loin Steaks.

Short Ribs CHUCK, RIBS, PLATE Pieces of flat rib bones cut from ends of ribs with alternating layers of lean meat and fat attached.

Shoulder Clod CHUCK Large, meaty outside shoulder muscle. Weighs 16 to 20 pounds. Used for Steaks, Roasts, Ground Beef, Stew. Alias *Cross Rib.*

Shoulder Clod Roast See Boneless Rolled Chuck Roast.

Shoulder Clod Steak See Boneless Chuck Steak.

Shoulder Filet See Chuck Tender Roast.

Shoulder Steak CHUCK Bone-in or boneless.

Silverside Roast ROUND Boneless Bottom Round roast so named because of silvery membrane covering side of muscle next to Sirloin Tip.

Sirloin Basic 22 to 25-pound hindquarter section between Short Loin and Rump. Considered to have most superior flavor of all beef cuts. Used mainly for steaks.

Sirloin Butt Roast See Sirloin Tip Roast.

Sirloin Cubes SIRLOIN Tender cubes cut to skewer for grilling. Alias *Kabobs.*

Sirloin Steak SIRLOIN Any steak cut from Sirloin section, usually boneless. Once popular terms—*Wedge Bone, Round Bone, Flat Bone, Pin Bone,* indicating part of hip bone contained in steak—are now obsolete. See Full Cut Sirloin Steak, Culotte Steak, Top Sirloin Steak, Chateaubriand Steak, Sirloin Tip Steak.

Sirloin Tip *(Sirloin Butt)* SIRLOIN, ROUND Bulging muscle between the Sirloin and Round. Tender, weighs 10 to 12 pounds. Cut for Steaks, Roasts.

Sirloin Tip Roast See above. Single muscle roast. May be split in half, rolled and tied and sometimes netted. Alias *French Roll Roast, BBQ Roast, Triangle Tip Roast, Sirloin Butt Roast.*

Sirloin Tips SIRLOIN Small, tender, boneless pieces. Alias *New York Tips.*

Sirloin Tip Steak Boneless steak cut from sirloin tip muscle below the Sirloin section. Alias *Tip Steak, Sir Tip Steak, Breakfast Steak, Sandwich Steak.*

Sir Tip Steak Retail name. See Sirloin Tip Steak.

Skirt Steak Coarse, fibrous muscles attached to diaphragm inside rib cage. One ¾-pound skirt steak on each side of carcass.

Smoked Breakfast Beef See Beef Bacon.

Smooth Tripe See Tripe.

Soup Bones ROUND, CHUCK, SHANK Bones with some meat attached. Sometimes cut vertically to expose the marrow. Alias *Beef Bones, Neck Bones, Bouillon Bones, Knuckle Bones.*

Soup Meat SHANK, PLATE, ROUND Less tender beef attached to bone.

Spareribs See Barbecue Ribs.

Spencer Roast *(Roll)* See Rib Eye Roast. May have Cap Meat, Rib Meat and streaking of fat in addition to eye of rib muscle.

Spencer Steak See Rib Eye Steak. May have Cap Meat as well as eye of rib muscle and streaking of fat.

Standing Prime Rib Roast See Standing Rib Roast.

Standing Rib Roast *(Prime Rib Roast)* RIB Entire section may be cut into roasts. 2 to 3 rib roasts are popular size. Deluxe roasts cut from Short Loin end. See 10-Inch Standing Rib Roast, 7-Inch Standing Rib Roast, 1st-5th Standing Rib Roast, 6th-7th Standing Rib Roast.

Standing Rump Roast RUMP Fairly tender triangular roast with considerable amount of rump and tail bones.

Steak Tartare Coarsely ground very lean tender beef. Eaten raw after seasoning.

Stew Lean meaty beef cut uniformly into 1½ to 2-inch chunks. Usually boneless.

Stroganoff ROUND, SIRLOIN Thinly sliced Top Round or Sirloin Tip cut for making Beef Stroganoff.

Strip Loin *(Loin Eye)* SHORT LOIN Tender flavorful muscle attached to back bone. Covered with an outside layer of fat. Cut for Steaks and Roasts. Appears in Club, T-Bone, Porterhouse and New York Steaks.

Strip Loin Roast SHORT LOIN Oval bone-in or boneless 12-pound roast cut from Short Loin section after Tenderloin has been removed. Alias *New York Strip Roast, Club Roast.*

Strip Loin Steak SHORT LOIN Cut from section after tenderloin is removed. Entire section may be cut into about 12 bone-in or boneless steaks. Alias *New York Steak, New York Strip Steak.*

Sukiyaki ROUND Thin slices of Top Round cut for making Oriental specialty.

Sweetbreads Two lobes of thymus gland found in neck of calves and young beef. Gray to white color, covered with thin membrane.

Swiss Steak ROUND, CHUCK Bone-in or boneless. Indicates cooking style (pound in flour, simmer in tomato-onion sauce).

T-Bone Steak SHORT LOIN Named for shape of T-bone (finger bone). Has strip loin muscle covered with fat on one side of bone and not less than ½-inch of tenderloin on other. May be cut with or without tail. A 1-inch steak weighs ¾ to 1 pound.

Tenderloin *(Beef Filet)* Most tender and expensive of all muscles. Fine texture, no bone. Tip starts near 13th rib and extends through Short Loin and Sirloin, ending at hip bone.

Tenderloin Butt TENDERLOIN Large end of muscle in Sirloin section. Slightly less tender than tip end.

Tenderloin Tips TENDERLOIN Small tender pieces cut from tip or front end of muscle. Alias *Filet Tips.*

10-Inch Standing Rib Roast RIB Standing Rib with Short Ribs attached.

Texas Broil Steak CHUCK Retail name for blade bone steak.

Tip Steak Retail name. See Sirloin Tip Steak.

Tongue Muscular 4 to 5-pound organ attached to floor of mouth. Calf tongue— ¾ to 1½ pounds. Gray to pink in color, covered with rough membrane. Available fresh, corned or smoked.

Top Round ROUND Most tender muscle in Round section. Cut for Steaks, Roasts, Ground Beef, Kabobs. Weighs 16 to 20 pounds. Alias *Inside Round.*

Top Round Roast See Top Round.

Top Round Steak See Top Round.

Top Sirloin Steak SIRLOIN Largest muscle of section. May be divided into 2 or more steaks. Alias *New York Cut Sirloin Steak.*

Tournedos TENDERLOIN Thin steaks cut from middle section of Tenderloin muscle.

Triangle Rump Roast See Rump Roast.

Triangle Tip Roast See Sirloin Tip Roast.

Tripe Lining of stomachs (cattle have 4) often blanched or precooked. Smooth Tripe—first stomach. Honeycomb Tripe second stomach, better quality.

Velvet Steak ROUND Tender, one-per-hindquarter steak. Weighs about a pound. Cut from above knee joint between Top and Bottom Round.

Watermelon Roast RUMP Retail name for boneless roast.

Wedge Bone Steak See Sirloin Steak.

Wedge Cut Rump Roast RUMP Triangular, boneless.

X-Rib Roast See Boneless Rolled Chuck Roast.

Yankee Pot Roast NECK Less tender, bone-in or boneless roast. May be rolled.

Appendix B

USDA Inspection

Meat and poultry are probably the biggest items in your family food budget, but they're hearty and nutritious ones. you can choose from a wide variety of products, and you can plan a meal around a home-made dish that takes hours or a convenience product that takes minutes to prepare. Inspection provides the best assurance that these meat and poultry products are wholesome and safe to eat.

Uniform Standard

Federal inspection is required in all plants that sell products across State lines or in foreign commerce. Many States are actively enforcing or developing their own programs for inspecting products produced in plants which sell totally within the State boundaries.

Congress passed the Wholesome Meat Act in 1967 and the Wholesome Poultry Products Act in 1968 to assure that all meat and poultry sold in the United States will meet a uniform standard of wholesomeness, whether it is inspected by Federal or by State inspectors.

Sanitary Plants

The U.S. Department of Agriculture must approve the layout of each Federally inspected plant, as well as the equipment and facilities, to assure that they lend themselves to proper cleaning and to sanitary operation. And the Federal inspector each day makes sure that the plant is kept sanitary.

Healthy Animals

The inspector, who in many cases is a veterinarian, checks all livestock and poultry before slaughter to make sure they are healthy. He examines each animal or bird again after slaughter, checking the internal organs and examining the eviscerated carcass as it is processed. At any point along the line, the carcass or parts are condemned if they are unfit for human food.

Processed Products

In many cases, the meat or poultry is processed further. Since they are highly perishable, the products are inspected again. Sausages, hams, soups, and convenience foods like frozen chicken dinners are among the processed products that undergo inspection.

Meat and poultry are reinspected at the processing plant to make sure they are still fresh and wholesome and that nothing has happened to contaminate them.

The complete formula a plant uses to make its product must be approved by USDA's Consumer and Marketing Service. The inspector has a copy of the formula, which he refers to while he examines all the steps in processing, from the weighing of the ingredients to the cooking, to the packaging, labeling, and sealing of the product. All the other ingredients besides the meat and poultry—from the spices in products to the vegetables in frozen dinners or pot pies—are also inspected.

Informative Labels

When the products reach you at the supermarket, they will be truthfully labeled. By approving every label before it can be used and by continually supervising its use, USDA makes sure the label on the package of every meat and poultry product gives you accurate information about the contents.

Every label must carry an accurate name or description of the product, a complete listing of the ingredients —with the ingredient weighing the most first, on down to the item weighing the least—the net weight of the product, the packer or distributor's name and address, and the mark of inspection.

Unseen Partners

Backing up the inspectors in plants are chemists, microbiologists, pathologists, and other laboratory personnel who examine product samples to assure that they are wholesome and properly prepared, or to confirm an inspector's decision. Home economists also analyze products to make sure that the label is right and help establish standards for products, so when you buy "corned beef hash," for example, you always get a product that contains at least 35 percent beef, plus potatoes and seasonings.

Also backing up the inspector is a staff of compliance officers who make sure that handling and distributing of meat and poultry products complies with the law.

Best Assurance

All these steps are taken to provide inspection for your protection, to give you the best possible assurance that the meat and poultry products you buy are wholesome.

Here are the Marks of Federal Inspection

This is the stamp put on meat carcasses. It is only stamped on the major cuts of the carcass, so it may not appear on the roast or steak you buy.

You will find this mark on every prepackaged processed meat product —soups to spreads—that has been Federally inspected.

```
U.S.
INSPECTED
AND PASSED BY
DEPARTMENT OF
AGRICULTURE
EST. 38
```

This is the mark used on Federally inspected fresh or frozen poultry or processed poultry products.

USDA Grading

Totally apart from the "inspection" of meat for wholesomeness is the "grading" of meat for quality. There is often confusion about the difference. Many people, it seems, think that all meat is graded—Not so! Virtually all meat is inspected but not all meat is graded.

There are some cities and states that have regulations making the grading of meat mandatory within their jurisdiction, but throughout most of the country, the grading of meat is a voluntary program provided by the USDA but paid for by the meat industry.

There was a time when all a consumer needed to know to be fairly certain of the quality and tenderness of the meat, notably beef, that came into the kitchen was the USDA *grade* stamped on the carcass. The grading of beef began way back when Grandma was a girl in 1916. But, it didn't really become a factor as far as aiding the consumer was concerned until it was changed from a voluntary program in September of 1942 to a compulsory program in order to make price control laws meaningful and enforceable during the war years. The grading system went back to a voluntary system between WW II and the Korean conflict, was again made mandatory from May 1951 to February 1953 and since then has been back on a voluntary basis.

During the periods of compulsory grading consumers began to rely on the purple shield stamp of USDA Grading as an accurate and reliable indication of quality. Since that time, every cookbook written that has even a chapter on meat has a listing and description of USDA quality grades: **prime, choice, good, standard, commercial, utility, cutter** and **canner**. Unfortunately, however, under the voluntary system that has evolved since 1953, all meat is not accurately marked. The only meat graded for quality these days is that which packers want graded in order that it will bring more money in the market place. That means only the top grades are ever even offered for grading. You never see USDA **standard** or **commercial** grade beef in your butcher's meat case, you may seldom see even **good** grade beef. If a carcass doesn't meet the qualifications of at least the **choice** grade it isn't graded at all.

Just over half of the beef slaughtered in this country is graded for quality by the USDA. Of that, only 6% makes the top **prime** grade, 80% grades **choice** and 12% qualifies for the **good** grade. However, much of what is not stamped with the USDA **good** purple shield, is sold to companies who then put their own purple stamp on the carcass. These private "house grades"— "Sam's Select," "Peter's Premium," or whatever else—are nothing more than the branding of merchandise. They carry no guarantee that any objective standards have been met.

It is this butcher's opinion that the United States Department of Agriculture's grading service, as a voluntary service paid for by the meat industry, has become of little use as a guide to quality for the consumer. Oh, **prime** beef is still the best and **choice** is still more tender than **commercial**, but the fact is, about all you ever see is **choice** and there is a tremendously wide range of quality within that grade.

The USDA is under constant pressure from segments of the meat industry to relax the standards by which meat is graded. Should the Department concede to the continual pressure for lowering certain standards, it would eventually result in grades so broad and all inclusive that they would be totally meaningless.

Here, in the hopes that they may still have meaning for some of you, are descriptions of the USDA Grades of beef. Lamb, mutton, veal, calf, pork and poultry are also sometimes graded, but as a consumer guide to quality those have already become all but meaningless.

Quality Grades

Beef varies in quality more than any other kind of meat. But you don't have to learn to judge beef quality for yourself. USDA grades are a reliable guide to meat quality —its tenderness, juiciness, and flavor. The grades are based on nationally uniform Federal standards of quality and are applied by USDA graders. Therefore, you can be sure that a USDA Choice rib roast, for example, will provide the same good eating no matter where or when you buy it.

How Beef is Graded

Meat grading is a voluntary service provided by USDA's Consumer and Marketing Service to meat packers and others who request it and pay a fee for the service. So not all meat is graded, although a large percentage of it is.

USDA graders, who are highly trained in determining meat quality, grade only whole carcasses or wholesale cuts. This is because quality differences are difficult, or impossible, to recognize in the smaller retail cuts. When the carcass is graded, a purple shield-shaped grade mark containing the letters USDA and the grade name—such as Prime, Choice, or Good—is applied with a roller-stamp. The grade shield is rolled on in a long ribbon-like imprint all along the length of the carcass and across both shoulders. Then when the carcass is divided into retail cuts, one or more of the grade marks will appear on most of these cuts.

Only meat which has first passed a strict inspection for wholesomeness may be graded. So you may be sure when you see the grade mark that the meat came from a healthy animal and was processed in a sanitary plant.

Each USDA beef grade is a measure of a distinct level of quality—and it takes eight grades to span the range. They are: USDA Prime, Choice, Good, Standard, Commercial, Utility, Cutter, and Canner. The three lower grades, USDA Utility, Cutter, and Canner, are seldom if ever sold at retail but are used instead to make ground beef and manufactured meat items such as frankfurters.

The highest grade, USDA Prime, is used mostly by hotels and restaurants, but a small amount is sold at retail and by dealers supplying freezer meat. The grade most widely sold at retail is USDA Choice. It is produced in the greatest volume and most consumers find this level of quality to their liking.

Pictured below are porterhouse steaks in each of the first five grades.

Pictured below are rib roasts in each of the first five grades.

 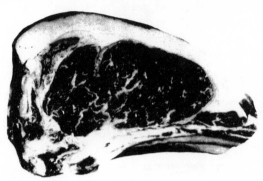

USDA Prime

Prime grade beef is the ultimate in tenderness, juiciness and flavor. It has abundant marbling—flecks of fat within the lean—which enhances both flavor and juiciness. Steaks of this grade are the best for broiling. Prime grade roasts are the best for dry-heat (oven) cooking.

 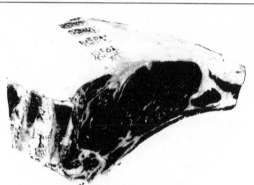

USDA Choice

Choice grade beef has slightly less marbling than Prime, but still is of very high quality and will be very tender, juicy, and flavorful. Steaks of this grade are best for broiling. Choice rib, rump, round and sirloin roasts, like Prime, can also be oven roasted.

 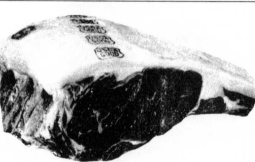

USDA Good

Good grade beef is somewhat more lean than the higher grades. It is relatively tender, but because it lacks marbling it lacks some of the juiciness and flavor of the higher grades.

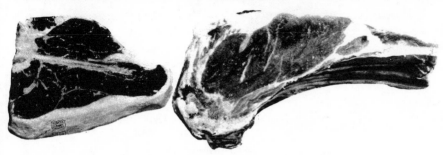

USDA Standard

Standard grade beef has a high proportion of lean meat and very little fat. Because it comes from young animals, beef of this grade is fairly tender. But because it lacks marbling, it is mild in flavor and most cuts will be somewhat dry unless prepared with moist heat.

USDA Commercial

Commercial grade beef is produced only from mature animals—the top four grades are restricted to young animals. it has abundant marbling (compare it with Prime grade above), and will have the rich, full flavor characteristic of mature beef. However, Commercial grade beef requires long, slow cooking with moist heat or a commercial tenderizer to make it tender. When prepared in this manner it can provide delicious and economical meat dishes.

Appendix C

Sources of Additional Information

We would both be fools if either of us assumed that now we know all there is to know about the meat we eat. There is much too much to know to ever know it all. For those of you who would like to learn more, here are a few of the many organizations that can help:

National Live Stock and Meat Board
36 South Wabash Ave.
Chicago, Illinois 60603

The Meat Board has a wealth of information available for little more than the cost of a stamp. Pamphlets on handling and storage, recipes, educational aids of all kinds, including films that can be borrowed. Write for their "Catalog of Educational Publications and Audio-Visual Aids."

Several departments of the federal government have tons of good information available. Booklets on everything from raising your own squab and butchering your own beef to recipes for cooking muskrat. It is difficult, however, to get what you need out of the government—have you noticed that? Write for lists of available material and prices to:

U.S. Department of Agriculture, Superintendent of Documents, Consumer and Marketing Service; Department of the Interior;

All at the same address:
Washington D.C. 20250

American Lamb Council
200 Clayton St.
Denver, Colorado 80206

For information on Poultry contact:

National Broiler Council
1155 15th St. N.W.
Washington, D.C. 20050

National Turkey Federation
Suite 302
Reston International Center
Reston, Virginia 22091

Many states where cattle are a big agricultural commodity have Councils or Commissions or Associations to promote beef. These can be a good source of much valuable information. Check for one in your state.

Alabama Cattlemen's Association
P.O. Box 1746
Montgomery, AL 36103

Arizona Beef Council
4851 East Washington St.
Phoenix, AZ 85034

California Beef Council
1436 Rollins Road
Burlingame, CA 94010

Colorado Beef Board
Rm 326
Livestock Exchange Building
Denver, CO 80216

Florida Beef Council
Box 1929
Kissimmee, FL 32741

Georgia Cattlemen's Association
P.O. Box 4986
Macon, GA 31208

Idaho Beef Council
2232 Main St.
Boise, ID 83706

Illinois Beef Industry Council
R.R. 2 Box 119
Lanark, IL 61046

Indiana Beef Cattle Association
7956 Silverleaf Dr.
Indianapolis, IN 46260

Iowa Beef Industry Council
P.O. Box 451
Ames, IA 50010

Kansas Beef Council
2044 Fillmore
Topeka, KS 66604

Louisiana Cattlemen's Association
Box 26 I-10 West
Port Allen, LA 70767

Michigan Beef Industry Commission
805 Stoddard Building
Lansing, MI 48933

Minnesota Beef Research & Promotion Board
10 East First St.
Morris, MN 56267

Mississippi Cattle Industry Board
121 North Jefferson St.
Jackson, MS 39209

Missouri Beef Promotion Foundation
P.O. Box 315
Ashland, MO 65010

Montana Beef Council
P.O. Box 1679
Helena, MT 59601

Nebraska Beef Industry Foundation
P.O. Box 537
Gibbon, NE 68840

Nevada Beef Promotion Fund
% Dept. of Agriculture
P.O. Box 1209
Reno, NV 89504

New Mexico Cattle Growers Association
P.O. Box 7517
Albuquerque, NM 87104

North Carolina Cattlemen's Association
P.O. Box 25756
Raleigh, NC 27611

North Dakota Beef Commission
107 South Fifth St.
Bismark, ND 58501

Ohio Beef Marketing Program
6649 North High St.
Room 103
Worthington, OH 43085

Oregon Beef Council
400 S.W. Broadway
Portland, OR 97205

South Dakota Beef Council
P.O. Box 219
Sioux Falls, SD 57101

Texas Cattle Feeders Association
2915 South Georgia
Amarillo, TX 79109

Texas and Southwestern Cattle Raisers Association
410 East Weatherford
Ft. Worth, TX 76102

Utah Beef Council
150 South 6th East
Salt Lake City, UT 84102

Washington State Beef Commission
P.O. Box 799
Ellensburg, WA 98926

Wyoming Beef Council
P.O. Box 206
Cheyenne, WY 82001

Many State Colleges and Universities have on going programs and much material available for any consumer concerned with knowing more about meat. Check them out.

Appendix D

Mail Order Meat

A good way to buy some of the best meat available these days is the same way Grandmother used to buy her "goods"—from a catalog.

Prime, corn-fed beef from the corn country around Omaha and Chicago. Great "country hams" and bacon from those places off the beaten path, where folks seem to have the time to take the time to make great hams and bacon by old-fashioned, traditional methods.

Following is a list of some of the companies around the country which provide good eating by mail order. They will be happy to send you a catalog. Their products are not inexpensive! You could likely build your own smoke house for the price of some, but they are good food.

- **Alewels' Old Missouri Country Meats**, South Saint Louis St., Concordia, Missouri, 64020—Country-cured hams, bacon, and sausage, as well as a "summer sausage" and a selection of cheese.
- **Aunt Lucy's Hams, Inc.**, 3 Fredrick St., Box 126, Walkersville, Maryland, 21793—"Country foods" of all kinds: hams, bacon, sausage, "scrapple" and "country puddin'," all prepared according to original Maryland farm recipes.
- **Early's Honey Stand**, Route 2, Spring Hill, Tennessee, 37174 —Some of the best sausage I have ever tasted. It comes packed in a 3-lb. old-fashioned cloth "poke," smoked to a golden brown over hickory wood, and tasting every bit as good as Aunt Gert used to make. (Maybe even better.) Early's also offers hams, bacon, sorghum, honey and a whole line of old-fashioned foods from the Tennessee hill country.
- **Harrington's**, Richmond, Vermont, 05477—This firm does its smoking like my Aunt Gert used to—with corn cobs. You can get ham (cooked or uncooked, boneless or bone-in), bacon, pork loins, sausage, dried beef, turkey and pheasant—all with the flavor that comes from long, slow, leisurely corn-cob smoking. They also have a nice line of smoked cheese, stone-ground flours and pure maple syrup.
- **Hudson Ham House, Inc.**, Route 3, Box 27, Culpeper, Virginia—Specializing in a "dry cured" Virginia-style ham which is not smoked. Cooking such a ham is a long slow process, but for a small charge the folks in Culpeper will do it for you.
- **Joyner Smithfield Hams**, Box 387, Smithfield, Virginia, 23430—Famous "Smithfield Ham," either cooked ready-to-eat or the old-fashioned way—in a cloth sack imprinted with a long list of cooking instructions.
- **Omaha Steaks International**, 4400 South 96th St., Omaha, Nebraska, 68127—Offering a selection of goodies, guaranteed to boggle the mind. Everything from caviar to corned beef (free if you buy an electric meat slicer).
- **Pfaelzer Brothers**, 4501 West District Blvd., Chicago, Illinois, 60632—A variety of beef, pork, lamb, veal, poultry and seafood specialties.
- **The Quail Kitchen**, Route 2, Valhalla Farm, Varsailles, Kentucky, 40383—Specializing in Bob White Quail, smoked and completely cooked in brick ovens with hickory wood. They are fantastic with French bread, a salad and a glass of white wine.
- **Signature Prime, Inc.**, 8030 Central Park Ave., Skokie, Illinois, 60076—An array of meat that would amaze the most jaded gourmet or gourmand. From **prime** Filet of Beef to Loin of South American Llama or Canadian Brown Bear. Even if you can't afford the meat, the catalog itself is an experience in good taste; beautifully photographed and illustrated.

Appendix E

How to Roast a Roast

"Put in lots of cobs to get the oven right hot, so as two or three minutes is all you can keep your hand in. The meat should be wiped, then dredged all over with salt, pepper and flour. Place bits of butter or lard over top and add enough boiling water to cover roaster 1½ inches. Place in a hot oven; baste every ten minutes. Allow twenty minutes to the pound. Don't shake the grate much, you want the cobs to burn slow."

That's how Grandma used to roast a roast in the oven of her wood burner in 1911. Times have changed a great deal since then, and so have the stoves and so has the meat we roast in them. And, over the years, how to roast a roast has become one of the greatest controversies in the meat eating world. Every cook, every butcher, every hotel chef can tell the best way and no two "best" ways will ever be the same.

One butcher recommends, "500 degrees for 35 minutes, then turn off the oven, but don't open the door for two hours." Another recommends, almost by rote, "350 degrees for two hours . . . good for anything." Then there is the "sear it quickly to seal in the flavor" school which recommends 450 degrees for 12 to 15 minutes per pound. All of these "modern" methods have something in common with the way Grandma used to do it. *They leave a great deal to chance.* It's not necessary any longer to put your hand in a hot oven and count to see how hot it is, today you simply set the thermostat and your oven is (within minutes) at the temperature you desire. Neither is it necessary to play guessing games with regard to how long to roast a roast no matter which method you might prefer.

Today there is but one thing you must do to roast a roast to perfection time after time: *use a meat thermometer!* A meat thermometer is the only accurate guide to the doneness of meat, especially roasts. Meat is done to the "rare" state when the internal temperature reaches approximately 140 degrees; "medium" at 160 degrees and "well done" at 170 degrees, and that is true no matter how it was cooked. The only way to measure that internal temperature is with a meat thermometer.

If you have found the perfect way to roast a roast, don't let anybody tell you differently. There are a variety of "best ways," but there is no such thing as a wrong way if that way works for you. I would, however, like to put a plug in for cooking meat at low temperatures. Nothing will save you more money at the meat counter than cooking the meat you buy there with low, slow heat. Meat cooked at a low temperature is always more tender, more juicy and more flavorful, but even more importantly, *you get more of it.* Meat cooked at a high temperature shrinks more than meat cooked at a low temperature. A roast cooked at 400 degrees to an internal temperature of 160 degrees will lose 17% more weight than the same size roast cooked at the same internal temperature in a slower, lower, 275 degree oven.

That means that 17¢ out of every dollar you spend on a roast is wasted if you are of the "sear it quick and roast it fast" school of roasting a roast.

There are other fringe benefits to low temperature roasting: You use less energy cooking at low temperatures, just as you use less gas in your car if you drive at slower speeds; the principle is the same. You have less of a mess when you are through; low temperatures cause less spattering of fat so your oven will be much easier to clean. But most important, your roast will be more flavorful, more tender, and considerably juicier if cooked at a low temperature. Take advantage of the modern age we live in—you don't have to stick your hand in the oven and count to get the temperature right—set the automatic temperature control. And for the most in economic and gastronomic benefits, set it low. Don't take a chance with all of the variables that can louse up anybody's "best way to roast a roast," buy a meat thermometer. To help you use it, the following time and temperature tables were provided by the National Live Stock and Meat Board.

Time and Temperature Tables for Beef Cookery

Timetable for Roasting

(300°F.-325°F. Oven Temperature)

CUT	Approx. Weight	Meat Thermometer Reading	Approx.* Cooking Time
	Pounds		*Min. per lb.*
Rib[1]	6 to 8	140°F. (rare)	23 to 25
		160°F. (medium)	27 to 30
		170°F. (well)	32 to 35
Rib[1]	4 to 6	140°F. (rare)	26 to 32
		160°F. (medium)	34 to 38
		170°F. (well)	40 to 42
Rib Eye[2] (Delmonico)	4 to 6	140°F. (rare)	18 to 20
		160°F. (medium)	20 to 22
		170°F. (well)	22 to 24
Tenderloin, whole[3]	4 to 6	140°F.(rare)	45 to 60 (total)
Tenderloin, half[3]	2 to 3	140°F. (rare)	45 to 50 (total)
Boneless rump (rolled) (high quality)	4 to 6	150°F.-170°F.	25 to 30
Tip (high quality)	3½ to 4	140°F.-170°F.	35 to 40
	6 to 8	140°F.-170°F.	30 to 35
Ground Beef loaf (9" x 5")	1½ to 2½	160°F.-170°F.	1 to 1½ hrs.

*Based on meat taken directly from the refrigerator.
[1]Ribs which measure 6 to 7 inches from chine bone to tip of rib.
[2]Roast at 350°F. oven temperature.
[3]Roast at 425°F. oven temperature.

Cooking in Liquid

CUT	Approx. Weight	Approx. Total Cooking Time
Fresh or corned beef	4 to 6 pounds	3½ to 4½ hours
Shank Cross Cuts	¾ to 1¼ pounds	2½ to 3 hours
Beef for stew	—	2½ to 3½ hours

Timetable for Broiling

CUT	Weight	Approximate Total Cooking Time	
		Rare	Medium
	Pounds	*Minutes*	*Minutes*
Chuck steak (high quality)—1 in.	1½ to 2½	24	30
1½ in.	2 to 4	40	45
Rib Steak—1 in.	1 to 1½	15	20
1½ in.	1½ to 2	25	30
2 in.	2 to 2½	35	45
Rib eye steak (Delmonico)—			
1 in.	8 to 10 ozs.	15	20
1½ in.	12 to 14 ozs.	25	30
2 in.	16 to 20 ozs.	35	45
Top loin steak—1 in.	1 to 1½	15	20
1½ in.	1½ to 2	25	30
2 in.	2 to 2½	35	45
Sirloin Steak—1 in.	1½ to 3	20	25
1½ in.	2¼ to 4	30	35
2 in.	3 to 5	40	45
Porterhouse steak—			
1 in.	1¼ to 2	20	25
1½ in.	2 to 3	30	35
2 in.	2½ to 3½	40	45
Tenderloin (Filet Mignon)	4 to 8 ozs.	10 to 15	15 to 20
Ground beef patties—1 in. thick by 3 in.	4 ozs.	15	25

*This timetable is based on broiling at a moderate temperature. Rare steaks are broiled to an internal temperature of 140°F., medium to 160°F., well-done to 170°F.

Timetable for Braising

Cut or dish	Approx. Weight or Thickness	Approx. Total Cooking Time
Pot-Roast	3 to 5 pounds	2½ to 3½ hours
Short Ribs	Pieces (2 in. x 2 in. x 4 in.)	1½ to 2½ hours
Flank Steak	1½ to 2 pounds	1½ to 2½ hours
Stuffed Steak	½ to ¾ inch	1½ hours
Round Steak	¾ to 1 inch	1 to 1½ hours
Swiss Steak	1½ to 2½ inches	2 to 3 hours
Fricassee	2-inch cubes	1½ to 2½ hours
Beef Birds	½ inch (x 2 in. x 4 in.)	1½ to 2½ hours

Time and Temperature Tables for Lamb Cookery

Timetable for Roasting

(300°F.-325°F. Oven Temperature)

CUT	Approx. Weight	Meat Thermometer Reading	Approx. Cooking Time
	Pounds		*Min. per lb.*
Leg	5 to 9	140°F. (rare)	20 to 25
		160°F. (medium)	25 to 30
		170°F.-180°F. (well)	30 to 35
Leg, Shank Half	3 to 4	140°F. (rare)	25 to 30
		160°F. (medium)	30 to 35
		170°F.-180°F. (well)	35 to 40
Leg, Sirloin Half	3 to 4	140°F. (rare)	20 to 25
		160°F. (medium)	25 to 30
		170°F.-180°F. (well)	30 to 35
Leg, Boneless	4 to 7	140°F. (rare)	25 to 30
		160°F. (medium)	30 to 35
		170°F.-180°F. (well)	35 to 40
Crown Roast	2½ to 4	140°F. (rare)	30 to 35
		160°F. (medium)	35 to 40
		170°F.-180°F. (well)	40 to 45
Shoulder, Square Cut	4 to 6	160°F. (medium)	25 to 30
		170°F.-180°F. (well)	30 to 35
Shoulder, Boneless	3½ to 5	140°F. (rare)	30 to 35
		160°F. (medium)	35 to 40
		170°F.-180°F. (well)	40 to 45
Shoulder, Cushion	3½ to 5	170°F.-180°F. (well)	30 to 35
Rib*	1½ to 2	140°F. (rare)	30 to 35
		160°F. (medium)	35 to 40
		170°F.-180°F. (well)	40 to 45
Rib*	2 to 3	140°F. (rare)	25 to 30
		160°F. (medium)	30 to 35
		170°F.-180°F. (well)	35 to 40

*Roast at 375°F. oven temperature.

Timetable for Cooking in Liquid

CUT	Average Size	Approx. Total Cooking Time
Lamb for Stew	1 to 1½-inch pieces	1½ to 2 hours

Timetable for Broiling

(Moderate Temperature)

CUT	Approx. Weight	Approx. Total Cooking Time
	Ounces	*Minutes*
Shoulder Chops		
¾ to 1 inch	5 to 9	10 to 12
Rib Chops		
1 inch	4 to 6	12
1½ inches	6 to 8	18
2 inches	8 to 12	22
Loin Chops		
1 inch	4 to 7	12
1½ inches	7 to 10	18
2 inches	8 to 14	22
Sirloin Chops		
¾ to 1 inch	6 to 12	12 to 14
Leg Chops (steaks)		
¾ to 1 inch	10 to 14	14 to 18
Cubes for Kabobs		
1 to 1½ inches		12 to 18
1½ to 2 inches		18 to 22
Ground Lamb Patties		
1 inch by 3 inches	4 ounces	18

Timetable for Braising

CUT	Average Weight or Thickness	Approx. Total Cooking Time
Neck Slices	¾ inch	1 hour
Shoulder Chops	¾ to 1 inch	45 to 60 min.
Breast, Stuffed	2 to 3 pounds	1½ to 2 hours
Breast, Rolled	1½ to 2 pounds	1½ to 2 hours
Riblets		1½ to 2½ hours
Shanks	¾ to 1 pound each	1 to 1½ hours
Lamb for Stew	1½-inch pieces	1½ to 2 hours

Time and Temperature Tables for Pork Cookery

Timetable for Roasting

(300°F.-350°F. Oven Temperature)

CUT	Approx. Weight	Meat Thermometer Reading	Approx.[1] Cooking Time
### Fresh	Pounds	Degrees F.	Min. Per. Lb.
Loin			
Center	3 to 5	170°F.	30 to 35
Half	5 to 7	170°F.	35 to 40
End	3 to 4	170°F.	40 to 45
Roll	3 to 5	170°F.	35 to 40
Boneless Top	2 to 4	170°F.	30 to 35
Crown	4 to 6	170°F.	35 to 40
Picnic Shoulder			
Bone-In	5 to 8	170°F.	30 to 35
Rolled	3 to 5	170°F.	35 to 40
Boston Shoulder	4 to 6	170°F.	40 to 45
Leg (fresh Ham)			
Whole (bone-in)	12 to 16	170°F.	22 to 26
Whole (boneless)	10 to 14	170°F.	24 to 28
Half (bone-in)	5 to 8	170°F.	35 to 40
Tenderloin	½ to 1		45 to 60
			Hours
Back ribs		Cooked	1½ to 2½
Country-style		Well	
backbones		Done	1½ to 2½
Spareribs			1½ to 2½
Pork loaf	2		1¾
### Smoked			
Ham			
(cook-before-eating)			
Whole	10 to 14	160°F.	18 to 20
Half	5 to 7	160°F.	22 to 25
Shank Portion	3 to 4	160°F.	35 to 40
Butt Portion	3 to 4	160°F.	35 to 40
Ham (fully-cooked)[2]			
Half	5 to 7	140°F.	18 to 24
Loin	3 to 5	160°F.	25 to 30
Picnic Shoulder			
(cook-before-eating)	5 to 8	170°F.	30 to 35
Picnic Shoulder			
(fully-cooked)	5 to 8	140°F.	25 to 30
Shoulder roll (butt)	2 to 4	170°F.	35 to 40
Canadian-style bacon	2 to 4	160°F.	35 to 40
Ham Kabobs	1″ to 1½″ cubes		45 to 60
Ham Loaf	2	160°F.	1½ hrs.
Ham Patties	1″ thick	160°F.	45 to 60

*325°F. to 350°F. oven temperature is recommended for fresh pork and 300°F. to 325°F. oven temperature for smoked pork.
[1]Based on meat taken directly from the refrigerator.
[2]Heat "fully-cooked" whole hams to 140°F. internal temperature. Allow 15 to 18 minutes per pound for heating.

Timetable for Broiling

(Moderate Temperature)

CUT	Approx. Thickness	Approx. Total Cooking Time
### Smoked		Minutes
Ham Slice	½ inch	10 to 12
Ham Slice	1 inch	16 to 20
Loin Chops	½ to ¾ inch	15 to 20
Canadian-Style Bacon		
Sliced	¼ inch	6 to 8
Sliced	½ inch	8 to 10
Bacon		4 to 5
Ham Patties	1 inch	16 to 20
### Fresh		
Rib or loin chops	¾ to 1 inch	20 to 25
Shoulder Steaks	½ to ¾ inch	20 to 22
Patties	1 inch	20 to 25
Pork Kabobs	1½ x 1½ x ¾ to 1 inch	22 to 25

Braising

CUT	Approx. Weight or Thickness	Approx. Total Cooking Time
Chops, fresh	¾ to 1½ inches	45 to 60 min.
Spareribs	2 to 3 pounds	1½ hrs.
Backribs		1½ to 2 hrs.
Country-style backbones		1½ to 2 hrs.
Tenderloin		
Whole	¾ to 1 pound	45 to 60 min.
Fillets	½ inch	30 min.
Shoulder steaks	¾ inch	45 to 60 min.
Cubes	1 to 1¼ inches	45 to 60 min.

Cooking in Liquid

CUT	Approx. Weight	Approx. Total Cooking Time
### Smoked	Pounds	Hours
Ham (old style and country-cured)		
Large	12 to 16	4½ to 5
Small	10 to 12	4½ to 5
Half	5 to 8	3 to 4
Picnic Shoulder	5 to 8	3½ to 4
Shoulder roll	2 to 4	1½ to 2
Hocks		2 to 2½
### Fresh		
Spareribs		2 to 2½
Country-style backbones		2 to 2½
Hocks		2½ to 3

Index

Abats de Boucherie, 159-165
Adobu, 99, 103
Age, of meat, 14, 15
  of lamb, 78
Aging of meat, 14, 15, 16
Aitch bone
  Beef, 57
  Lamb, 81, 82
  Pork, 108
  Veal, 117
American leg of lamb, 82
Arm, 41
Arm bone
  Beef, 63
  Lamb, 87, 88
  Pork, 104
  Veal, 117
Arm pot roasts, beef, 61, 62
Arm roast, beef, 62-63
Arm steaks
  Beef, 62-63
  Veal, 118
Arrowroot, 157

Baby beef, 120
Backbone, 49
Back strap, 53
Bacon, 95, 104, 109
Ball tip, beef, 52
Barbeque beef ribs, 54
Barbeque lamb ribs, 91
Barbeque steak, beef, 63
Barding, 31
Beauty steaks, beef, 54
Beef, 45-72
  Aitch bone, 57
  Arm bone, 63
  Arm pot roast, 61-62
  Arm roast, 62-63
  Arm steaks, 62-63
  Baby beef, 120
  Back ribs, 54
  Ball tip, 52
  Barbeque ribs, 54
  Barbeque steak, 63
  Beauty steak, 54
  Bell tip, 51
  Bifteck, 48
  Blade chuck, 63, 64-65
  Blade cut chuck roast, 65-66
  Blade end, 52

Boiled tongue, 162
Boneless club steak, 48
Boneless cross rib, 63
Boneless rib eye steaks, 54
Boneless short ribs, 54
Bones, 151
Bottom cuts, 57
Bottom round, 56, 58-59
Bottom round roasts, 58
Bottom round steak, 59
Bottom sirloin, 51
Bourguignon, 62
Braising, 70
Breakfast steaks, 59
Brisket, 61, 62, 70, 90
Butcher's steak, 71
Butterball steak, 58
Butter steak, 64
Cap meat, 55
Carving, 173-179
Center cut chuck, 66
Chateaubriand, 46, 47-48
Chicago round, 51, 57
Chine bone, 53, 54, 66, 79
Choice porterhouse, 48
Chuck, 52, 54, 61-66
Chuck roast, 61, 66
Chuck roll, 65
Chuck short ribs, 63
Chuck tender, 64-65
Club steaks, 46
Corned beef, 70, 189-190
Coulotte steak, 51
Crescent, 60
Cross rib roast, 61, 62, 63, 67
Cube steak, 51
Delmonico steak, 48, 54
Denver pot roast, 59
Diamond round, 51, 57
Dictionary of beef cuts, Appendix A
Double bone sirloin, 49
Essex steak, 60
Extra lean ground beef, 72
Eye, 54
Eye cuts, 57
Eye muscle, 54
Eye of round, 56, 59
Eye of round steak, 59
Family steak, 60, 63
Feather bone, 53, 54
Filet de boeuf, 47
Filet mignon, 46, 47-48
Filet steak, 48

Flank, 46, 49, 67-68
Flank steak, 67
  Butterflying, 67-68
Flanken short ribs, 63
Flap, 51
Flat bone sirloin, 49
Flat cut, 70
Flat iron, 64, 65, 66
Fluff steak, 63
Fore shank, 70
French tenderloin, 48
Full cut round, 59
Full cut round steak, 57
Ground beef, 58,59,65,67,69,70,72
Ground chuck, 63, 72
Ground round, 72
Ground sirloin, 72
Hamburger, 71-72
Hamburg steak, 72
Hanging tender, 71
Head filet, 50
Head loin, 50
Heel of round, 59
Hind bone, 57
Hindquarter, 71
Hindshank, 70
Hip bone, 49
Hock, 57
Hotel steak, 48
Inside steak, 71
Jerky, 190-191
Jewish filet, 64-65
Kabobs, 51, 58, 60
Kansas City strips, 46, 48
Kidneys, 71, 165
Knuckles, 60
Lean ground beef, 72
Lean ground chuck, 63
Leg, 40
Leg bone, 57
Leg socket, 49
Liver, 164
Loin, 50, 52, 60, 63
London broil, 58, 60, 67, 71
Market steaks, 54, 55, 65, 66
Medallions, 47
Middle plate, 63, 69
Mock tender, 64-65, 66
Muscle boned chuck, 63
New York strip, 46, 48
Outside round, 58
Patio steak, 63
Petite steak, 64

Pike's peak, 59
Pin bone, 49
Pin bone sirloin, 49
Plate, 69
Point cut, 70
Porterhouse, 39, 46, 47, 48, 49
Pot au feu, 62
Pot roasts, 62-63, 64, 65, 66
Primal cuts, 45-72
Primal rib cut, 52
Prime porterhouse, 48
Prime rib, 52
Rib bones, 54-55
Rib cap muscle, 54
Rib caps, 54
Rib eye, 54, 55
Rib eye muscle, 65, 66
Rib eye steaks, 66
Rib filets, 54
Rib lifters, 54-55
Rib roast, 54
Rib steak, 53-54
Ribs, 52-55, 56, 61, 62, 63, 65, 69
Rolled roast, 60
Rolls in Beer, 170
Roulades, 171
Round, 51, 56-60
Round bone, 49, 57
Round bone sirloin, 49
Round steak, 57, 72
Round tip, 60
Rump, 50, 58
Rump bone, 57
Rump roast, 58, 59
Scotch tender, 64-65
Seven-bone chuck, 66
Shank bone, 57
Shanks, 61, 62, 63, 70, 91
Shell steak, 48
Short loin, 46-48, 49, 50, 52, 53, 54, 56, 58, 67
Short ribs, 63-69
Shoulder clod, 63
Sirloin, 49-51, 54, 56, 58
Sirloin; bone-in, 49
Sirloin; boneless, 50
Sirloin butt, 50
Sirloin club steak, 48
Sirloin steak, 60
Sirloin tip, 51, 60
Sirloin tip roast, 51, 60
Sirloin tip steak, 67
Skirt steak, 67, 71
Spencer steak, 54, 55, 65
Square cut chuck, 61-63
Standing rib roast, 53

Standing rump roast, 57
Stew, 54, 58, 60, 65, 66, 69, 70
Stock, 151
Stroganoff, 58, 60, 66
Stuffed flank, 67-68
Sukiyaki, 60
Super lean ground beef, 72
Swiss steak, 58, 62, 66
Tail, 46-47, 49
Tail bone, 57
Tartar steak, 72
T-Bone, 49
T-Bone steak, 39, 46, 60, 67
Tenderloin, 47-48, 50, 64-65
Tenderloin muscle, 47, 49, 59
Timetable, 207
Tip, 56, 57, 60
Top cuts, 57
Top loin, 54
Top loin muscle, 49
Top round, 56, 58, 67
Top round steak, 58, 59
Top sirloin, 49, 50, 54
Tournedos, 46, 47, 48
Triangle tip, 51, 60
Underblade, 65
Wafer steak, 59, 60
Wedge bone, 49, 56
Wedge bone sirloin, 49
Wellington, 50
Wholesale rib cut, 52
Yankee pot roast, 69
Bell tip, beef, 51
Beurre Manie, 157
Bifteck, 48
Blade bone, 39-40
    Lamb, 85, 86, 87, 88, 90
Blade chops, lamb, 86-87
Blade chuck, beef, 63, 64-65
Blade cut chuck roast, beef, 65-66
Blade end
    Beef, 52
    Pork, 96, 99
Blade end pork loin, 99
Blade end roasts, pork, 96
Blade steaks, veal, 118
Blocks, lamb, 86
Blond roux, 155
Boiled tongue, beef, 162
Bologna, 29
Bone-in, lamb, 86
Bone-in rump, veal, 117
Boneless butt, pork, 102
Boneless chops, lamb, 83, 89, 90
Boneless club steak, beef, 48
Boneless cross rib, beef, 63

Boneless hams, 108
Boneless lamb steaks, 82
Boneless loin, pork, 98
Boneless loin roll, lamb, 79-80, 85
Boneless pork chops, 98
Boneless pork loin, 98-99
    Butterflying, 98
Boneless rib eye steaks, beef, 54
Boneless rib lamb chops, 85
Boneless, rolled double loin
    lamb chops, 80
Boneless rolled roast, lamb, 83
    Carving, 179
Boneless rolled shoulder roast, lamb, 89
Boneless short ribs, beef, 54
Boneless shoulder, lamb, 86, 88, 89
Boneless stuffed chicken legs, 131
Boneless turkey breast roll, 139-140
Bones, 38-40
    Beef, 151
    Chicken, 148
    Lamb, 152
    Pork, 152
    Veal, 152
Boning
    Chicken breasts, 128-129
    Chickens, 135-136
    Leg of lamb, 82-83
    Pork shoulder, 102
    Pork sirloin end, 99
    Shoulder of lamb, 87-89
Boning knife, 22, 35
Boston butt, pork, 95, 102-103, 104, 110, 168
Boston shoulder, pork, 102-103
Bottom cuts, beef, 57
Bottom muscle, lamb, 83
Bottom round,
    Beef, 56, 58-59
    Carving, 179
    Veal, 117
Bottom round roasts, beef, 58
    Carving, 179
Bottom round steak, beef, 59
Bottom sirloin, beef, 51
Braising, 17
    Beef, 70
    Lamb, 82
Brains, 160
Breakfast steaks, beef, 59
Breast
    Chicken, 127
    Lamb, 86, 90-91
    Veal, 119
Brisket, beef, 61, 62, 70, 90
Broiling, 16

Brown roux, 155
Brown sauce, 155
Brown stock, 151
Butcher's bordelaise sauce, 156
Butcher's heart, 51
Butcher's knots, 36
Butcher's steak, beef, 71
Butterball steak, beef, 58
Butterfly chops, pork, 96, 98
Butterfly leg of lamb, 83
Butterflying
    Boneless pork loin, 98
    Flank steak, 67-68
    Leg of lamb, 83
    Pork blade ends, 99
    Pork chops, 96, 98
Butter steak, beef, 64

Canadian bacon, 110
Canned hams, 108
Cap meat, beef, 55
Capons, 141
Carving, 173-179
    Boneless roasts, 179
    Bottom round, 179
    Chuck pot roast, 179
    Cross ribs, 179
    Crown roasts, 178
    Flank steak, 179
    Hotel rounds, 179
    Lamb roasts, 179
    Legs, 178
    London broil, 179
    Porterhouse, 179
    Pot roasts, 179
    Rack of lamb, 178
    Rib roast, 178
    Rib roast, beef, 177, 178
    Rolled ribs, 179
    Rolled veal, 179
    Rump, 179
    Sirloin tip roasts, 179
    Standing rib roast, 177
    T-Bone, 179
    Top round, 179
    Top sirloin, 179
Carving knives, 20
Center cut, veal, 118
Center cut chuck, beef, 66
Center cut leg, veal, 117-118
Center cut pork chops, 96
Center loin, pork, 96, 97
Chateaubriand, beef, 46, 47-48
Chef's knife, 35
Chicago round, beef, 51, 57

Chicken, 123-137
    Bones, 148
    Boning, 135-136
        Breasts, 128-129
    Breasts, 127
        Stuffed, 129-130
    Capons, 141
    Chicken stuffed chicken, 136
    Chinese chicken wings, 133
    Cutting up, 126-128
    Gizzards, 128
    Hearts, 128
    Legs, 126, 131
        Boneless stuffed, 131
    Livers, 128
    Necks, 128, 131-132
        Stuffed, 131-132
    Quartering, 134-135
    Splitting, 134-135
    Stewed, 137
    Stock, 148-149
    Thighs, 126
    Wings, 126, 133
Chili, 70
Chine bone, 39
    Beef, 53, 54, 66, 79
    Lamb, 81, 84, 85, 86, 87, 88
Chinese chicken wings, 133
Chinese cleaver, 21
Choice porterhouse, beef, 48
Chopper, 20
Chopping blocks, 27-28
Chopping knife, 20
Chop suey, 103
Chorinzo, pork, 98
Chow mein, 99, 103
Chuck, beef, 52, 54, 61-66
Chuck roast, 29
    Beef, 61, 66
    Carving, 179
Chuck roll, beef, 65
Chuck short ribs, beef, 63
Chuck tender, beef, 64-65
Chump chops, lamb, 80
Clarifying stock, 153
Cleaver, 20, 30
Club steaks, beef, 46
Color, of meat, 14
Corned beef, 70, 189-190
Cornstarch, 157
Cottage roll, pork, 110
Coulotte steak, beef, 51
Country style sausage, 168
Country-style spare ribs, 96, 99
Crescent, beef, 60
Crisp fried pork skin squares, 104

Crock mincemeat, 188
Crocks, 188
Cross rib roasts, beef, 61, 62, 63, 67
    Carving, 179
Crown roasts
    Carving, 178
    Lamb, 85
    Pork, 96
Cube steak, beef, 51
Curry, lamb, 82, 87, 88
Cushion roast, lamb, 88
Cushion shoulder, lamb, 90
Cushion shoulder roast, lamb, 87
Cutting boards, 27-28

Deglazing, 157
Delmonico steak, beef, 48, 54
Denver pot roast, beef, 59
Diamond round, beef, 51, 57
Double bone, beef, 49
Double bone sirloin, beef, 49
Double cut rib chops, lamb, 84
Double loin chops, lamb, 79
Dry heat cooking, 16, 17
    Lamb, 78
Ducks, 124, 143

Eight-rib racks of lamb, 85
Electric meat slicer, 30
English chop, lamb, 79
English knife, 20
Escalopes, 117
Essex steaks, beef, 60
Extra lean ground beef, 72
Eye
    Beef, 54
    Lamb, 83
Eye cuts, beef, 57
Eye muscle
    Beef, 54
    Lamb, 83
Eye of round
    Beef, 56, 59
    Veal, 117
Eye of round steak, beef, 59

Family steaks, beef, 60, 63
Fat, 14, 15
Feather bone, 39
    Beef, 53, 54
    Lamb, 80, 87, 88
    Pork, 100

Fell, lamb, 85
Filet de boeuf, 47
Filet mignon, beef, 46, 47-48
Filet steak, beef, 48
Finger bone, 39
Flank, beef, 46, 49, 67-68
Flank steak, 67
   Butterflying, 67-68
   Carving, 179
Flanken short ribs, beef, 63
Flap, beef, 51
Flat bone, 40
   Beef, 49
Flat bone sirloin, beef, 49
Flat cut, beef, 70
Flat iron, beef, 64, 65, 66
Flour paste, 157
Fluff steak, beef, 63
Fore shank, 14
   Beef, 70
   Lamb, 91
Four blade chopper, 20
Four-rib yoke, lamb, 78
Freezing, 181-186
French chef's knife, 22, 35
Frenching, 85
French tenderloin, beef, 48
Frenched lamb chops, 84
Frenched leg, lamb, 82
Fresh leg of pork, 105
Fresh picnic, pork, 104
Fresh picnic shoulder, pork, 104
Fresh side of pork, 95, 104
Frying, 16
Full cut leg of lamb, 82
Full cut round, beef, 59
Full cut round steak, beef, 57
Full leg, lamb, 81
Full loin, lamb, 79

Geese, 124, 143
Gizzards, chicken, 128
Glands, lamb, 76, 89
Grading of meat, 198-200
Grinding, 23
Ground beef, 58, 59, 65, 67, 69, 70, 72, 73
Ground chuck, 29
   Beef, 63, 72, 73
Ground lamb, 86
Ground round, beef, 72, 73
Ground sirloin, beef, 72
Ground veal, 119

Half leg, lamb, 81
Hamburger, beef, 71, 72, 73
Hamburg steak, beef, 72
Ham hocks, 111
Hams, 95, 96, 106-109, 110
Ham shanks, 111
Hanging tender, beef, 71
Head filet, beef, 50
Head loin, beef, 50
Hearts, 163
   Chicken, 128
Heat, 16, 17
Heel of round, beef, 59
Hind bone, beef, 57
Hindquarter, beef, 71
Hind saddle, veal, 117-118
Hind shank, 14
   Beef, 70
   Lamb, 91
Hip bone, 40
   Beef, 49
   Lamb, 81
   Pork, 99, 100
   Veal, 117
Hock
   Beef, 57
   Pork, 104, 105, 111
Honeycomb tripe, 164
Honing, 23-25
Hotel steak, beef, 48

Inside steak, beef, 71
Inspection of meat, 197-198
Italian style sausage, 168

Jerky, beef, 190-191
Jewish filet, beef, 64-65

Kabobs
   Beef, 51, 58, 60
   Lamb, 82, 83, 86, 88, 90
   Pork, 99, 101, 102, 104
   Turkey, 140
Kansas City strip, beef, 46, 48
Kidneys, 165
   Beef, 71, 165
   Lamb, 80, 165
   Pork, 165
   Veal, 116, 165
Kidney chops, veal, 116
Kielbasa, pork, 98, 168
Kip, veal, 120

Kipper calf, veal, 120
Knee, 40
Knee joint, 83
Knife racks, 26
Knives, 19-26
   Boning knife, 22, 35
   Carving knives, 20
   Chef's knife, 35
   Chinese cleaver, 21
   Chopping knife, 20
   Cleaning, 26
   Cleaver, 20, 30
   English knife, 20
   Grinding, 23
   Holding, 35
   Honing, 23-25
   Meat cleaver, 20, 30
   Racks, 26
   Selecting, 22
   Sharpening, 23-25
   Steak knife, 22
   Steeling, 23, 24
   Types of edges, 23
   Types of steel, 22, 25
Knots, 36
Knuckles
   Beef, 60
   Veal, 117

Lamb, 75-91
   Age, 78
   Aitch bone, 81, 82
   American leg, 82
   Arm bone, 87, 88
   Barbeque ribs, 91
   Blade bone, 85, 86, 87, 88, 90
   Blade chops, 86-87
   Blocks, 86
   Bone-in, 86
   Boneless chops, 83, 89-90
   Boneless loin roll, 79-80, 85
   Boneless rolled double loin chops, 80
   Boneless rolled roast, 83
   Boneless rolled shoulder roast, 89
   Boneless shoulder, 86, 89
   Bones, 152
   Boning
      Leg, 82-83
      Shoulder, 87-89
   Bottom muscle, 83
   Braising, 82
   Breast, 86, 90-91
   Butterfly leg, 83
   Carving, 173-179
   Chine bone, 81, 84, 85, 86, 87, 88

Chump chops, 80
Crown roast, 85
Curry, 82, 87, 88
Cushion roast, 89
Cushion shoulder, 90
Cushion shoulder roast, 87
Double cut rib chops, 84
Double loin chops, 79
Dry heat cooking, 78
Eight rib racks, 85
English chop, 79
Eye, 83
Eye muscle, 83
Feather bone, 80, 87, 88
Fell, 85
Fore shank, 91
Four rib yoke, 78
Frenched leg, 82
Full cut leg, 82
Full leg, 81
Full loin, 79
Glands, 76, 89
Ground, 86
Half leg, 81
Hind shank, 91
Hip bone, 81
Kabobs, 82, 83, 86, 89, 90
Kidneys, 80, 165
Leg, 80, 81-83, 87, 91
Leg bone, 81, 83
Leg chops, 80
Liver, 164
Loin, 78, 79-80, 84, 91
Loin chops, 79
Loin end steaks, 80
Loin roll, 85
Long saddle, 78
Neck, 86
Pre-carved shoulder, 86-87
Pre-carved roast, 86-87
Prescapular gland, 89
Primal cuts, 78-91
Rack, 84-85
Rib bones, 84-88
Rib chops, 84-85
Rib eye muscle, 85, 89
Riblets, 91
Rib rack, 84-85
Ribs, 84, 86, 90
Rolled rib roast, 85
Round bone, 87, 88
Saddle, 79
Saratoga chops, 87, 89
Scotch chops, 91
Scotch roast, 91
Shank, 86, 90-91

Shank bone, 81, 82, 83
Short cut leg, 82
Short leg, 81
Short loin, 82
Short saddle, 78
Shoulder, 84, 86-90
Shoulder chops, 87
Shoulder roast, 87
Sirloin, 80, 81, 82
Sirloin chops, 80, 82
Sirloin steak, 80
Small loin chops, 79
Spare ribs, 91
Spinal cord, 87
Spring lamb, 77
Square cut shoulder, 86-87
Stew, 82, 86, 89
Stock, 152-153
Tail, 82-83
Tail bone, 81
Tenderness, 78
Three quarter leg, 81, 82
Three rib yoke, 78
Timetable, 207
Top leg muscle, 83
Whole leg lamb, 81
Yoke, 86
Larding, 31, 104
Larding needles, 31
Large loin lamb chops, 80
Lean ground beef, 72
Lean ground chuck, beef, 63
Leg
    Beef, 40
    Carving, 178
    Chicken, 126, 131
    Lamb, 80, 81-83, 87, 91
    Turkey, 140
    Veal, 117-118
Leg bone
    Beef, 57
    Lamb, 81, 83
Leg chops, lamb, 80
Leg socket, beef, 49
Liver, 164
    Beef, 164
    Chicken 128
    Lamb, 164
    Pork, 164
Loin, 14, 16, 38-39, 40
    Beef, 50, 52, 60, 63
    Lamb, 78, 79-80, 84, 91
    Pork, 95, 96-101, 110, 168
    Veal, 116
Loin chops, 39
    Lamb, 79

Loin end steaks, lamb, 80
Loin lamb roast, 79-80
Loin roll, lamb, 85
London broil, beef, 58, 60, 67, 71
    Carving, 179
Long Island duck, 143
Long saddle, lamb, 78

Mail order meat, 204
Mallets, 30
Marbling, 14, 15
Market steaks, beef, 54, 55, 65, 66
Meat cleaver, 20, 30
Meat grinder, 28-29
Meat saw, 30
Meat slicer, 30
Meat tenderizers, 30
Meat thermometer, 29
Medallions, beef, 47
Middle plate, beef, 63, 69
Minestrone, 150
Mock tender, beef, 64-65, 66
Moist heat, 16, 17
Muscle-boned chuck, beef, 63

Neck, 14, 40
    Lamb, 86
    Chicken, 128, 131-132
Neck bone, 87, 88
New York strip, beef, 46, 48

Offal, 159-165
Oiseaux sans Tetes, 171
Osso Buco, 119
Outside round, beef, 58

Pan broiling, 16
Patio steak, beef, 63
Petite steak, beef, 64
Pickled pig's feet, 191-192
Picnic ham, 104, 108-109
Picnic shoulder, pork, 95, 104
Pike's peak, beef, 59
Pig's feet, 95, 105, 191-192
Pin bone, 40
    Beef, 49
Pin bone sirloin, beef, 49
Plate, beef, 69
Point cut, beef, 70
Polish style sausage, 168
Pork, 93-111
    Aitch bone, 108

Arm bone, 104
Bacon, 95, 104, 109
Blade end, 96, 99
Blade end pork loin, 99
Blade end roast, 96
Boneless butt, 102
Boneless chops, 98
Boneless hams, 108
Boneless loin, 98-99
Bones, 152
Boning
  Shoulder, 102
  Sirloin end, 99
Boston butt, 95, 102-103, 104, 110,168
Boston shoulder, 102-103
Butterflying
  Blade ends, 99
  Chops, 96, 98
  Pork loin, 98
Canadian bacon, 110
Canned hams, 108
Carving, 173-179
Center cut pork chops, 96
Center loin, 96, 97
Chorinzo, 98
Cottage roll, 110
Crisp fried pork skin squares, 104
Crown roast, 96
Cutlets, 101, 103
Feather bone, 100
Filet, 99
Fresh leg, 105
Fresh picnic, 104
Fresh picnic shoulder, 104
Fresh side of pork, 95, 104
Ham hocks, 104, 105, 111
Hams, 95, 96, 106-109, 110
Ham shanks, 111
Hip bone, 99, 100
Kabobs, 99, 101, 102, 104
Kidneys, 165
Kielbasa, 98, 168
Liver, 164
Loin, 95, 96-101, 110, 168
Pickled pig's feet, 105-106
Picnic ham, 104, 108-109
Picnic shoulder, 95, 104
Pig's feet, 95, 105, 191-192
Primal cuts, 95-111
Rib end, 96-97, 168
Rib end, pork loin, 97
Rib end roast, 97
Salt pork, 104
Sandwich steaks, 101

Sausages, 95, 98, 99, 167-171
Shank bone, 111
Shoulder, 95, 102-103, 104
Shoulder blade, 102
Side pork, 103-104
Sirloin, 101
Sirloin end, 96, 99, 101
Sirloin end roast, 99-100
Slab bacon, 109
Smoked hams, 106-109
Smoked picnic shoulder, 108
Smoked pork, 106-109
Smoked pork butt, 110
Spare ribs, 95, 98, 99, 103, 104
Steaks, 102-103
Stir fry pork, 99, 103
Tenderloin, 96, 99, 100-101
Teriyaki, 103
Timetable, 208
Top sirloin, 100, 101
Tournedos, 101
Porterhouse, beef, 39, 46, 47, 48, 49
  Carving, 179
Pot au feu, beef, 62
Potato flour, 157
Potato starch, 157
Pot roasts
  Beef, 62-63, 64, 65, 66
  Carving, 179
  Veal, 118
Poultry, 123-143
  (see chicken, duck, geese, turkey, etc.)
Pre-carved lamb shoulder, 86-87
Pre-carved roast, lamb, 86-87
Prescapular gland, lamb, 89
Preserving of meat, 188-191
Primal cuts
  Beef, 45-72
  Lamb, 78-91
  Pork, 95-111
  Veal, 115-120
Primal rib cut, beef, 52
Prime porterhouse, beef, 48
Prime rib, beef, 52

Quartering of chicken, 134-135

Rack of lamb, 84-85
  Carving, 178
Rack of veal, 116
Refreezing, 184
Rib bones, 41
  Beef, 54-55

Lamb, 84, 88
Rib cap muscle, beef, 54
Rib caps, beef, 54
Rib chops, 39
  Lamb, 84-85
  Veal, 116
Rib end, pork, 96-97, 168
Rib end pork loin, 97
Rib end roast, pork, 97
Rib eye, beef, 54, 55
Rib eye muscle
  Beef, 65, 66
  Lamb, 85, 89
Rib eye steaks, beef, 66
Rib filets, beef, 54
Riblets
  Lamb, 91
  Veal, 119
Rib lifters, beef, 54-55
Rib rack, lamb, 84-85
Rib roast, beef, 54
  Carving, 177-178
Rib steak, beef, 53-54
Ribs, 16, 39-40
  Beef, 52-55, 56, 61, 62, 63, 65, 69
  Lamb, 84, 86, 90
Roast leg of fresh pork, 105
Roasting, 16, 205-208
  Timetables, 206-208
Rock Cornish game hens, 124, 142
Rolled leg roast, veal, 118
Rolled pork sirloin roast, 101
Rolled rib roast, lamb, 85
  Carving, 179
Rolled roast, beef, 60
Roulades, beef, 171
Round, 40, 41
  Beef, 51, 56-60
Round bone, 40, 41
  Beef, 49, 57
  Lamb, 87, 88
Round bone sirloin, beef, 49
Round steak, beef, 57, 72
Round tip, beef, 60
Rump
  Beef, 50-58
  Carving, 179
  Veal, 117, 118
Rump bone, beef, 57
Rump roast, beef, 58, 59

Saddle of lamb, 79
Salt pork, 104
Sandwich steaks, pork, 101
Saratoga chops, lamb, 87, 88, 89

Sauces, 154-157
  Blond roux, 155
  Brown roux, 155
  Brown sauce, 155
  Butcher's bordelaise sauce, 156
  White roux, 154
  White sauce, 154
Sausages, 95, 98, 99, 167-171
  Country style, 168
  Italian style, 168
  Kielbasa, 168
  Polish style, 168
  Stuffing, 169-171
Scallops, veal, 117
Scaloppini, veal, 117
Schnitzel, veal, 117
Scotch broth, 82, 153
Scotch chops, lamb, 91
Scotch roast, lamb, 91
Scotch tender, beef, 64-65
Seasonal purchasing, 187
Seven-bone chuck, beef, 66
Seven-bone cuts, 40
Sewing, 37
Sewing needles, 31
Shank bone
  Beef, 57
  Lamb, 81, 82, 83
  Pork, 111
Shank half of leg, veal, 118
Shanks
  Beef, 61, 62, 63, 70, 91
  Lamb, 86, 90-91
  Veal, 119
Shell steak, beef, 48
Short cut leg of lamb, 82
Short leg, lamb, 81
Short loin
  Beef, 46-48, 49, 50, 52, 53, 54,
    58, 67
  Lamb, 82
Short ribs, beef, 63, 69
Short saddle, lamb, 78
Shoulder, 39
  Lamb, 84, 86-90
  Pork, 95, 102-103, 104
  Veal, 117, 118
Shoulder blade, 39
  Pork, 102
Shoulder chops, lamb, 87
Shoulder clod, beef, 63
Shoulder roast, lamb, 87
Side pork, 103-104
Simmering, 17
Sirloin, 40
  Beef, 49-50, 54, 56, 58

Lamb, 80, 81, 82
Pork, 101
Veal, 117
Sirloin; bone-in, beef, 49
Sirloin; boneless, beef, 50
Sirloin butt, beef, 50
Sirloin chops, lamb, 80, 82
Sirloin club steak, beef, 48
Sirloin end, pork, 96, 99, 101
Sirloin end pork roast, 99-100
  Boning, 99-100
Sirloin roast, veal, 117
Sirloin steak
  Beef, 60
  Lamb, 80
Sirloin tip, 31
  Beef, 51, 60
  Veal, 117
Sirloin tip roast, beef, 51, 60
  Carving, 179
Sirloin tip steak, beef, 67
Skirt steak, beef, 67, 71
Slab bacon, pork, 109
Small loin chops, lamb, 79
Smoked hams, 106-109
Smoked picnic shoulder, pork, 108
Smoked pork, 106-109
Smoked pork butt, 110
Spare ribs, pork, 95, 98, 99, 103, 104
Spencer steak, beef, 54, 55, 65
Spinal cord, lamb, 87
Spring lamb, 77
Square cut chuck
  Beef, 61-63
  Veal, 118
Square cut shoulder
  Lamb, 86-87
  Veal, 118
Standing rib, beef, 53
Standing rib roast, beef, 53
Standing rump roast
  Beef, 57
  Veal, 117
Steak knife, 22
Steeling, 23, 24
Stew
  Beef, 54, 58, 60, 65, 66, 69, 70
  Lamb, 82, 86, 88
  Veal, 118
Stewed chicken, 137
Stewing, 17, 70
Stewing hens, 137
Stir-fry pork, 99, 103
Stock, 148-153
  Beef, 151
  Chicken, 148-149

Clarifying, 153
Lamb, 152-153
White, 152
Stockpot, 29
  Recipes, 145-157
Straight bladed chopper, 19-20
Stroganoff, beef, 58, 60, 66
Stub tender, beef, 50
Stuffed beef hearts, 163
Stuffed breasts, chicken, 129-130
Stuffed butterfly chops, pork, 98
Stuffed chicken legs, 131
Stuffed flank, beef, 67-68
Stuffed pork loin, 98
Stuffing, 169-171
Stuffing tube, 30
Sukiyaki, beef, 60
Super lean ground beef, 72
Sweetbreads, 161
Swiss steak, beef, 58, 62, 66

Tail, 14
  Beef, 46-47, 49
  Lamb, 82, 83
Tail bone
  Beef, 57
  Lamb, 81
Tartar steak, beef, 72
T-Bone, beef, 49
T-Bone steak, beef, 39, 46, 60, 67
  Carving, 179
Tenderizing, 16
Tenderloin
  Beef, 47-48, 50, 64-65
  Pork, 96, 99, 100
  Veal, 117
Tenderloin muscle, beef, 47, 49, 59
Tenderness, 13-17, 38-40
  Lamb, 78
Teriyaki, pork, 103
Thermometers, 29
Thighs
  Chicken, 126
  Turkey, 140
Three quarter leg, lamb, 81, 82
Three rib yoke, lamb, 78
Timetables, 206-208
  Beef, 207
  Lamb, 206
  Pork, 208
Tip, beef, 56, 57, 60
Tongue, 162
Top cuts, beef, 57
Top leg muscle, lamb, 83
Top loin
  Beef, 54

Veal, 117
Top loin muscle, beef, 49
Top round
  Beef, 56, 58, 67
  Carving, 179
  Veal, 117
Top round steak, beef, 58, 59
  Carving, 179
Top sirloin
  Beef, 49, 50, 54
  Carving, 179
  Pork, 100, 101
  Veal, 117
Tournedos
  Beef, 46, 47, 48
  Pork, 101
Triangle tip, beef, 51, 60
Tripe, 164-165
Tube steak, 212
Turkey, 124, 138-141
  Boneless breast roll, 139-140
  Carving, 174-175, 176-177
  Cutting up, 138-139
  Kabobs, 140
  Legs, 140
  Thighs, 140
  Wings, 140
  Wishbone, 130
Tying knots, 36

Underblade, beef, 65
USDA grading, 199-200
USDA inspection, 198
Utensils, 19-31

Variety meats, 159-165
Veal, 113-120
  Aitch bone, 117
  Arm bone, 117
  Arm steaks, 118
  Baby beef, 120
  Blade steaks, 118
  Bone-in rump, 117
  Bones, 152
  Bottom round, 117
  Breast, 119
  Carving, 173-179
  Center cut, 118
  Center cut leg, 117-118
  Chops, 116
  Cutlets, 116, 117, 118

Eye of round, 117
Ground, 119
Hind saddle, 117-118
Hip bone, 117
Kidneys, 116, 165
Kidney chops, 116
Kip, 120
Kipper calf, 120
Knuckles, 117
Leg, 117-118
Loin, 116
Osso Buco, 119
Pot roasts, 118
Primal cuts, 115-120
Rack, 116
Rib chops, 116
Riblets, 119
Roast, 117
Rump, 117, 118
Scallops, 117
Scaloppini, 117
Schnitzel, 117
Shanks, 119
Shoulder, 117, 118
Sirloin, 117
Sirloin tip, 117
Square cut chuck, 118
Square cut shoulder, 118
Standing rump, 117
Stew, 118
Tenderloin, 117
Top loin, 117
Top round, 117
Top sirloin, 117
Vegetable knives, 19
Veiny, beef, 60

Wafer steak, beef, 59, 60
Wedge bone, 40
  Beef, 49, 56
Wedge bone sirloin, beef, 49
White roux, 154
White sauce, 154
White stock, 152
Whole leg lamb, 81
Wholesale rib cut, beef, 52
Wings
  Chicken, 126, 133
  Turkey, 140
Wishbone, 130
Wooden mallets, 30

Yankee pot roast, beef, 69
Yoke, lamb, 86